The Tenderness of Silent Minds

The Tenderness
of Silent Minds

Benjamin Britten and his *War Requiem*

MARTHA C. NUSSBAUM

OXFORD
UNIVERSITY PRESS

Oxford University Press is a department of the University of Oxford. It furthers
the University's objective of excellence in research, scholarship, and education
by publishing worldwide. Oxford is a registered trade mark of Oxford University
Press in the UK and certain other countries.

Published in the United States of America by Oxford University Press
198 Madison Avenue, New York, NY 10016, United States of America.

Library of Congress Cataloging-in-Publication Data
Names: Nussbaum, Martha C. 1947– author.
Title: The tenderness of silent minds : Benjamin Britten and
his War requiem / Martha C. Nussbaum.
Description: [1.] | New York, NY : Oxford University Press, 2024. |
Includes bibliographical references and index.
Identifiers: LCCN 2024021400 (print) | LCCN 2024021401 (ebook) |
ISBN 9780197568538 (hardback) | ISBN 9780197568552 (epub) |
ISBN 9780197568569
Subjects: LCSH: Britten, Benjamin, 1913–1976. War requiem. |
Britten, Benjamin, 1913–1976—Criticism and interpretation. |
Music—20th century—History and criticism. |
Music and war—History—20th century. |
Pacifism. | Coventry Cathedral. | Pears, Peter, 1910–1986.
Classification: LCC ML410.B853 N87 2024 (print) |
LCC ML410.B853 (ebook) | DDC 780.92—dc23/eng/20240508
LC record available at https://lccn.loc.gov/2024021400
LC ebook record available at https://lccn.loc.gov/2024021401

DOI: 10.1093/oso/9780197568538.001.0001

Printed by Sheridan Books, Inc., United States of America

"Their flowers the tenderness of silent minds"
        —Wilfred Owen, "Anthem for Doomed Youth"

To the citizens of Ukraine, both living and dead, with a wish for a future just peace

Contents

Acknowledgments

The idea of writing about Britten's *War Requiem* has been in my mind for a long time. In the period of silence and contemplation that Yom Kippur marks out in my emotional calendar, I have listened to the work often, in between synagogue services. When I began to think about the presidential address I would deliver in April 2000 to the Central Division of the American Philosophical Association (APA), my first plan was to write about the *War Requiem* and its critique of retributive aggression. I had already chosen this title— "The Tenderness of Silent Minds"—and I had in mind some of the arguments about anger and aggression that I would develop much later in *Anger and Forgiveness* (2016). As I pondered the idea, however, I began to feel that a lecture so contemplative, requiring an emotionally receptive audience, would be ill suited to the noisy gathering that is a plenary session of the APA. Nor were my thoughts ready to unfold at that time. And given the infrequent election of a woman to that office, it seemed like a good time to give a feminist lecture—as I did, with "The Future of Feminist Liberalism," later published in the *Proceedings and Addresses of the American Philosophical Association* 74 (2000), 47–79. But I never let go of the other project, and a conference on War in Law and Literature at the University of Chicago Law School in spring 2018—part of our long law-literature series—gave me a fine opportunity to move it back to the center of my attention—and, later, to enlarge a long article[1] into

---

[1] Subsequently published as "Crucified by the War Machine: Britten's *War Requiem* and the Hope of Postwar Resurrection," in *Cannons and Codes: Law, Literature, and America's Wars*, edited by Alison L. LaCroix, Jonathan S. Masur, Martha C. Nussbaum, and Laura Weinrib (New York: Oxford University Press, 2021), 135–63.

the present book. I am very grateful to Peter Ohlin for suggesting the expansion and for supporting the project all along the way.

Another publication that contributed to the present book is my long article "Mercy."[2] There I treat the end of the *War Requiem* as one example of music representing the presence or absence of divine mercy—along with numerous other works, including the Verdi *Requiem*. All three editors were immensely helpful during the process of revision, especially in the section dealing with Britten, suggesting further readings and contesting some of my interpretations.

This book has had feedback from my colleagues at the University of Chicago Law School at various stages: the long article that was the basis for my book proposal, and three work-in-progress workshops about the book manuscript itself. I owe thanks especially to Douglas Baird, Dhammika Dharmapala, Lee Fennell, Tom Gallanis, Tom Ginsburg, Todd Henderson, Aziz Huq, Alison LaCroix, Brian Leiter, Saul Levmore, Dorothy Lund, and Tom Miles. I also presented versions of the paper as a Berggruen Lecture at the American Philosophical Association, and at Brown University. Others who have helped with their comments are Paul Guyer, Anne Robertson, and Colin Ure, as well as an anonymous referee for Oxford University Press. But above all I owe tremendous thanks to Philip Kitcher—who was the commentator at the APA–Berggruen session and the other reviewer for OUP, in both cases supplying valuable written comments, and eventually showing me an unpublished manuscript of his own, which I have his permission to cite, as I frequently do. His generosity, insight, and rare combination of musical and philosophical gifts helped me more than I can say.

For first-rate research assistance I am extremely grateful to Julian Gale, Andrew Biondo, and Nima Mohammadi. For meticulous and extremely helpful comments, I am grateful to Philip Rupprecht.

---

[2] *Oxford Handbook of Western Music and Philosophy*, edited by Tomas McAuley, Nanette Nielsen, and Jerrold Levinson (New York and Oxford: Oxford University Press, 2020), 803–22, actually published in 2021.

1

Introduction: Britten and Coventry

War is one of the great evils of human life. Unlike earthquakes, tornadoes, and wildfires, in which both human and nonhuman factors play a causal role, war is a purely human-made evil. (Human wars affect other animals too, but, although other species engage in various forms of hostility and at times violent intraspecies competition, no other species shows patterns even vaguely resembling humans' obsession with war-making.) Ever since Homer's *Iliad*, and no doubt long before, war has been decried for the horrendous capacity of its human aggressors to bring "thousandfold pains" upon more than one entire people. (Indeed, Homer's focus is on how Achilles' anger caused suffering for his own side; the suffering he caused for the Trojans is taken as obvious.) Solutions are sought, peace is temporarily made. Achilles joins with Priam, his enemy, in lamenting the fragility of human life. And yet wars do not stop happening. The suffering they inflict renews itself and continues.

Wars are fought with bodies, both human and animal. For most of human history, most of the combatant bodies in human wars have been both human and male—breakable, fierce, brave, bleeding. The strength, commitment, daring, and compassion of male bodies, both as combatants and in a variety of support functions, has been a central means to wars' ends, as has been the strength, daring, and compassion of female bodies at the front (as nurses or other support personnel and, more recently, as combatants). Nor should we omit the courage and strength of the countless animals (horses

The Tenderness of Silent Minds. Martha C. Nussbaum, Oxford University Press.
© Oxford University Press 2024. DOI: 10.1093/oso/9780197568538.003.0001

especially) that have also been combatants, though they are always unwilling conscripts.[1]

A further means to wars' ends has been the fortitude of both male and female bodies at home. Meanwhile, the torment and destruction of combatant bodies, both male and female, is wars' toll, as is the profound pain of those who wait at home, suffering anxiety, deprivation, and, too often, bereavement. When the war is an invasion of the home territory, as today in Ukraine and in much of Europe during World War II (including Britain, bombed though not invaded), noncombatants are exposed to wounds, death, and destruction of cities, as well as anxiety and bereavement.

Political debates about war are not expert at incorporating bodily experience or the reality of bodily pain. The makers of policy often live very far from the place where, as Wilfred Owen wrote, "shell-storms spouted reddest spate," nor do they even "[see] God through mud" or "hea[r] music in the silentness of duty."[2] If they do imagine common soldiers at all, they have often tended to romanticize them, preferring a false poetics of heroic gallantry, unaware that "they are troops who fade, not flowers / For poets' tearful fooling."[3] A truthful poetics of war might, however, be able to supplant this false poetics, producing poetry that "is [not] about deeds, or lands, nor anything about glory, honour, might, dominion, or power, except War."[4]

---

[1] Both Homer and Tolstoy are outstanding in their attention to the use and suffering of animals in war.

[2] All quotes in this sentence are from Owen's "Apologia Pro Poemate Meo." I cite Owen's poems from *The Collected Poems of Wilfred Owen*, edited by C. Day Lewis (London: Chatto & Windus, 1963) The edition includes numerous textual variants found in Owen's drafts, and at times Britten selects a different reading from the one the editor prints; I'll note such changes.

[3] Owen, "Insensibility." Paul Fussell, *The Great War and Modern Memory* (Oxford, UK: Oxford University Press, 1975) offers a marvelous commentary on Owen's poetry, juxtaposing it with the rhetoric of World War I recruitment posters, which never faced the body and always spoke in romantic abstractions such as "gallant lads," and used poetic euphemisms for bodily parts: blood is the "red wine of youth," and so on (see pp. 21–22).

[4] Owen, preface to his collected poems.

What would that poetics be like? The makers of policy and the makers of war have tended not to devote intense or specific thought to the body, the seat of war's suffering (both on and away from the battlefield). Bodies are embarrassing for people invested in their own invulnerability, as leaders all too often tend to be. Confronting bodily pain and penetrability is perilously close to being unmanly. So a true poetics of war, counteracting these denials, must also, perhaps, be an unmanly poetics (i.e., not manly in a conventional way), revealing the softness and at the same time the hardness of the body at war, and the equal vulnerability of the suffering bodies at home— and making its audience feel what those bodies feel: longing, desire, exultation, sensuous pleasure, hope for the future, unbearable pain. (President Volodymyr Zelenskyy, ignorantly criticized for appearing before the US Congress in the attire of a common soldier, used his own body as a symbol of a shared vulnerability that few leaders have dared to acknowledge, preferring attire connoting triumphalist masculine toughness.)

If that poetry could somehow be joined to music, along with dance the most kinetic, dynamic, hence bodily of the arts, the two arts together could perhaps transform the consciousness of the makers of war in our world, producing real thought about future wars and an opening to a stable peace—through what Owen calls the "tenderness of silent minds," a reflective and receptive mode of listening and emotional experience that people are rarely willing to assume in daily life. Britten (who chose that variant version of Owen's poetic line, inclusive of the home front, from among several in Owen's notebooks[5]) thus links the audience with those who suffer bereavement at home—and are left to think, and feel, about their loss and to imagine a better possible future.[6]

---

[5] See Part II.

[6] I am very grateful to Paul Guyer for insisting on the central importance of those who suffer at home. My reaction to his comments could be seen by comparing this version with the version of this material in Alison L. LaCroix, Jonathan S. Masur, Martha C. Nussbaum, and Laura Weinrib, eds., *Cannons and Codes* (New York: Oxford University Press, 2021).

Such was the project of composer Benjamin Britten (1913–1976), drawing on the war poetry of Wilfred Owen (1893–1918).

World War I saw an outpouring of distinguished poetry about the futility and waste of war. Among the best of the war poets was Owen, an officer decorated for "conspicuous gallantry and devotion to duty," who was killed in action on November 4, 1918, one week before the signing of the Armistice. Owen was not a total pacifist, but he deplored the pointlessness of World War I and its needless sacrifice of so many fine young men.

In 1962, Britain's Coventry Cathedral—bombed during World War II, and subsequently restored in such a way as to preserve the bombed-out shell alongside a soaring new structure—was rededicated. The occasion was solemnized by the premiere of Britten's *War Requiem*, indisputably one of the great musical works of the twentieth century, which uses Owen's war poetry, cutting into and sometimes against the Latin text of the Requiem Mass, to articulate a scathing critique of wars and the human forces that create them, and to gesture ambiguously toward a future of reconciliation and European peace. Britten pointedly assigned the leading roles to an Englishman (Peter Pears), a German (Dietrich Fischer-Dieskau), and a Russian (Galina Vishnevskaya, who was replaced by Heather Harper at the premiere due to visa difficulties, but who subsequently sang the work and made the debut recording). The work has great insights but might also be charged with serious blind spots, not the least being its tacit assumption that World War I and World War II are basically the same, and equally, and similarly, pointless. Britten was a complete pacifist, as was his lover and collaborator for thirty-nine years, the great singer Peter Pears (1910–1986), whose tenor solo role in the *War Requiem*, composed for him as were many of Britten's works, includes the pivotal song depicting Christ as a common soldier crucified by obtuse and greedy elites. Despite my serious objections to Britten's wartime stance, I believe that the work itself survives that critique. Focused on creating a better future, especially through a sharp critique of traditions that encourage retributive anger and other errors of aggression, it can to a great extent make common cause with many of those who participated in World War II, seeing it as a just war of national self-defense.

This book offers a reading of the *War Requiem* and its use of Owen's poetry, pondering both the work's insights and one (as I see it) grave ethical error—namely, Britten's lifelong unwillingness to accept the idea that there could ever be such a just war. Three connected insights, I argue, survive our critique of the error. First: law and policy need to retain at all times a vivid sense of the human body, its beauty and its vulnerability, as the seat of human striving and whatever is valuable in human striving. Second: nations, after a devastating war, should not remain stuck in a posture of division and blame, but should move forward together toward a new future of cooperation—based, in fact, on the commonality of bodies, their needs and their beauties. Third: music and poetry can assist the search for future peace by their bodily immediacy and sensuous/sensory pleasures, revealing the true spirit of a human and very bodily Christ, in what musicologist Heather Wiebe calls an "incarnational aesthetic."[7]

Britten connected these insights to his triple outsider status, as an artist, a pacifist, and a homosexual.[8] But he lacked, indeed rejected, the somewhat disdainful attitude that Wilfred Owen sometimes expressed toward both women and straight British culture: Britten's aesthetic was fully inclusive. He is conspicuous for his support of female friends and of women's careers, including making his former assistant Imogen Holst director of the Aldeburgh Festival, probably the first woman to direct a major arts festival in Britain. Moreover, he had the good fortune to live on into what E. M. Forster, looking

---

[7] Heather Wiebe, *Britten's Unquiet Pasts: Sound and Memory in Postwar Reconstruction* (New York: Cambridge University Press, 2012), 56. See further below.

[8] Throughout this book I avoid using the word *gay*, because both Britten and Pears disliked it—they thought it let a persecutory society off the hook by denying the unhappiness created by repressive laws and customs. For more on his sense of outsider status, see Chapter 3.

to the future, called "a happier year,"[9] since before the *Requiem*'s premiere, the Wolfenden Commission had recommended the decriminalization of same-sex acts, and only five years after the premier, in 1967, the decriminalization took place.[10] Thus Britten is able to gesture not only toward European unity but also toward a future in which the pacifist, the artist, and the same-sex lover can become reconciled with traditional British culture, an obsessive theme in his postwar works (for example *Albert Herring* and *Saint Nicolas*)— a future made institutional through the Aldeburgh Festival, a music festival founded by Britten and Pears in 1948, that to this day holds performances in various historic venues in the Tudor-era Suffolk town in which they lived (see Chapter 6). Said Britten in 1964, "My music now has its roots in where I live and work. . . . I am firmly rooted in this glorious county. . . . I treasure these roots, my Suffolk roots." Any reading of the *War Requiem* must include this desire for home and belonging, for a regeneration of the Britain that estranged and excluded. In 1976, shortly before his death, he became Baron Britten of Aldeburgh. When he died, the Queen sent a personal letter of condolence to Pears, just as she would to any prominent grieving spouse.[11]

I hope that this specific case study of one outstanding work will offer a way of meditating about what a musical/poetic work can offer law and policy as we think about the future of nations aspiring to live with both peace and freedom.

This book is above all an exploration and interpretation of the *War Requiem*. But it sets that study within a philosophical

---

[9] Forster (1879–1970) used "To a Happier Year" as the dedication for his novel *Maurice,* which concerns an ultimately happy same-sex relationship; the novel was written in 1913–1914, but Forster believed that it could not be published in the Britain of that time, since its happy ending would appear to recommend crime. It was published after his death, in 1971.

[10] The history of this period is recounted in Chapter 4. Britten's work, then, is situated at the beginning of what, borrowing from another work about oppression, one might call the "long walk to freedom."

[11] https://www.huffingtonpost.com/kevin-childs/benjamin-britten_b_4318555.html.

framework, and also within the context of Britten's developing insights about war. Britten's earlier works on this theme offer rich illumination to the interpreter of the *War Requiem*, and are important in their own right.

First, then, we need to ask why we should think that music can help us reflect about war. Given the prominence of war as a theme in literature, people are likely to grant that there is something to be gained by turning to literature in an effort to understand war. But music can seem too abstract to offer us much. Chapter 2, Music as Representation of Bodily Striving and Failure, investigates this question, with Schopenhauer's powerful theory of musical experience as a guide, though rejecting Schopenhauer's pessimism.

Britten began his career as composer in the run-up to World War II, and thoughts about war and what causes it were with him from the very beginning—as were thoughts about human abuse of non-human animals and our related flight from acknowledgment of our own animality. I think an interpreter of the *War Requiem* can gain a lot from a study of some of these earlier works, especially those written in collaboration with the poet W. H. Auden. In Chapter 3, Britten, Auden, and the Spirit of War: Persecuting Bodies, I study a group of these collaborative works, particularly the song cycle *Our Hunting Fathers* (1936), but also *Ballad of Heroes* (1939), *Sinfonia da Requiem* (1940), and *Paul Bunyan* (1941), Britten's first opera. We find Britten attaining confident maturity as a composer, with some well-developed ideas about the origins of warlike aggression, and subtle command of their musical expression—even when his librettist does not do his best work.

But in order to conclude that we ought to care about the sufferings of soldiers in battle, and the equal suffering of people on the home front, we need to ask and answer Schopenhauer's question: is human striving worth anything, and are human beings worth caring about? Unlike Schopenhauer, Britten consistently answers both of those questions in the affirmative. Despite his skepticism about the nation and about political enterprises, he maintained a resolute optimism about the lovability of the human heart and body. In Chapter 4, Britten and Pears: the Beauty and Nobility of Human Love, I discuss three song cycles Britten wrote for his life partner and for himself as pianist: *Seven Sonnets of Michelangelo* (1940), *Holy Sonnets of John Donne* (1945), and *Winter Words* (1953). I set these works in the context of their thirty-nine-year partnership, as revealed in letters the two men gifted to the nation. Despite the terrible persecution of same-sex lovers during most of their life together, the two men not only lived with dignity and stability, but also affirmed the worth of their love publicly in many ways—and connected this human love, in the wake of the Holocaust and Britten's visit to Belsen, to reflections about Christ's mercy for sinful human beings.

Britten was a pacifist who refused even supportive national service during World War II. In Chapter 5, Pacifisms and the Music of Peace, I examine the views he and Pears held, their intellectual and social context, and their testimony to the tribunal assessing them for national service. Although I am very critical of their absolutist Gandhian stance in the context of World War II, I argue that the most important aspect of Britten's view is defensible: that is, what I call his "emotional pacifism," his opposition to retributive aggression and his insistence on inner discipline to overcome the sources of war in each person. I then study a group of works in which Britten finds a musical language to express the emotions essential to creating and sustaining a world of peace, some more successful than others: *The World of the Spirit* (1938), *Spring Symphony* (1949), *Voices for Today* (1965), and *Owen Wingrave* (1971), (the latter two postdating the *War Requiem*).

Unlike Auden, Britten was interested in the community as well as the individual, and if he found much to criticize in the nation as it was, he retained a profound attachment to British life and especially to Suffolk, his home county. In the lead-up to composition of the *War Requiem*, he set out to shed his outcast status and to become reconciled—on terms of dignity and tough criticism—with his country and region. Chapter 6, Reconciliation: Aldeburgh, Wolfenden, Coventry, discusses this period of emotional homecoming, especially the creation of the Aldeburgh Festival by Britten and Pears as a musical offering to the nation that endures to this day. During this same period, the nation was also moving toward them, through the Wolfenden Commission, which recommended the decriminalization of same-sex acts between men in 1957, and the subsequent slow progress toward decriminalization, which occurred, as I have mentioned, in 1967. Finally I study the history of the rebuilding of the Coventry Cathedral and the decision to invite Britten to compose a major new work for the rededication ceremony in 1962.

Thus, although this book culminates in a close reading of the *War Requiem*, its scope is far broader, both contextually and within Britten's musical career. I have been selective, omitting many other works of importance, and especially two central works treating the themes that concern me: the operas *Peter Grimes* (1945) and *Billy Budd* (1951). To do anything like justice to these wonderful works would unbalance the book. In any case I plan to discuss them in a future book on opera.[12] In Chapter 6 I make an exception to my no-major-opera principle for *Albert Herring* (1947), which I think one of Britten's best operas, fully worthy to be ranked alongside *Peter Grimes* and *Billy Budd*—because it is too closely linked with the founding and aims of the Aldeburgh Festival to be omitted in a chapter that focuses on that festival. For similar reasons I make some remarks in Chapter 5 about the 1971 opera *Owen Wingrave*, whose central theme is pacifism, although I do not offer a full interpretation and consider it an inferior work.

I turn now to the central issue: how can music speak about war, and how does this matter in our search for understanding and appropriate action?

---

[12] *The Republic of Love: Opera, Breath, and Freedom*, under contract to Yale University Press.

PART I

MUSIC, BODIES, BEAUTY, VULNERABILITY

2

Music as Representation of Bodily Striving and Failure

What does music have to do with war and the understanding of war?[1] Not much, one might think. In Mozart's *The Marriage of Figaro* the young Cherubino, about to leave the female world of amorous sighs, courtly dances, and, crucially, music, is taunted by Figaro, who describes the world of war as the antithesis of that gentle world. Instead of dancing the fandango, he says, you will march through mud, *il fango*. And this world is also a world of anti-music: Cherubino will march "to a concerto of blunderbusses, / shells, and cannons / whose shots, on all pitches, / make your ears whistle."[2] If we follow Figaro, we might suppose that the idea of writing music about war is a self-defeating task: it means turning something that subverts the very being of music into music, which it absolutely is not. In the opera, not surprisingly, Cherubino never does go to war; the action remains confined to a world in which music is audible.

And yet many composers have written music on war-related themes. If one is already a composer and a pacifist, as Britten was,

[1] For comments on this part of my book project, I am especially grateful to Paul Guyer and Brian Leiter. And for able research assistance in this and subsequent chapters, I am indebted to Julian Gale.

[2] "Al concerto di trombone, / Di bombardi, di cannone / Che le palle In tutti i tuoni/ All'orecchio fan fischiar." The words *concerto* and *tuoni* are musical words used for the anti-musical noises of war. The word *trombone* is frequently translated as trumpets or bugles. But it is also the word for blunderbuss, and I think Da Ponte is clearly having fun with its double meaning, both musical and anti-musical. *Fischiar* can mean either ring or whistle.

The Tenderness of Silent Minds. Martha C. Nussbaum, Oxford University Press.
© Oxford University Press 2024. DOI: 10.1093/oso/9780197568538.003.0002

seeking to reveal the damages of war and to move listeners toward peace and reconciliation, it would be natural to approach the topic of war with one's own tools and modes of expression. Surely, war itself does not promote an understanding of war. As Figaro says: it just makes your ears ring. And far worse.

But there are deeper reasons why all people seeking an understanding of war and peace should turn to music.

In this chapter I will develop a philosophical view about music and war—not in the belief that any composer would apply a philosophical program, but, rather, in the belief that philosophers have sometimes had insight into the human significance of art in general, and music in particular. I shall draw my examples from Western classical music, but I believe the general framework is applicable to the music of other cultures and to Western popular music.

Many philosophers of art have not been interested in music, but there is one Western philosopher above all who, whatever his perversities and shortcomings, has unsurpassed insight into the role of music in human life: Arthur Schopenhauer (1788–1860). Not surprisingly, composers have often turned to Schopenhauer to articulate in words their own projects: in particular, Gustav Mahler and Richard Wagner were greatly influenced by his ideas. Schopenhauer attracted them, and many others, not only by the power of his overall view of life and suffering, but also because he gives music a special place in the understanding of life. I have serious criticisms to make, but Schopenhauer is so insightful that his views are a valuable starting point.

Will and Representation: Music as Representation of the Will

For Schopenhauer, human beings make contact with the world outside themselves in two ways. First, through our cognitive faculties (*Vorstellung*) we attain ideas of the world by representing external objects to ourselves.[3] The activity of representation is calm and detached. But we also move in the world, toward objects we want. This dynamic principle of wanting or seeking he calls Will (*Wille*). Will is present in all of nature, an often-blind force seeking the preservation of life.[4] Desire, joy, planning, effort, all this is Will, but Will also operates in nonsentient and even nonliving Nature. Humans and other animals[5] are aware of being moved by Will, but plants and inanimate objects are moved by it as well.

Will uses us for its own ends (the continuity and propagation of natural entities), but human happiness is not among them. Human beings, like all animals, are doomed to suffering. Most of the time we fail to attain our ends. If we do, our satisfaction is brief and quickly changes to boredom and misery. This is Schopenhauer's famous pessimism, and although we can gain insight from Schopenhauer's view of art without accepting his pessimism, we must first understand it.

Strongly influenced by Buddhism, Schopenhauer believes that the best we can do in life is to detach ourselves from our personal projects and, ultimately, from our own individual egos.[6] In this endeavor the arts give us great assistance. The arts—he discusses painting, sculpture, architecture, literature, and music (never dance)—are representations of human striving and failure. Engaged with a work of art, we are lifted out of our own personal projects for a time, and can study the world dispassionately and see how it works, while being moved by generic emotions not related to

[3] Schopenhauer is an idealist: he holds that what we perceive is made by our faculties. But the intricacies of his epistemology and his attempt to grapple with external reality need not concern us here.

[4] Schopenhauer denies that there are individual human beings and animals at all: strictly speaking, they are illusory, forms of the Will in action. Nonetheless, he continues to talk about them, and so shall I.

[5] It is important for my later discussion of Britten on animal bodies that Schopenhauer emphasizes the similarity of humans and other animals. A zealous defender of animal rights, he lived with a succession of poodles (each named Atman for the universal soul), and nobody else for much of his life, once he and his mother (a celebrated writer) had quarreled and severed contact.

[6] Which, we must recall, are phenomenal illusions.

any personal goal. In this way we come to see how futile all human projects are, and we learn to seek detachment from Will in all its manifestations in our extra-aesthetic lives.

Schopenhauer sees value in all the arts, and he has especially eloquent things to say about literary tragedy, which, he says, teaches us explicitly about the vanity of human endeavors. But there is one art to which he ascribes unique and paramount importance: music. Music, in his view, offers us a representation of the Will itself, uncluttered by any reference to specific objects. While poetry and other art forms approach Will only indirectly, through images, music depicts it directly, with a powerful and searing effect, showing us "the "many different forms of the Will's efforts," especially the inner experience of our passions (a central instance of the Will's efforts) and how they lead us to disaster and suffering in a world of ungovernable chance events. Music does this through rhythm, accent, dynamics, and melody, all being forms of bodily movement that have, in turn, a direct effect on the listener's body.[7] Musical experience is detached but not dry; it is perceptual and not conceptual, and inexhaustibly rich.

Schopenhauer clearly loved music and was deeply moved by it. Because his discussion of music in *The World as Will and Representation* was published in 1819, the music he loved was utterly unlike the music of composers later influenced by him. (Rossini is a particular favorite of his, and he interestingly singles out Mozart's *Don Giovanni* as one of the world's greatest works of art.) Although he is not convincing when he speaks of music as a "universal language" of the emotions,[8] and although many of his particular observations about musical representation are eccentric, by and large he speaks knowledgeably and lovingly about the way music achieves its effects.

---

[7] Arthur Schopenhauer, *The World as Will and Representation*. Trans. E. F. J. Payne (New York; Dover, 1958), vol. I, sec. 52.

[8] See my discussion in Nussbaum, *Upheavals of Thought: The Intelligence of Emotions* (New York: Cambridge University Press, 2001), ch. 5.

In life, Schopenhauer holds, the bodies of others give rise to desire and also, when we are satiated, to disgust. In hearing music, by contrast, he plausibly claims, we never are moved to either desire or disgust, because we are never in touch with a particular. (Consider the jealous husband in Tolstoy's *The Kreutzer Sonata*: he shows his mental instability when he claims that the first movement of Beethoven's sonata inspires sexual desire in both the listener and the musicians.) Music does not represent particulars. But it can contain a nonparticular representation of desire, perhaps even of disgust (think of what Mahler calls the "cry of disgust" in his Second Symphony). And these representations help us to understand what desire and disgust really are and why we must exit from the life of striving and failure that they construct.

Similarly, in life, Schopenhauer claims, the failure of our projects negates any worth these projects might have been thought to have. Before a musical work, by contrast, we think of neither achievement nor failure, and we begin to appreciate why we must subtract ourselves from the frenzied hunt after success.

Schopenhauer believes that the basis of all morality is compassion for suffering—a compassion that includes all beings in its scope.[9] As he imagines compassion, the experience delivers a person from bondage to the ego: in compassion for suffering we imagine ourselves as one with the whole world of suffering beings, and we lose the focus on our own specialness that is, in his view, the source of all immoral action. His famous essay on compassion was written more than twenty years after *The World as Will and Representation*, with its discussion of art.[10] I know of no text in which he brings the insights of the two works together. But it is

---

[9] Again: strictly speaking there are no individuals, only Will; but he speaks of compassion as an ethical imperative, and a connection to both other humans and nonhuman animals, indeed to all of nature.

[10] Schopenhauer, "Prize Essay on the Basis of Morals," in *The Two Fundamental Problems of Ethics*, edited and translated by Christopher Janaway (Cambridge, UK: Cambridge University Press (1840/2009).

not difficult to do so. Before a work of art—most of all a musical work—we learn the structures of human aggression and victimization, of seeking and frustration, of longing and doom—all the while being unaware of our own egos. Thus we acquire a powerful motive for general compassion and for a time embody it. From the grasp of suffering in the experience of art, we can (if we choose) move back into our lives with a new nonegoistic attitude. We can give up our typical self-obsession, cultivating a generalized compassion for all suffering beings.

Now think about war, the central theme of this book. People who plan wars, or who vote them into being, typically have a distanced intellectual concept of war, apprehending it as a set of strategies and objectives. But they are always at one remove from the bodies of soldiers, on which war is inscribed, so to speak. For the makers of war, war is words. For soldiers, it is written in their flesh, often fatally.[11] To understand the cost of war, therefore, it is necessary to confront the flesh and blood of soldiers, the ripping of their flesh by bullets and bayonets—but also the equally violent wounding of their psyches (also physical of course) by shell-shock and other wartime traumas. (To this we should add, as Britten will, the damages to the bodies and psyches of those who suffer at home, from deprivation and grief.) We must confront these things not just intellectually, and at the same time not by really going there and being in the midst of battle—for then, as Schopenhauer saw, we would be too preoccupied with our own immediate survival to understand anything. Instead, we should confront them with the nondetached detachment, the powerful but nonpersonal emotions, with which we respond to music, which digs into us with its percussive beatings and clangings, its rhythmic dashings, its wide range of both pitches and dynamics. The ensuing understanding of vulnerability and futility ought to lead to what Wilfred Owen called Pity with a capital

---

[11] Consider Kafka's "In the Penal Colony" (1919) in which the convicted person's punishment is literally inscribed into his flesh, eventually killing the person.

P—a powerful emotion embracing all the vulnerable bodies and seeing their suffering as fully real—and then (back in our lives) with compassionate action to avoid future wars. This was the "warning" that Owen, in his Introduction (to be discussed later), said poets could give and that he thought his poetry did give. Thus Owen's poetics deploys quasi-musical techniques to get through to the reader: the battering of consonants, the gaping sound of vowels. Britten, using both words and actual music, is able to go even further, as we shall see.

Although Schopenhauer does not discuss the role of voice in music, voice is an embodied instrument and thus bears an especially intimate connection to the ways human beings endure bodily desire and suffering. The human voice has often been thought suspect in performance, and singing on the stage has long been thought to be akin to "a kind of publick prostit[ut]ion," as Adam Smith decrees.[12] In the article "A Wicked Voice" (1890), the popular aesthetics writer Vernon Lee (really Violet Paget) writes, "Singer, thing of evil, stupid and wicked slave of the voice, of that instrument which was not invented by the human intellect, but begotten of the body, and which, instead of moving the soul, merely stirs up the dregs of our nature!"[13] In Schopenhauerian terms, however, we should say that the singer helps us to experience a representation of our bodily nature more than any other musician. Britten is aware of the special ability of the human voice to depict bodily vulnerability and longing, and writes with this idea almost constantly in mind.

In a late addition to Part II of *The World as Will and Representation*, talking about the links between his views and Buddhism, Schopenhauer says that they are also fully consistent with Christianity: *Wille* "is, so to speak, the crucified Saviour, or

---

[12] Adam Smith, *An Inquiry into the Nature and Causes of the Wealth of Nations.* Two volumes (Carmel, IN: Liberty Fund, 1981–1982).

[13] Vernon Lee, "A Wicked Voice," in Hauntings. Project Gutenberg, 1890. I owe this reference to Jess Peritz.

else the crucified thief, according as it is decided."[14] This provides a hint to a central achievement of the *War Requiem*: its portrayal of the crucified Christ as a soldier—a fully human body—put to death by a corrupt war-making society.

Schopenhauer's Failure and a Way Forward

Schopenhauer offers us deep insight into the ways music contributes to human life. But his insights are flawed by a blind spot at the heart of his pessimism. Schopenhauer thinks that human projects are worthwhile only if they achieve stable success. Since they never do, he concludes that all our aims are worthless, and we ought to detach ourselves from them. No mortal project, by definition, could meet his austere standard. But he never sufficiently investigates the possibility of a characteristically mortal happiness: of a life that is doomed to end, and doomed, no doubt, to contain much suffering along the way, but that still embodies projects of value and constitutes the human agent as a person of value.

One particular area in which this blind spot appears is in his verdict on human love, which is unremittingly negative.[15] Because love is unstable, and typically upset either by aggression and jealousy or by boredom, therefore, he concludes that love itself is worthless, as are all particular human relationships.[16] Romantic/erotic love comes in for special contempt and condemnation. He ignores the possibility that love might be beautiful and yet not enduring or perfect. Because he sets the bar so high, everything human is condemned to failure. Nor would he grant, ultimately, that human

[14] Schopenhauer, *The World as Will and Representation*, vol. II, p. 645. Presumably he means that the *Wille* can animate the good nonegoistic person (Christ) as well as the selfish person (the thief).

[15] See especially II. 531–67.

[16] Occasionally he speaks better of friendship, but in contexts where he is heaping opprobrium on romantic love. All particular relationships, investigated deeply enough, would eventually turn out to be flawed and hence (in his view) worthless.

or even animal bodies may have beauty or worth. Infected with the failures of their projects, and with the suffering those projects cause, they become ugly.

These large failures undermine his treatment of the arts. Schopenhauer certainly seems to grant that works of art can have aesthetic value. But how, precisely, can a representation have beauty and worth if what it represents is squalid and ugly to the person who sees things correctly? And if the representation is not beautiful and worthwhile, why should we engage with it or care about it? Consider tragedy. A familiar view of Greek tragedies and related works follows Aristotle: the leading figure suffers a reversal and comes to grief. This inspires the onlooker with compassion. But, importantly, the leading figure must be good, even "better than us" (*Poetics* 1448a15) as Aristotle says, in order that the downfall should seem worthy of compassion, rather than censure or contempt or indifference.[17] As Aristotle puts it, "the noble [or beautiful] shines through, *dialampei to kalon*" (EN 1100b30), despite the batterings of fortune. Aristotle agrees with Schopenhauer in holding that works of art show us general possibilities in human life, "things such as might happen" (*Poetics*, ch. 9). But how would we see general human possibilities in them (implicating our own efforts), if the person is worthless or contemptible? The projects of such a person are not good cases of human effort, with which we identify our own. Tragedy moves us to compassion against a background of admiration, even a kind of wonder-suffused love.

---

[17] For Aristotle, the hero should fall through a mistake in action (*hamartia*), which may be either innocent or somewhat culpable: but this mistake must not be a vicious trait of character. Aristotle distinguishes here between a fall that is explicable and one that is *paralogon*, simply absurd or inexplicable. But he omits cases in which the fall, though explicable, is not caused by any mistake made by the leading figure. Most tragedies of war are like this, and Euripides' *The Trojan Women* is a fine example of tragic suffering in which the mistakes are those of the commanders, not of the suffering women. So Aristotle's account needs to be broadened in order to fit our topic.

Music is not different.[18] Mahler was fond of writing programs for his symphonies that he immediately disowned, saying they were but "a crutch for a cripple."[19] But they do give us a general idea to work with. His symphonies depict, he typically says, the struggles of a "hero" who encounters various reversals. When Schopenhauer says that music represents the Will, he means something like that: that a musical work depicts, in a highly generalized way, the strivings of a generalized human (or other animal) being, meeting with success and ultimately (he thinks) with failure. But he knows that musical works awaken deep emotions because of their beauty (and other fine characteristics). How can music be alluring if that which it represents is tawdry or even ugly? Of course in our daily lives the projects to which Will directs us are alluring; Schopenhauer certainly grants that. But he thinks that when we understand Will in its true nature—as we do in engaging with a work of art—we see how base and worthless its projects are. How is this compatible with the enthusiasm he plainly has for that experience and the aesthetic values it discloses? How, in other words, can there be aesthetic value without human value, if we accept Schopenhauer's general picture that the arts represent human desire and effort?[20] Mahler's struggling "hero," like Aristotle's tragic hero, is portrayed as noble amid life's catastrophes, as worth admiring and caring about. That is how the catastrophes that befall the "hero" can come to awaken a generalized compassion.

Mahler portrays this clearly in the sequence of emotions in his Second Symphony. At one point, the struggles of humanity seem worthless, and the onlooker is encouraged (in the satirical third movement) to view human beings as base and not worth engaging

---

[18] And of course Greek tragedy was musical: even dialogue had a musical accompaniment, and the choral odes were sung.

[19] See my detailed account in Nussbaum (2001, ch. 5), with references.

[20] His metaphysical answer would likely be that music connects us to Will, erasing the illusion of individuality and individual projects. But absorption in the flow of Will is one thing, his evident contempt for human projects quite another.

with. This is where the famous "cry of disgust" occurs. But it is followed, not by more disgust, but by a movement back to humanity in the fourth movement, "Urlicht." The contralto, vibrant with compassion, sings "O little red rose, Humanity lies in the greatest need." And this movement leads in turn to the final triumph of the human heart in the fifth "resurrection" movement.[21]

Let me give a further example, using a work that Schopenhauer knew and greatly admired. I went to a performance of the Beethoven Ninth on the day Russian armies first invaded Kyiv. The world around me gave plentiful reasons for thinking human projects doomed to frustration and failure. What was in the music, however, was a powerful representation of the beauty and worth of human striving and hope—even when striving does not succeed. Kant thought that we have a moral obligation to stir up hope in ourselves, in order to motivate ethically good actions, even though the world cannot prove to us that hope is justified. I felt that I had followed Kant's wise advice that afternoon. Schopenhauer at one point grants that a symphony of Beethoven (he doesn't say which one, and perhaps he means that these properties belong to all) moves us to create beauty and harmony in the world, but he then says, obscurely, that we would be wise not to do that, but rather to listen to the work as a pure abstraction (II. 450). However, even then: it is not an ugly abstraction, but a powerfully beautiful and meaningful one, containing resonant images of hope. (He grants that point, saying that a Beethoven symphony represents all the human passions—II. 450). And how could it be like that, if it represents human Will and if Will has the properties he imputes to it?

In short, the movement from musical experience to generalized compassion cannot take place if the striving of the "hero" is seen as contemptible and foolish.[22] But that is how it must be seen from the

---

[21] I study the sequence in detail in Nussbaum (2001, ch. 14).

[22] Strictly speaking, the "hero" is an illusion for Schopenhauer. And yet, in his discussion of tragedy he draws attention to the striving of heroes and their failure, and urges us to learn from them.

point of view of detachment, given Schopenhauer's view of life. This problem has vexed all views that try to combine detachment from human projects and their worth with a generalized concern for humanity. Consider the Greek and Roman Stoics, who urge us to see the struggles of the tragic hero as contemptible and even ridiculous. Epictetus says: "Behold how tragedy comes about: when chance events befall fools." And he engages in imaginary conversations, full of contempt, with tragic heroes such as Oedipus and Medea. It's difficult to see how the Stoic can pivot to compassion, even if the attempt is made.

Stoics carry that attitude into their confrontation with war. Marcus Aurelius, as Emperor, leading his army into battle, records in his *Meditations* that the soldiers seem to him like "crazed mice running for shelter." Apart from the obvious question of whether this is a proper attitude for a commander to have, it is a very bad perspective from which to assess the damages war does to human bodies (since Marcus plainly thinks mice base and worthless). Marcus's posture of superiority leads to contempt, even though intermittently he suggests that some type of general compassion for human foolishness is warranted.

Schopenhauer would no doubt reply that what music represents is beautiful, not ugly and pathetic, because it is utterly separated from real life. In fact, he does say this: "The inexpressible depth of all music, by virtue of which it floats past us as a paradise quite familiar and yet eternally remote, and is so easy to understand and yet so inexplicable, is due to the fact that it reproduces all the emotions of our innermost being, but entirely without reality and remote from pain" (I. 264). However, how can this really be true, if we are to see in music the representation of Will and the manifold failures and frustrations to which it always leads? Again and again Schopenhauer hammers home this point in talking about literary tragedy, and it is crucial to his entire case for the practical significance of art that we do see in it the failures we are bound to encounter if we allow ourselves to be led by Will and fail to detach ourselves. We do not see our own suffering, to be sure, but we see a general form of life-suffering caused by Will. And he must insist on this, or else why would music help us seek detachment, as he thinks we should?

So Schopenhauer and the Stoics fail at their own aim: to lead people to a generalized compassion for human suffering. We might instead follow Mahler and Aristotle, not Schopenhauer, seeking in music a representation of the often tragic struggles of human life, but struggles in which, as Aristotle says, "the noble (beautiful) shines through." The listener must never succumb to disgust or contempt, denying all worth to human projects. And indeed the very beauty of musical works is our ally in our efforts not to succumb. For fine music awakens, typically, not these emotions at all, but a different emotion: *wonder*, which, I claim, is a key element in much of our aesthetic experience.[23]

Wonder is a detached emotion in a sense, in that it is nonpersonal, not connected to our own particular well-being. But it responds to signs of beauty and meaning, and, more active than awe, it moves us outward toward the beauty it sees, as if to protect it. Fear, grief, anger, jealousy, envy, pride—all these emotions make reference to the self and how the self's attachments are doing in the world. Wonder is different: it takes us out of ourselves and toward the other. It is connected to our original joy at life itself. It is at the furthest remove from narcissism or pride. Schopenhauer is right that in responding to a musical work we are detached from our own projects. But he is wrong about the conclusion that, from our detached perspective, we see only worthlessness. (As I said, it is difficult to believe that he consistently endorses that conclusion, given the delight, indeed wonder,

---

[23] See Ronald W. Hepburn, *"Wonder": And Other Essays: Eight Studies in Aesthetics and Neighbouring Fields* (Edinburgh, UK: University of Edinburgh Press, 1984); I discuss wonder in Nussbaum, *Justice for Animals: Our Collective Responsibility* (New York: Simon & Schuster. (2022), and connect it, as here, to both compassion and outrage.

that he expresses in musical beauty.) Instead, music itself helps us overcome the tendency to see worthlessness in human life and to turn from it in disgust. There is marvelous beauty there, and it moves us to wonder. The *kalon* shines through. Next door to wonder, I think, is a wish to protect the beauty that inspires the wonder. When the beauty we hear is assailed by life's events, wonder leads to compassion.

And when the suffering we witness is inflicted wrongfully, not by blind necessity but by human malice and stupidity, we are also, very likely, awakened to anger. Much human anger is retributive: it simply seeks to pay back, and thus to destroy the destroyer, with the thought, "an eye for an eye." There might be a work of art about war that inspired retributive anger: indeed a lot of the martial bugle-blowing military type of music tries to do just that. (Britten's *War Requiem* will deal extensively, and critically, with that type of anger.) That sort of anger, however, could not lead to future peace or reconciliation, but only, as the Greeks saw, to an endless sequence of retributive acts, pain for pain. But there is another type of anger, which I call by the made-up term *Transition-Anger*, in order to emphasize that it turns around and moves toward the future. Its content is, "That's outrageous. That must not happen again." And then this anger seeks to find ways to prevent the bad actions and events in the future. This sort of constructive future-directed anger lies at the heart of all nonviolent justice movements, including those of Gandhi and Martin Luther King Jr., both of whom reject retributive anger and seek a future of justice and reconciliation (see Chapter 5). To get ahead of my story, this is a type of anger that Britten the pacifist can accept and create.

When a musical work engages with the subject of war, then, it can awaken compassion—and associated action to promote peace and reconciliation—only if it finds a way of seeing beauty and worth in the struggles of at least some of the participants, and awakening listeners to wonder at that beauty. If the work awakens anger as well, toward those whose malice or stupidity inflict suffering, it will enable future efforts toward peace and reconciliation (in my view) only if it is Transition-Anger, not retributive anger.

Writing Music about War

Let me now return to Mozart. Figaro's aria sets a problem before the composer embarking on a musical depiction of war: How can it be music if it represents war, which, in effect, is anti-music, lacking melody or harmony? This is part of a perennial and more general question: How can music, which aims at beauty and order, enticing the listener, contain ugliness and disorder? Lessing's *Laocoon* (1766) is a noteworthy philosophical attempt to grapple with this issue in literature and fine art, but the issue arises in music too.

Composers must grapple with it each in their own way. But in general the route that has seemed promising to many is Lessing's: hold on to form and order in some way, abstracting from what would elicit disgust in the listener, but gesturing to the disorder that has inflicted suffering. (Thus Lessing approves of Philoctetes' abstract metrical cry of pain in Sophocles' tragedy—a scream would be too ugly[24]—and of Laocoon's distanced and aesthetically fascinating anguish in the famous sculpture.) Music has an easy time here compared to other arts, since, as psychologists of disgust have noted, there is no aural portal for disgust. A composer depicting war may include some representations of disorder, in the form of dissonance, percussive rhythms that are reminders of cannons and gunfire, and brass instruments that are reminders of bugles. But just as Haydn's *Creation* could begin with a representation of Chaos through a limited use of musical dissonance only

---

[24] This valuable device of Greek tragedy, which has a number of different metrical ways of expressing pain through syllables with no semantic content, is unfortunately untranslatable into any modern language I know, so at that point one must either omit the outcry or instruct the actor to scream. (When we performed *The Trojan Women* at our Law School, the leading actors switched to ancient Greek at the relevant moments.)

because order would shortly burst forth, so a compassionate work about war must also find a way of inspiring wonder through the manifest beauty of some of the human beings and actions it depicts. If no wonder, then no compassion and no outrage.

There is a music of war with which we are all too familiar. It is martial music, often in the rhythm of a march, and often using trumpets and other brass instruments as if the orchestra ere a military band marching with soldiers into battle. A real "concerto" of musical *trombone* (Italian plural) to accompany the blunderbuss "trombone." The marches of John Philip Sousa and the *1812 Overture* of Tchaikovsky are perennially popular examples of this sort of pro-war music, the latter with real cannons at the end. These works march the listener off to battle, so to speak, representing war as a glorious endeavor (for example, Russia's successful resistance to Napoleon's invasion) that will be crowned, or has already been crowned, with success. National anthems, including "The Star-Spangled Banner" and "La Marseillaise," are often war music of this sort, and we can find countless examples in popular film scores and even video game scores. I note that Schopenhauer does not consider this sort really music, because it is too directly representational of a specific life event. "All this is to be rejected," he says (I. 264).

Britten, being a pacifist, would object to this type of music for different reasons: because it glorifies war and urges people on to war. (Thus when he includes such music, it is in a context that invites critical scrutiny.) I am not a pacifist. I think that there are wars that are just and that resistance to tyranny (whether Napoleon's or Hitler's) is one occasion for a just war. People need to stiffen their resolve if they are going to fight such a war, so isn't that a good use for conventional martial music? This music, however, still hides the real pain and chaos of war. Indeed, its purpose is to conceal the suffering, so that people will leap ahead and eagerly take part. I object to this mendacity. With Winston Churchill, I think resistance to tyranny is best faced with a full awareness of the need for "blood, toil, tears, and sweat." Even ex post, with tyranny successfully resisted, taking the full measure of war's pain and cost is crucial in order to orient listeners correctly to the possibility of future wars. So I can agree with Britten that the music of ex post reflection about World War II, with an emphasis on the future, must put suffering front and center—although in Chapter 5 I shall be very critical of his refusal to engage in even supportive civilian functions during that war.

There can also be a music of war that is genuinely Schopenhauerian, representing war and its human costs as worth nothing and the human participants as fools. We might call this Stoic war music. We can find it, for example, in the satirical war music of Prokofiev's *Lieutenant Kije Suite* (originally a film score). (Lieutenant Kije is just a fraud, a nullity, a bureaucratic fiction—and all who believe in his adventures are fools.) Shostakovich is so devious and complicated that I shall not attempt to pronounce which of his works might fit this category, and there are many other examples. During the Vietnam War there was a lot of popular music of this sort. I grew up to the tune of Country Joe and the Fish singing: "And it's one, two, three,/ What are we fighting for? / Don't ask me, I don't give a damn,/ Next stop is Vietnam; / And it's five, six, seven, / Open up the pearly gates, / Well there ain't no time to wonder why, / Whoopee! we're all gonna die." The music of the song, with its false bonhomie, bouncy beat, and cheerful banjo strumming, perfectly conveys the satirical message even without the words. In both of my examples, so different in genre, the surface good humor is accompanied by an underlying melancholy about the real human cost of what is falsely glorified. But there is nothing noble shining through, and nothing beautiful that does not get tarnished by ridicule. The people duped by Kije are fools, and anyone who goes off to fight in Vietnam is also a fool.

Both the glorifying Sousaesque music of war and the sardonic mocking of war are bound to lack serious aesthetic value, if my argument is correct. The glorifying sort is false, obscuring what it purports to represent. And the sardonic belittling sort makes human beings look like Marcus's "crazed mice running for shelter."

There may be a kind of tragic war music that is profoundly pessimistic in its conclusions about what a war has done and the diminished worth of what survives. I think Elgar's Cello Concerto, for example, is in this category, and it has considerable aesthetic value. But Elgar's music attributes worth both to human beings and to the culture that preceded World War I, which war has allegedly destroyed. Humans remain, but as lonely mourners. However, they are not seen as base or absurd.

It would certainly have been theoretically possible for Britten to compose a work of the sardonic belittling sort. But that would have been a scandalous use of his *War Requiem* commission, dooming him to social ostracism henceforth. More important, to write war music in this way would have been false to the love of flawed human beings that is integral to Britten's musical personality, as of Mahler's. This love prevents him even from writing in the Elgar tragic-pessimistic mode, though perhaps in *Owen Wingrave* he approaches it (see Chapter 5) In the early works that I shall shortly discuss, he is always pursuing some deeper and potentially constructive insight, even when he depicts the makers of war with scathing negativity, as in *Our Hunting Fathers*. Moreover, when Britten writes satire or scathing denunciation, it always has some real affection in it: either gentle comic love of all the flawed participants, as in *Albert Herring*, or deep sympathy for the tragically persecuted outcast, as in *Peter Grimes* and *Billy Budd*, and even for at least some of the persecutors (Captain Vere). Britten is no Schopenhauerian, and he would have been incapable of writing Stoic or Schopenhauerian war music, portraying all human striving as worthless.

This remains to be shown, of course. But for now I claim only that there is an open space beyond Sousa and Prokofiev, even beyond Elgar: a space in which the suffering of war is represented truthfully, with all its bodily and emotional costs, but in which the beauty of the human mind, body, and voice (and the mind and body through the voice) "shine through" despite the ongoing presence of the deep, possibly ineliminable, aggression in the psyche that leads human beings to make war, again and again.

War music of this sort (unlike the rah-rah or satirical sorts) can be great music. For Mozart is correct: music in its nature summons us to beauty and enriches our lives by a confrontation with beauty. If seeing beauty truthfully also means seeing persecution, aggression, and ugliness, we still need the beauty, or we don't need the music. Or to put it otherwise: in the perpetual struggle of life against death, meaning against emptiness, music must ultimately be on the side of life.[25]

The view I just expressed is my own. It is also that of Britten—and of Mahler, a kindred spirit. Discussing the last movement ("Der Abschied," "Farewell") of Mahler's *Das Lied von der Erde*, Britten wrote this a letter to a friend in 1937, a rare account of his own personal response to music:

> It is cruel, you know, that music should be so beautiful. It has the beauty of loneliness & of pain; of strength & freedom. The beauty of disappointment & never-satisfied love. The cruel beauty of nature, and everlasting beauty of monotony.
>
> And the essentially "pretty" colours of the normal orchestral palette are used to paint this extraordinary picture of loneliness.

---

[25] Compare Ricardo Muti's speech before the first big Chicago Symphony Orchestra (CSO) concert after the pandemic, at which he conducted Beethoven's "Eroica" Symphony: "Culture is not entertainment. You are not here tonight because you did not know how to spend your evening. You are here tonight because you need music. You need to hear live your fantastic musicians. That is the reason why we are here. We are here to give you emotions, to give you the sound of beauty, of harmony—that sound the world is forgetting. Without music the world will become more and more savage. . . . So I'm asking you to stay close to the Orchestra, . . . not just to hear the music, but to receive through music beauty, harmony, and, as Beethoven said, brotherhood. This is what I wanted to tell you." CSO, *Program Book—Muti Conducts Vivaldi & Handel Water Music* (Chicago: Chicago Symphony Orchestra, 2022), p. 9.

... And there is nothing morbid about it ... I cannot understand it—it passes over me like a tidal wave—and that matters not a jot either, because it goes on for ever, even if it is never performed again—that final chord is printed on the atmosphere.[26]

Even when music addresses death and emptiness, it conveys beauty and value. Schopenhauer understood many things about music, but this—although perhaps he intuitively felt it, lover of music as he was—he could not concede. He was wrong, and Britten (with Mozart and Mahler) are right.

This is a huge topic, which we have not exhausted. It would be worthwhile to examine many more works that grapple with war. But it is now time to turn to Britten. The next two chapters will put to work these Schopenhauerian ideas, showing how in music written during the onset of World War II, Britten explored the roots of war and the body at war and, so to speak, represented the Will on its way to war. Chapter 3 deals with the sources of aggression. In a group of collaborations with the poet W. H. Auden, Britten explored European society's longstanding commitment to aggression against both human and animal bodies, especially targeting those who figure in the social imaginary as "other" or "outsiders." Auden and Britten trace aggression to fear of one's own body, its vulnerability and its unruly desires. Chapter 4 then asks the question I asked of Schopenhauer: is the body, war's target, worth caring about? Here I study parts of three song cycles, two written during the early days of Britten's collaboration and personal love affair with the singer Peter Pears. The early ones are *Illuminations* (the movement "Being Beauteous" was dedicated to Pears, though sung by him only later) and *Seven Sonnets of Michelangelo*, written specifically for Pears as the singer and for Britten as the pianist. These works show the body as fragile, beset by a hostile world, but also as extremely beautiful

---

[26] Quoted in Humphrey Carpenter, *Benjamin Britten: A Biography* (New York: Charles Scribner's Sons, 1992), p. 215.

and lovable, thus casting doubt on Schopenhauer's hostile depiction of love. In *Holy Sonnets of John Donne*, written in 1945 after Britten's return from Belsen, he confronts with agony the wickedness of which humans are evidently capable, and finds a hint of possible mercy in the beauty of the human form.

3

Britten, Auden, and the Spirit of War: Persecuting Bodies

Only Hate was happy, hoping to augment
his practice now, and his dingy clientele
　who think they can be cured by killing
　and covering the garden with ashes.
　　　—W. H. Auden, "In Memory of Sigmund Freud" (1940)

Fido, A Dog. and Moppet and Poppet, Two Cats:
　　From a Pressure Group that says I am the Constitution,
　　From those who say Patriotism and mean Persecution,
　　From a Tolerance that is really inertia and delusion . . .

Chorus:
　　Save animals and men
　　　　　　　　　　—Auden, Libretto for the Auden/Britten
　　　　　　　　　　　　operetta *Paul Bunyan*, 1940

Violence against the body is a constant theme in Benjamin Britten's work.[1] A committed pacifist, he addressed the ubiquity of violence—against both humans and animals—in works from at least the early song cycle *Our Hunting Fathers*, with libretto by W. H. Auden, to the very late *Owen Wingrave* (1970). To understand the

---

[1] See Donald Mitchell, "Violent Climates," in *The Cambridge Companion to Benjamin Britten*, edited by Mervyn Cooke (Cambridge, UK: Cambridge University Press, 1999), 188–216.

The Tenderness of Silent Minds. Martha C. Nussbaum, Oxford University Press.
© Oxford University Press 2024. DOI: 10.1093/oso/9780197568538.003.0003

War Requiem, we must try to understand his lifelong pursuit of this preoccupation.

Like his early collaborator, W. H. Auden, Britten sought the roots of violence in his culture, which treated blood sports (fox hunting, hawking) as great fun and as definitive of the dominant classes. But, again like Auden, he then traced the glorification of violence to something deeper in the human psyche, something that Auden, in the poem that opens *Our Hunting Fathers*, calls "pride," an arrogant assertion of dominance that masks an inner fear—a fear of the unruly aspects of the body and spirit that comprise our vulnerability and mortality—longing, sexual desire, bodily frailty, and the anticipation of death. By hunting animals, our fathers (who are, Auden reminds us, both "our past and our future") pretend that they are not mortal animals. By banding together as a class, as a crowd, they suppress dissident voices of protest. "O pride so hostile to our charity," Auden concludes the Prologue. "But what their pride has retained, we may by charity more generously recover."

Who is this "we"? Repeatedly, both Britten and Auden identify themselves with, and as, outsiders, as "other"—consequently as targets of the pride of the hunters.[2] They were outsiders as opponents of war in a bellicose culture, as men drawn to same-sex relationships[3] in a culture that made their sex lives illegal, as artists in philistine British culture that trusted only tame, docile artists, as leftists in the middle-class Tory culture from which both men came and to whom their music must inevitably be addressed; above all as lonely individuals in a solidaristic culture.

And what is "our charity"? We must answer this question later on, but briefly here: it is the unsparing clear-eyed look of the artist at human desire and frailty, a compassionate yet truthful gaze that

---

[2] See Paul Kildea, "Britten, Auden and 'Otherness,'" in *The Cambridge Companion to Benjamin Britten*, edited by Mervyn Cooke (Cambridge, UK: Cambridge University Press, 1999), 36–53.

[3] Throughout, I avoid the word *gay* because both Britten and Pears disliked it, feeling that it trivialized the pain society inflicted on people through its aggression.

Auden associates with the work of Sigmund Freud in his great poem "In Memory of Sigmund Freud" (1940), to which I shall return. Britten and Auden take the side of the outsider and see human weakness with compassion.

In this chapter I will examine the early Britten–Auden partnership, focusing on *Our Hunting Fathers*, which Britten called "my real Opus 1," but also dealing more briefly with *Sinfonia da Requiem*, *Ballad of Heroes*, and *Paul Bunyan*. I will argue that the work of the two is not political in the obvious overt sense suggested by Donald Mitchell in his wonderful book *Britten and Auden in the Thirties: The Year 1936*[4]—that is, the song cycle is not, or is only tangentially, a warning about the rise of Nazism. Instead, the work delves deeper to excavate the roots of violence, finding it in the fear of self and the consequent fearful clinging to one's group.

I shall also argue that the dark vision of the song cycle has nothing at all to do with Britten's sexual history. So many of his interpreters have felt a discomfort about homosexuality that they then project onto Britten, reading parts of the cycle as agonized expressions of guilt and torment. But there is no sign of torment in the man (whose diaries and letters are all published), nor is there gay panic in the music. The panic is a human panic about mortality and fragility, a panic characteristic above all of the "fathers," though Auden and Britten would be hypocrites if they asserted, as they do not, that they stood above this universal human fearfulness. In Auden's vision, as we shall see, sexuality, and, more generally, human finitude, human longing, is what makes certain people become marked victims, outsiders; but it is also what, if faced with generosity and honesty, even love and delight, makes for a "charity" that might enable people somehow to rebuild Europe's flawed and self-devouring culture. When Freud died, wrote Auden, "Only Hate was happy,

---

[4] Donald Mitchell, *Britten and Auden in the Thirties: The Year 1936*, The T.S. Eliot Memorial Lectures Delivered at the University of Kent at Canterbury in November 1979 (1981/2000).

hoping to augment / his practice now, and his dingy clientele / who think they can be cured by killing / and covering the garden with ashes." War wells up from a sense that human frailty is intolerable, a disease that only slaughter can cure.

Is this happy regeneration possible? This question hangs over the song cycle, over even the American cheeriness of *Paul Bunyan*; it hangs, still, over the *War Requiem* in 1962, with its project of postwar reconciliation.

In this chapter we see Britten attaining confident maturity as a composer. His collaboration with Auden did much to deepen his insights into politics and human desire. And yet I shall repeatedly express exasperation with Auden, for the way in which, again and again, he failed to do his best work in this partnership, trying to get away with lazy and inferior writing for the performed collaborative works, while at the same time producing some of his most wonderful poems. Part of the reason for this failure seems to have been his contempt for audiences, and in general for "the masses," an attitude unworthy of someone seeking to advise the public on important matters, an attitude that Britten never shared. (Some of his most wonderful songs are arrangements of familiar English folk songs.) But my exasperation springs even more from the feeling that if a task is not worth doing seriously, with one's best work, it should not be undertaken at all. Britten always did his best work, and it is fortunate that in some cases the brilliance of the music transcends the sloppiness of the libretti. With the *War Requiem*, he wisely chose, in Wilfred Owen, a dead great poet and one whose work he could adapt to his own purpose.

Britten, Auden, and the Onset of War

Benjamin Britten (1913–1976) was born in Suffolk, the county that he loved and always called home. He was, in his own words, "very ordinary middle-class," the son of a dentist. The youngest of four siblings, he had at the age of three months a serious bout of pneumonia that almost killed him and left him with a damaged heart.[5] (He recovered sufficiently to lead an active life, but it was eventually of heart disease that he died at the relatively young age of sixty-three.) During the Great War he was a small boy, and there is no record of any impact of that war on his psyche. He was doted on by his mother and his sisters, and had a happy, pampered childhood. His mother, an excellent amateur singer[6] and a stager of musical soirées, began teaching him, and his talent was soon recognized. (He remained close to his mother as long as she lived, and to his siblings, especially his sister Beth [1909–1989].[7])

Going to prep school as a day boy, he recalled being ordinary and basically happy[8]—with one exception. He later said that his interest in pacifism began with his horrified reaction to the regime of corporal punishment at the school:

> I can remember the first time—I think it was the very first day that I was in school—that I heard a boy being beaten, and I can remember my absolute astonishment that people didn't

---

[5] See Carpenter (1992, p. 6). His source is Britten's older sister Beth. See also the fine biography by Paul Kildea, *Benjamin Britten: A Life in the Twentieth Century* (London: Allen Lane, 2013), superior to Carpenter on musical matters and able to use all the diaries and letters.

[6] People in the Britten circle knew that his mother sang a lot to him as a boy, and they noticed (or imagined) a striking resemblance between his mother's vibrant contralto and Peter Pears's high tenor. Thanks to Colin Ure for this recollection.

[7] Beth's daughter, Sally Schweizer, played a role in the Britten centenary in 2013.

[8] In 1956 he wrote a record-jacket note for a recording of his *Simple Symphony* portraying his young self: "Once upon a time there was a prep-school boy. He was called Britten mi., his initials were E. B., his age was nine, and his locker was number seventeen. He was quite an ordinary little boy . . . ; he loved cricket, only quite liked football (although he kicked a pretty "corner"); he adored mathematics, got on all right with history, was scared by Latin Unseen; he behaved fairly well, only ragged the recognized amount, so that his contacts with the cane or the slipper were happily rare (although one nocturnal expedition to stalk ghosts left its marks behind); he worked his way up the school slowly and steadily. . . . But—there was one curious thing about this boy: he wrote music. His friends bore with it, his enemies kicked a bit but not for long (he was quite tough), the staff couldn't object if his work and games didn't suffer. He wrote lots of it, reams and reams of it." Quoted in Carpenter (1992, p. 9). This account is doctored for the occasion, of course, but does seem to be the record of a basically happy time at school.

immediately rush to help him. And to find that it was sort of condoned and accepted was something that shocked me very much. Whether or not it all grew from that I don't know. [In the context, "it" is clearly his pacifism.[9]]

Britten's long-time life partner and great love, the tenor Peter Pears (1910–1986), believed that this occasion was indeed the origin of Britten's pacifism—though we could also say that being loved as a child and not beaten is an even deeper origin. Pears reports that Britten organized some type of protest against corporal punishment in the school, "and he got into a certain amount of trouble about that."[10] This period ended abruptly, it seems, when, in an assigned graduation essay on "Animals," he wrote an attack on hunting for sport and even suggested that their brutalizing effect was a cause of war. The essay was not even marked, and he left school.[11] His next school was a boarding school, Gresham's at

---

[9] A newspaper interview of 1971, quoted in Carpenter (1992, p. 10). Britten's sister Barbara, however, reports that Britten avoided being bullied for such attitudes because he was "quite good with his fists." See Carpenter (1992, p. 12).

[10] Quoted in Carpenter (1992, p. 10). Carpenter also spends some time on a report by Britten's ex-friend Eric Crozier (dropped by Britten in the 1950s and henceforth ignored) that he reported having been sexually abused by one of the masters at the school; he apparently used the word *rape*. Crozier is the only source for this story, and most of Britten's friends view it with great skepticism, all the more since Crozier was one of the former friends who had been suddenly "dropped" by Britten. It seems to me decisive that Pears, who spoke very openly about sexual matters, did not mention it, and in the nature of their long relationship he surely would have known of any such incident. It would appear from Carpenter's account of his interview with Crozier that Crozier was trying to find some cause for Britten's being gay, as if sexual abuse could have produced delighted love of male bodies and a happy thirty-seven year marriage. Far more pertinent to the sexual banter he and Pears exchange is the happy experience of being the baby of the family, doted on and fondly held by all. Pears frequently addresses him as "Dear Pussy Cat" and draws pictures of a cat in his love letters. See Chapter 4.

[11] Stevenson (n.d.), "Benjamin Britten: Our Hunting Fathers, Song Cycle for High Voice & Orchestra, Op. 8." *https://www.allmusic.com/composition/our-hunting-fathers-song-cycle-for-high-voice-orchestra-op-8-mc0002373256*. The author is Joseph Stevenson, and in the manner of such notes he does not identify his source. The same anecdote is reported by Graham Johnson, *Britten, Voice and Piano: Lectures on the Vocal Music of Benjamin Britten* (London: Routledge, 2017). Oddly, Carpenter does not mention either this incident or the end of Britten's time at the prep school: at this point, he turns to Britten's early musical compositions.

Norfolk, which he did not like very well. W. H. Auden (1907–1973), who attended Gresham's a few years earlier, said that he understood fascism through his experience there: its repression of dissent and individuality made it "a Fascist State."[12]

Meanwhile, however, by the time he was 14 (in 1927), Britten had already been introduced by a friend of his mother to the composer Frank Bridge, who began to teach him, recognizing Britten's prodigious talent. In 1930 he received a scholarship to the Royal College of Music. His first musical works soon began to be performed in public.

In 1935, he was engaged to write music for the UK General Post Office's (GPO) documentary film division. There he met Auden and formed a close friendship with the slightly older man, at first asymmetrical and worshipful, but with Britten gradually asserting himself as an equal. Britten's diaries show keen awareness of the Nazi threat, the situation of Europe's Jews, and the war against fascism in Spain. In the increasingly fraught climate of public anxiety about the Nazi threat, the two embarked on a series of collaborations, both in Britain and, after the two both left separately for the United States in 1939, in America as well. The two shared the view that artists have a public responsibility, a view that Auden later gave up, but Britten never did. And whereas Auden was also ready for actual service, driving an ambulance in Spain and later volunteering to return from the United States to serve (he was denied because of his age), Britten became a conscientious objector (see Chapter 5) and maintained consistently that the best thing artists could do in time of war was to address the issues in their work.

A constant theme in the friendship was their shared awareness of being outsiders—because of their left-wing views, their rebellion against middle-class conformity, their vocation as artists, and their homosexuality. Auden, happily and relatively openly

---

[12] See Kildea (1999).

living a same-sex sexual life, encouraged Britten to have an active sex life and seems to have been infatuated with him. Britten was not attracted to Auden, and was hesitant and celibate at the time. Because he kept detailed diaries of both professional and personal matters, we know that his first sexual affair was with the slightly younger Wulff Scherchen,[13] a budding poet from a prominent musical family.

Meanwhile, Pears and Britten were sharing a flat, and Britten's diaries show that he thought of Peter as a fine person and friend. But the two did not become physically intimate until the move to the United States, a move that Pears strongly urged, perhaps in the hope of separating him from Scherchen. The Pears–Britten sexual relationship began in 1939 in Grand Rapids, Michigan, on a visit to Pears's friends—an event Pears remembered as a turning point in both of their lives (perhaps with slight amusement about the unromantic nature of the place).[14] Britten was slower to fall deeply in love

---

[13] Scherchen (1920–2016) was the son of conductor Hermann Scherchen, a friend of Schoenberg. Britten first met him while traveling with his parents in 1934, but then didn't see him again until 1938, when Scherchen was living in England. They had a very passionate, but brief, affair, which more or less ended with Britten and Pears's departure to the United States, though passionate letters continued, overlapping slightly the beginning of the Pears–Britten affair. Scherchen commented that Britten always seemed extremely boyish to him, and he had no awareness of a meaningful age difference. Sadly, Scherchen was later embittered by his experience of internment as an enemy alien; Britten found him unpleasant and "vindictive" after the war and did not renew any social tie (Kildea, 2013, p. 217). Scherchen changed his name to John Woolford, taking the surname of the woman whom he married; he died in Australia in 2016 at the age of ninety-six, shortly after his wife died. In 2015, the Australian composer Lyle Chan obtained permission from the ninety-five-year-old Scherchen to make a song cycle out of the letters between him and Britten. The work, *Serenade for Tenor, Saxophone, and Orchestra* ("My Dear Benjamin"), was premiered by the Queensland Symphony Orchestra in 2016. The work was awarded the Orchestral Work of the Year Award at the 2017 Australasian Art Music Awards. The relationship between Scherchen and Britten is extremely well covered in Kildea's biography, with ample quotations from the letters, though that final chapter postdates the publication of the biography in 2013.

[14] Pears wrote the following January, "I shall never forget a certain night in Grand Rapids"; and thirty-five years later, in 1974, "It is *you* who have given *me* everything, right from the beginning, from yourself in Grand Rapids!" Vicki P. Stroeher, Nicholas Clark, and Jude Brimmer, *My Beloved Man: The Letters of Benjamin Britten and Peter Pears*. Aldeburgh Studies in Music 10 (Woodbridge, UK: Boydell & Brewe, 2016, letter number 8 [January 9, 1940], letter number 351 [November 21, 1974]).

with Pears: he continued to write passionate letters to Scherchen for some months. In *Les Illuminations* (1939), one song, "Antique," was dedicated to Scherchen and one, "Being Beauteous," to Pears. Soon, however, Pears won out, and for thirty-seven years the two men lived and worked together with deep devotion, forming one of the great creative/romantic partnerships in musical history, perhaps in all history.[15]

Even though Britten became sexually active relatively late and may have worried, before her death, about his beloved mother's likely reaction (she died in 1937), there is no sign of deep psychological trauma, self-hatred, or oppressive guilt, often though others mention these ideas in order to explain dark themes in Britten's music—as if a gay man *must* be tormented, a common homophobic trope. Britten adjusted to his new life with joy and delight, and seems always to have connected his own sex life with ideas of beauty, joy, and creative freedom.

This is the context, in Britten's life, for the series of early works in which he and Auden explored aggression against the body and the underlying causes of war. Among the collaborations is the song cycle, *Our Hunting Fathers* (1936), an important work that explores the roots of violent aggression and compares English blood sports to war, with explicit reference to the German persecution of Jews. There were also two film scores, a choral work celebrating the Republicans in the Spanish Civil War, in which Auden was an ambulance driver (*Ballad of Heroes*, 1940), and an operetta depicting a mythic America and exploring themes of liberty and exile (*Paul Bunyan*, 1941). The two men then grew apart, differing about pacifism, about the public role of the artist, and about the importance of the artist in maintaining an ironic distance from middle-class life and domesticity (Auden romanticizing outsider status, and

---

[15] The letters of the two were left by Pears to the nation and are in a museum at Aldeburgh. They are published in Stroeher, Clark, and Brimmer (2016). As we'll see in Chapter 4, the love continued, deep and unbroken, until Britten's death.

Britten prospering in his newly settled domestic life, of which Auden disapproved). As we shall see, they differed all along about some key aesthetic issues. Auden, in addition to being a terrible librettist who devoted minimal effort to the task, also had a smug esoteric disdain for the "masses" that undercut even the useful texts he supplied. Britten never had that type of arrogant cleverness, and his music, though sometimes sandbagged by a terrible text, as in *Paul Bunyan*, never fails to delve deeply into real human issues, successfully in *Our Hunting Fathers*, a work that was badly received at its premiere but whose value has now become widely evident.

Our Hunting Fathers, Opus 8

Our Hunting Fathers was written for high voice and has been sung by both sopranos and tenors. Sophie Wyss, a singer whose lyric soprano Britten admired, sang at the premiere, but it was later recorded by Peter Pears, and today is sung by both voices. Britten repeatedly described it to others, and in his diary, as a work about animals. It consists of five movements: three central movements setting earlier texts chosen but not composed by Auden, framed by a Prologue and an Epilogue written by Auden. Throughout, Auden's contributions are obscure, fortunately redeemed by the fact that most of the text is not by him. Britten's musical setting shows extraordinary maturity and daring, harmonic, rhythmic, and emotional.

The Prologue, by Auden, is sung as recitative: "They are our past and our future. . . . / O pride so hostile to our charity. / But what their pride has retained, we may by charity more generously recover." The first line and especially the last lines are significant; the rest is obscure and artificial, so I shall not quote the whole text.

The first of the three central movements, Rats Away!, is a musical and emotional tour de force. It has both dazzled and puzzled interpreters. Let us begin with the text, an anonymous medieval prayer of exorcism:

> I command that all the rats that are hereabout
> That none dwell in this place, within or without;
> Through the virtue of Jesus that Mary bore,
> Whom all creatures must ever adore;
> And through the virtue of Mark, Matthew, Luke and John,
> All four Archangels, that are as one;
> Through the virtue of Saint Gertrude, that maid clean,
>> God grant in grace
>> That no rats dwell in the place
>> That these names were uttered in.
>> And through the virtue of St. Kasi,
>> That holy man who prayed to God Almighty
>>> Of the scathes they did
>>> The meadows amid
>>> By day and night
> God bid them flee and go out of every man's sight.
> Dominus, Deus, Sabaoth, Emmanuel, great name of God,
> Deliver this place from rats and from all other shame.
> God save this place from all other wicked wights
>> Both by days and by nights,
> Et in nomine Patris et Filii et Sancti Spiriti, Amen.

It seems to be a straightforward prayer. The music, however, is doing things that are far more complicated. It begins with an explosive crash from brass and timpani, followed by rapid, short ascending runs from the woodwinds and later the strings, often with piercing shrillness (punctuated by other explosions from brass and timpani), that give a definite impression of scurrying—the rats moving around in the house. Before long, the runs invade the whole orchestra. When the singer enters, it is not on the words of the prayer at all, but on the single word "Ra. . . . . a. . . . . a. . . . . . ts," as the voice imitates the upward runs of the orchestra and ascends melismatically in a long sequence of runs—punctuated by rests—from middle C to a high A. Referring to the complexity of the orchestration and the virtuosic use of the voice, as like another orchestral instrument, Donald Mitchell remarks, "I think we may be confident that nothing quite like this music had been heard before in the UK of 1936."[16]

The voice now sings the prayer rather simply, against a sparse orchestration. Peace appears to be restored. By the time we get to Saints Gertrude and Kasi, however, occasional scurrying sounds can again be heard from the orchestra. As the prayer continues, the rat motif invades the orchestra more and more, and eventually also the voice, which begins to sing "Rats" again, starting just before "and from all other shame." The syllable interrupts the prayer more and more frequently, until the ending is like this:

> *Et in nomine* (Rats!) *Patris et* (Rats!)
> *Filii* (Rats!) *et Sanc-* (Rats!) *ti Spiriti,*
> (Rats! Rats! Rats! Rats! Rats!) *Amen.*

The rats, it seems, have won, frustrating the exorcism. Mitchell draws attention to the way in which, as the rat motif reforms itself in the orchestra, a "baleful tuba solo is added to the texture, the most subversive and menacing sound of all."[17] He admits he speaks from hindsight, in the light of the use of the tuba in Britten's *Death in Venice* (1973) as the bearer of the plague. But I would agree with Mitchell that we are justified in hearing an ominous meaning in the tuba, even in this early work.

We now face two questions: who is asking for help to evict rats from the house, and what do the rats themselves represent? Since Mitchell gives a superb description of the music, and since, more generally, he is one of Britten's greatest interpreters, it is natural,

---

[16] Mitchell (1981/2000), p. 36.
[17] Ibid., p. 37.

first, to turn to him. In Mitchell's view, the rats are Nazis, and the way the rat motif suffuses the orchestra is like the way Nazism is seen to be spreading in Europe. The speaker, then, speaks from a subject-position like that of Britten and Auden: someone who sees the danger and wants the rats out of the house.

It is an odd way to hear the music, since the music depicts the speaker as hysterical and out of control, through the shrill runs and outbursts and the sudden occurrences of "Rats" inside what is supposed to be a sober prayer. It seems that the speaker is a terrified person who desperately wants to drive out something that is all too near and who is not reluctant to use divine powers to kill this ratlike something. This seems an unlikely position for two nonconformist artists to represent themselves as occupying.

But there are further reasons to reject Mitchell's reading, many of them set out cogently in a fine article by Joanna Bullivant.[18] First of all, Nazis were not represented as rats at this time: on the contrary, it was Nazis who depicted Jews as rats. This was well known and would have been known to Auden. "Rats," then, is a pejorative description of a hated outsider, used to justify persecution and extermination.

Second, by invoking the Trinity and the Saints, and speaking the Latin of the traditional liturgy, the speaker sets him- or herself on the side of Christian conventionality, not on the side of Auden and Britten, atheists and outsiders. (In Auden's Freud poem, it is the "cultures of conceit" that call upon God.) Britten's own account supports this:

> [It is] very satirical, and likely to cause a good amount of comment—especially the prayer to God to rid the house of rats. It has always puzzled me to think what the rats [sic] opinion must

[18] Joanna Bullivant, "'Practical Jokes': Britten and Auden's Our Hunting Fathers Revisited." In *Literary Britten: Words and Music in Benjamin Britten's Vocal Works*, edited by Kate Kennedy. Aldeburgh Studies in Music 13 (Woodbridge, UK: Boydell & Brewer, 2018).

be of God (naturally the same God—vide the Bible and sparrows etc.) while being poisoned in the name of the Lord. Consequently you can imagine the setting isn't reverent.[19]

I would further comment that here Britten anticipates his practice in the *War Requiem*, where the voices of soldiers, war's victims, are set against the background of the Latin mass, whose conventionality they call into question. Latin is on the side of tradition, the tradition of a hunting, war-making, outsider-persecuting culture.

To Bullivant's sound point I can add others. Animals throughout the cycle are depicted as victims (even if occasionally used by proxy to damage other animals) and are seen with sympathy. Hunting evinces "a pride so hostile to our charity," and the "our" clearly includes Auden and Britten, who aim "by charity" "more generously" to "recover" what pride has left behind. In *Paul Bunyan* too, the dog and the cats are chosen as primary voices of sympathy, both given and received. More generally, Auden elsewhere (for example, in the Freud poem) uses references to animals to signify the ungovernable insides of human desire, which the dominant culture suppresses, often by a terrified aggression. It is not from the point of view of the hunted outsider, whether Jewish or homosexual (Auden often compares the two persecutions), that outsiders look like vermin: it is the persecuting culture, the culture of "our hunting fathers," who see outsiders as vermin and seek to drive them out and exterminate them.

One further argument, not in the text, is supplied by the music. The ascending runs on the exclamation "Rats!," representing the scurrying of rats, are picked up again with the syllabus "rret" of the hunting cry "Whurret" in the "Dance of Death." It is Britten's setting that carves off the "rret" from "Whu" and repeats it obsessively on an ascending run. The speaker of "Rats Away," then, is the

---

[19] Donald Mitchell and Philip Reed, eds., *Letters from a Life: The Selected Letters and Diaries of Benjamin Britten 1913–1976.* Vol. 1: 1923–1939 (London: Faber & Faber Reed, 1991), vol. I, p. 409).

same subject as the hunter of the "Dance of Death," and that hunter represents our hunting fathers, seeking to kill animals, including Jews, who, as we shall see, are repeatedly named as prey in that movement. I think this clinches the case against seeing the speaker in "Rats" as a representative of Auden and Britten.

So: the speaker is not an Englishman trying to fend off Nazis. Nor is he or she a representative of the young Britten, said by some critics to be fearful about his own sexuality.[20] The speaker is a representative of our hunting fathers, seeking to exterminate an outsider seen as deviant and impious.

But why is the tone of the voice so terrified? What is really being expressed in this musically extraordinary outburst? A standard Auden theme during this period is that persecution stems from fear of one's own insides, seen as frightening and deviant, the rats in the house. Freud's death made "Hate" glad because it stopped a source of self-knowledge and self-toleration that might possibly undermine fear and thus mitigate hatred. Through Freud, the "unhappy Present" might become "life-forgiven and more humble, / able to approach the Future as a friend / without a wardrobe of excuses, without / a set mask of rectitude." Freud showed us, Auden continues, that evil is not "deeds that must be punished" but "our dishonest mood of denial." We can debate, and later, with Britten's *War Requiem*, we shall, whether this is a sufficient account of the evils of war. But it seems clear to me that this is the account of evil that is represented in "Rats Away!"

The other two middle movements can be more briefly analyzed. "Messalina" depicts the grief of the Roman empress over the death of her pet monkey. The music is very serious and not at all satirical. The musical depiction of her weeping—in a long cadenza on

[20] See Carpenter (1992, pp. 82–6); Philip Brett, "Auden's Britten," in *Music and Sexuality in Britten: Selected Essays*, edited by Philip Brett and George E. Haggerty (Berkeley: University of California Press, 2006), the former in terms of "sublimated sadism" (see summary in Brett), the latter suggesting, instead, anger at the dominant culture that will not permit him to express his feelings.

the syllable "Fie"—is operatic, an eloquent expression of a terrible grief.[21] Some critics have thought that Britten's aim is to depict perverse or deformed grief. They think this for two reasons: first, they think grieving so much over the death of an animal is perverse. That, however, is the view of *Our Hunting Fathers* and cannot possibly be that of Britten, who was willing to be expelled from school for defending the rights of animals.[22] Second, they note that Messalina is known for sexual excess. But of course it is clearly Auden's aim to discredit those who label the sexuality of others as excessive or perverse. As Bullivant says, "[I]f Messalina's grief repels the reader, Auden does not condone such a reaction, but rather turns a spotlight on the conventions—like those of the Oxford Don—that show horror at excessive love."[23] (Here she refers to another early Auden poem, "The Orators," in which an Oxford Don says, "I don't feel quite happy about pleasure.")

Here Mitchell's usually unerring sense for the music leads him to a similar conclusion. He sees the audience as shocked at first: all this *for a monkey*? But "the music, by audaciously inverting the scale of feeling and discharging it with such irresistible conviction . . . adds a whole new dimension to the text: the shock of it should shake one into a new perception of what men and animals might mean to each other."[24] He is right that all this is done by the music; by itself the text might lend itself to a more satirical and less earnest setting. And his conclusion is not precisely the same as Bullivant's, endorsing Auden's pro-pleasure stance. For Mitchell (and I believe he is correct), the music is utterly sincere and is all about grief and

[21] See Philip Rupprecht, *Britten's Musical Language. Music in the 20th Century* (Cambridge, UK: Cambridge University Press, 2001, pp. 6–14), who interprets the cycle. He is especially interesting on "Messalina," pointing to the interplay between the voice and orchestral instruments—flute, oboe, clarinet, saxophone—in gestures of lamentation. He suggests that the instruments mimic the wordless utterances of the animal world, especially in the flute's birdlike calls.

[22] He and Pears were great dog-lovers, and Pears even wrote a book about dachshunds.

[23] Bullivant, " 'Practical Jokes' " (p. 215). By contrast, Kildea's biography twice calls the movement a "mad scene." See Kildea (2013, pp. 119–20).

[24] Mitchell (1981/2000, p. 41).

deep attachment. The reference to pleasure is not in the music. Auden and Britten have different sensibilities, and Britten is beginning to become himself.

Finally, we arrive at the spectacular "Dance of Death (Hawking for the Partridge)," a movement of great harmonic daring and rhythmic invention. The poem by Thomas Ravenscroft (1588–1635), slightly revised by Auden, depicts a hunter gleefully goading on his birds and dogs, repeatedly calling "Whurret." (Although it is hawking that is depicted, Britten didn't really notice, and later he described the movement as being about fox hunting—with which he was of course better acquainted.[25]) The dogs and birds all have names, prominently including "German" and "Jew." These two names are actually in Ravenscroft, but they are repeated and given special prominence in Britten's musical setting: at the end, as if a coda, there are two final, hushed "Whurrets"—and, following them, sotto voce, the words *German. Jew.*[26] (Of course, strictly speaking, giving the name "Jew" to an aggressive animal is inappropriate, but the mysterious whispered text conveys clearly enough the meaning of pursuer and prey.)

This movement takes us closer to our topic of war. The "pride" of our hunting fathers includes an idea that masculinity requires a type of tough imperviousness to bodily pain and vulnerability—the performance that is often called "manning up," being a "real man," where this means not being soft, in pain, or even in desire.[27] Our "fathers" went hunting, engaging in cruel blood sports, because they wanted to show how tough they were, and they goad on their

---

[25] See ibid., pp. 53–54 n. 30; in a 1936 program note, Britten still refers to birds, but by 1950 he refers only to dogs, "suggesting . . .that what may have been uppermost in Britten's mind all along was the traditional form of hunting—the one, by the way, with which his audience would have been presumed to be most familiar."

[26] Mitchell plausibly says that this coda is probably Britten's idea, since it is not in Ravenscroft's or Auden's text.

[27] See Michael Warner, "Manning Up," in *American Guy: Masculinity in American Law and Literature*, edited by Saul Levmore and Martha C. Nussbaum (New York: Oxford University Press, 2014).

birds and dogs to inflict carnage in the service of an ideal of manly sport. The "Dance of Death" (a repeated obsession in Britten's works of this period) is the performance of a particularly manic and unstable version of masculine toughness. The speaker calls on his birds and dogs, and they charge after the prey—but the whole exercise, in Britten's rhythmically and harmonically daring composition, quickly gets out of control and spirals into death and disaster, in a wild tarantella. In a program note, Britten drew attention to the way in which the hunt repeatedly breaks down.[28] The drive to use animals to inflict carnage on other creatures (real animals, our own animality, other humans whom we represent as animals) is inherently unstable, leading not only to unspeakable crimes (the killing of Jews by Germans) but also to an implosion, a collapse of the self.

"Hawking" depicts a single hunter, but the activity of hunting has already been established as corporate, as that of "our fathers." It is important that for both Auden and Britten, persecution is a crowd phenomenon, the masses ganging up on the "deviant" individuals or groups that fail to conform. Britten's later depiction of persecution by the crowd in works ranging from the tragic *Peter Grimes* to the comic *Albert Herring* follows this same pattern. In short: as Auden writes in the Freud poem, "To be free / is often to be lonely." And the lonely are all too likely to be victims of group hatred.

Our Hunting Fathers ends with an Epilogue, a poem Auden published separately in 1934. It is highly obscure, not among his best works. It is difficult to make much sense of it or to connect it to the cycle, and I shall not try here. Mitchell and many others have felt it is not only obscure per se but especially unfortunate in a musical work, which must be comprehensible in performance. Mitchell says that he understands it better after reading Edward Mendelson's account of it in *Early Auden*, but he still thinks it a poor choice for a performed work. I don't love it even separately, even after reading Mendelson; I think that Auden's Freud poem,

---

[28] See Carpenter (1992, p. 88), referring to Mitchell and Reed (1991).

nearly contemporaneous, gives us much better access to the themes of the cycle.[29]

Britten seems to have been dissatisfied too, since he added a purely orchestral Epilogue to the Epilogue, an ironic Mahlerian funeral march, the first of several he would compose in this period. Mitchell brilliantly describes it as "a kind of spectral hunting music, a requiem for those who were danced, hunted, to death."[30]

The surprising complexity and novelty of the music[31] caused resistance at the first rehearsal. Soprano soloist Sophie Wyss reports that the musicians openly made fun of the music for "Rats Away!" at the first rehearsal and even "ran about pretending they were chasing rats on the floor."[32] Britten wrote in his diary that at this point he felt "pretty suicidal . . . the most catastrophic evening of my life."[33] Senior composer and respected authority Ralph Vaughan Williams had to intervene to reprove the musicians (not a wonderful situation for a young composer to be in), and from that point on they played very well. Britten was ultimately satisfied with the quality of the performance. (He noted that his mother really disliked "Rats."[34]) The reviews were silly and did not try to grapple seriously with the work. Britten was chided for juvenile cleverness, for "dire nonsense," and a lot more of what Kildea rightly calls "cloth-eared pontificating."[35] Nobody confronted the serious content of the work or its meaning for its ominous year. Critical opinion has by now completely reversed itself, and the work is generally seen as one of his best early works.

---

[29] See Mitchell (1981/2000, p. 54, n. 3) and Edward Mendelson, *Early Auden* (London: Faber & Faber, 1981, pp. 200–201). Mendelson treats the poem in isolation and in general completely ignores Auden's work as librettist, probably a wise choice for one who admires Auden.

[30] Mitchell (1981/2000, p. 49).

[31] Britten was very interested in Stravinsky at this time, as well as Mahler.

[32] Carpenter (1992, p. 88), quoting from her account.

[33] Mitchell and Reed (1991).

[34] Ibid., diary entry of June 11, 936: "She disapproves very thoroughly of 'Rats', but that is almost an incentive—no actual insult to her tho'."

[35] Kildea (2013, pp. 120–21).

Our Hunting Fathers depicts, to use Schopenhauer's language, the Will at work in the world: the aggressive desires of a whole class, seeking to inflict destruction on their victims, both animals and humans. It asks us to take up a position of detachment from our own fears and desires in order to comprehend the roots of this aggression in others and in ourselves. It moves us to outrage and inclines us toward compassion for the victims of aggression. And yet, the bodies of victims do not really appear, or, in "Rats!," appear only from the point of view of the fearful exorcist and therefore appear as disgusting. We are never asked to see victim bodies as lovable or worth defending—or only in a highly abstract way. So a part of our compassion remains incomplete. This aspect of war—the beauty and worth of victims—is central to the *War Requiem*. And Britten begins to address this theme already in works of the early 1940s, as we shall see in the following chapter.

From Auden to *Peter Grimes*

Three other works of this period shed more light on Britten's early approach to war; two are his final collaborations with Auden. I pass over lesser compositions: two film scores with Auden and two short works that Kildea rightly calls "awkwardly martial"[36]: *Advance Democracy* with poet Ronald Swingler, and the jaunty *Pacifist March* with an inferior text by Ronald Duncan.[37]

Ballad of Heroes (Op. 14, 1939) was written rapidly, in a period of several days, for a Festival of Music for the People, commemorating British members of the International Brigade who had died defending the Republican cause in Spain. It is an underrated work that deserves performance. Britten was ambivalent about the war in Spain, but, led on by Auden, he apparently reconciled it with

[36] Kildea (2013, pp. 128–29).
[37] "March, March, stride to resist, / strong with force not with fist."

his pacifism, up to a point, by thinking that the Republicans were underdogs and were in the right. In this work he takes a next step beyond *Fathers*, addressing the worth of the victims' lives in mourning them and setting texts by poet Ronald Swingler and by Auden.

Ballad is a cantata for tenor soloist, chorus, and orchestra. The first movement is another funeral march, an obsession of Britten's when confronting the topic of war in this period. This opening movement sets a text by Swingler in which the chorus asks English people, depicted as currently uninvolved, to drop their detachment and honor the fallen:

> . . . To you we speak, you numberless Englishmen,
> To remind you of the greatness still among you
> Created by these men who go from your towns
> To fight for peace, for liberty, and for you.
> They were men who hated death and loved life,
> Who were afraid and fought against their fear,
> Men who wished to create and not to destroy,
> But knew the time must come to destroy the destroyer.

As in *Fathers*, the music of the march is Mahlerian, prefaced by muted fanfare from the brass that prefigures the *War Requiem*. It is a fine movement, heavy with sadness, using the march for mourning, not for glory.

The second movement is entitled, once again, "Dance of Death." Auden supplies the text, a poem he had addressed earlier to Britten, expressing the imperative of departing from the cozy middle-class life. With its rapid anapaestic rhythm, it expresses sheer terror rather than solemn mourning.

> It's farewell to the drawing room's civilized cry
> The professors' sensible where-to and why,
> The frock-coated diplomat's social aplomb,
> Now matters are settled with gas and bomb . . .

The middle of the poem contains an apocalyptic vision of the Devil appearing, to destroy the order of British life, and thus the ending:

> So goodbye to the house with its wallpaper red,
> Goodbye to the sheets on the warm double bed,
> Goodbye to the beautiful birds on the wall,
> It's goodbye, dear heart, goodbye to you all.

The music is a wild Danse Macabre, with a nod to Saint-Saens, and perhaps, even more, to the Witches' Sabbath movement of Berlioz's Symphonie Fantastique. Here for the first and virtually only time, Auden gives Britten a seriously good text of his own that is worthy of the wild things the setting does with it. The only flaw is comprehension: the chorus proves unable to make the text clear over the heavy orchestration; a soloist would have been a better choice.

The text for the final movement is by both Auden and Swingler. First, the tenor sings a recitative on this Auden text:

> Still though the scene of possible Summer recedes
> And the guns can be heard across the hills
> Like waves at night: though crawling suburbs fill
> Their valleys with the stench of idleness like rotting weeds,
> And desire unacted breeds its pestilence.
> Yet still below the soot the roots are sure
> And beyond the guns there is another murmur,
> Like pigeons flying unnotic'd over continents
> With secret messages of peace: and at the centre
> Of the wheeling conflict the heart is calmer,
> The promise nearer than ever it came before, than ever before.
> Honour, honour them all.

This is not Auden's finest poem, but it is serious work, and it is comprehensible in performance, as his texts for *Hunting Fathers* are not. It contains his characteristic themes of the period: the corrupting influence of habit and convention, of the repression of desire, and yet the hope of a more authentic relationship to the world.

The chorus enters beneath the tenor line, with a banal but serviceable text by Swingler ("To build a city where / The will of love is done / And brought to its full flower / The dignity of man. . . . Honour, honour them all"). Because this text is sung beneath the tenor, who continues singing the Auden text, it cannot be heard at all, but that is no loss.

Musically, the recitative is sung to distant fanfares and explosions from the timpani, and then virtually *a capella*, as the chorus enters beneath. The whole movement is hushed and very solemn. Trumpet calls lead to "Honour, honour them all." At the conclusion, Tenor and chorus unite to sing the words of the first movement, to music of increasing weight and solemnity, ending with "To fight for peace, for liberty, and for you." The work ends on a long, sad fanfare that points ahead to the "Bugles" song in the *War Requiem*.

Ballad is a serious work, with some excellent musical ideas. If not as original as *Hunting Fathers*—after all, it was for a solemn popular occasion—it is a work that confronts the costs of war with moving music of mourning and with honor to the fallen. In a very un-Schopenhauerian way, both Auden and Britten indicate that their striving is far from futile. It ushers in a future of peace.

Sinfonia da Requiem, **Op. 20 (1940, premiere in New York, 1941)**. In 1940 the Japanese government paid Britten a commission to create a work for celebration of the 2600th anniversary of the Emperor's dynasty. Britten disapproved of Japanese military expansion and bellicosity, but his choice of a requiem for the celebratory occasion was not an intentional critique. There had been a long delay in sending the contract, and when it finally arrived there was no time to start a new work, so Britten, already at work on the symphony, asked the local Japanese consul if the symphony would be all right. He believed that the affirmative answer meant that the consul had checked it out with the government back home. He then fulfilled the commission in a way that harmonized with his sentiments, finishing his requiem for those who had died. Because the work is purely orchestral, there is no specific reference to war or even to death, but it is named a Requiem, and the movements have names taken from the Requiem Mass: *Lacrymosa, Dies Irae,* and *Requiem Aeternum.* The Japanese were not happy. They refused the work, saying that both its spirit of mourning and its Christian references were inappropriate to the occasion (though they did not ask Britten to give the money back). The work was premiered the following year in New York, conducted by John Barbirolli. It was a success, and a subsequent performance in Boston under Serge Koussevitsky led to the invitation from the Koussevitsky Music Foundation that became *Peter Grimes* (1945), Britten's first important opera and one of his finest.

This work is obviously a significant piece of the background to the *War Requiem*. It has roughly the same arc, from mourning to a wild *Dies Irae* (with the baneful tritone so central to the *War Requiem*) and finally to an equivocal reconciliation. It is the longest Britten work that is purely orchestral, with no soloist.

Once again, as with *Ballad,* the work opens with what Britten called "a slow marching lament," which leads without a break into the *Dies Irae,* which Britten called "a form of Dance of Death." The final movement is called "the final resolution." The orchestral writing has been consistently admired. The overall tone is somber. Britten dedicated it to the memory of his parents, and, written from exile in the United States, it also expresses his gloom at the darkening political situation. When I analyze the *War Requiem,* I will return to this important early precursor.

***Paul Bunyan*, Op. 17, first performed 1941 at Columbia University, reperformed in a revised version 1976.** *Paul Bunyan* is Britten's first opera, and despite its deserved failure at its debut, he remained strongly attached to it. Shortly before his death, he supervised a reworked version to considerable success. It is not surprising that Britten continued to value it, because it contains some lovely music, and also some very interesting ideas—about the role of the lonely individual in a democracy, about the relationship between human beings and animals, about the relationship between developed society and the prehuman world of nature. It does not deal with the theme of war directly, but by expressing these two exiles' view of the possibilities of the United States, it comments optimistically on a possible postwar future. Unfortunately, however, its libretto is unsalvageable, short of a total replacement.

The basic story is that of the mythic birth of the United States through the magical figures of Paul Bunyan, the enormous logger (represented by a voice offstage), and his blue cow Babe. The opening is the most successful part, with trees and birds narrating their experiences before the arrival of Bunyan, and then comes the sudden, almost miraculous, moment when the moon turns blue and along comes a being who wants to change the order of things. The epiphany is set to stirring music and the words, sung by the Wild Geese: "It isn't very often the conservatives are wrong. . . . Society is right in saying nine times out of ten / Respectability's enough to carry one along. / But once in a while the odd thing happens, / Once in a while the dream comes true, / And the whole pattern of life is altered, / Once in a while the moon turns blue." It is doggerel, but serviceable doggerel, and if we overlook the fact that the "odd thing" is human deforestation of the wilderness, we can see it as a paean to the work of the extraordinary individual. There are also some good moments later in the work: proclamations of freedom of speech and choice, and of a mutual compassion that does not cramp personal autonomy. Some of the best bits are entrusted to the animals: the dog, Fido, and the two cats, Moppet and Poppet, are central exemplars of an intelligent sympathy.[38] (Auden's fascination with dogs had already showed up in his play *The Dog Beneath the*

---

[38] Auden's fascination with dogs showed up already in his 1935 play *The Dog Beneath the Skin*, co-authored with Christopher Isherwood; and the 1971 poem "Talking to Dogs" continues the interest.

Skin, co-authored with Christopher Isherwood; and the later poem "Talking to Dogs" continues the interest.)

Unfortunately, things soon degenerate. The story moves from lumberjacks to agriculture and from agriculture to urban culture, all without introducing any characters the audience can care about, and with not much wit or humor. Auden writes so badly that he seems to have given up trying. Thus, felling trees with an axe is described as "melting the forests away." For no particular reason the itinerant narrator/ballad singer alludes to the "Yiddish Alps." The so-called characterization is nothing but a series of offensive stereotypes, especially that of the dumb Swede; Americans are caricatured just as much as the Americans in Dickens's *Martin Chuzzlewit*. Dickens, however, was a one-time visitor. Auden chose the United States over Britain and became an American citizen. So his disdain appears hypocritical.

Yet worse, Auden sprinkles in esoteric references that the audience is not expected to understand—little bits of Latin, for example. And then there is this, the (repeated) chorus of the Lumberjacks:

> We rise at dawn of day,
> We're handsome, free, and gay.

Naturally, Auden cannot be blamed for this lyric's hilarious evocation of the Monty Python lumberjack song (which debuted in 1965), after which no reference to manly lumberjacks can ever be the same. (Watch it on YouTube if you don't know it.) It is, however, very surprising that nobody seems to have told Britten about the skit when he was preparing the opera for performance in 1976. I have inquired through friends, and an inside figure in the Britten circle says he had no memory that it was ever mentioned, and thinks Britten didn't have a sense of humor.[39] (The brilliant Beyond the Fringe parody of Britten and Pears, with Dudley Moore

[39] Thanks to Colin Ure for forwarding my question.

playing like Britten and singing like Pears, was known to them. Pears enjoyed it, Britten hated it.) But what I want to draw attention to is the game that Auden was playing with the audience. Experts in gay history have established that by this time the use of "gay" to mean "homosexual" was firmly established in confidential gay circles, and to some extent beyond. Cary Grant in *Bringing up Baby* (1938), putting on a feathered robe, ad libbed the line, "I'm going gay," and the same experts agree that he knew and intended the double entendre.[40] Historian George Chauncey traces the usage back to the end of the nineteenth century, and even the Oxford English Dictionary traces it to 1950. So Auden is asking the amateur performers at Columbia to say a line many of them would not have understood, in front of an audience most of whose members would also not understand it—just to have some fun for himself at the audience's expense, while undercutting the whole emotional trajectory of the libretto for anyone who does understand it. For of course in its context the lumberjacks are entirely serious, indeed heroic, in their good cheer, and in this particular choral lyric too. I conclude that Auden was pretty bored by the whole exercise and was playing around, in a way that typifies his snide condescension to "the masses."

As for Britten, in later life he was firmly opposed to the use of "gay" to designate homosexuality, on the grounds that society had made their lives anything but "gay." He continued to use the word, in letters to Pears, in its original meaning of "cheerful." Pears, too, disliked the usage for similar reasons.[41] If Britten understood the double entendre at the time, he would likely have objected. Camp was not his type of humor. But perhaps he just went along with the libretto he was given.

<hr>

[40] Thanks to David Halperin for helpful correspondence on this point.

[41] In a 1979 interview he said, "I hate the word 'gay', actually . . . because, well, it's a terribly un-gay condition really: it gives quite a false impression." Quoted in Christopher Headington, *Peter Pears: A Biography* (London: Faber & Faber, 1993, pp. 287–88).

If *Paul Bunyan* had been a satire, my evaluation of Auden's role might be different. But it is, if lighthearted, dead serious about the values of individualism and freedom that lie at its heart. So Auden is undermining his own enterprise, with or without Britten's awareness.

What about the music? It is, of necessity, eclectic, given the lurching of the text from ballad to bluesy lament, and so on. There are bits that draw on Cole Porter (much admired by Auden), bits that echo Kurt Weill, bits that are rather like Gilbert and Sullivan, bits that sound like Copland—all knitted together in a mainly Brittenesque English idiom. A lot of the music is lovely: the opening, the love duet, the bluesy lament, the lyrical music of the dog and cats, and a lot more. And to my ear none of it is meant for the sake of satire or putting the audience down. Britten's humor—and he does have humor—is never like that anyway. He remarks during this period that he greatly admires Verdi's *Falstaff* and his own comic masterpiece, *Albert Herring*, owes more to the joyful reconciliatory ethos of *Falstaff* than to Auden's snideness. Musicologist Heather Wiebe, in her article about *Paul Bunyan*,[42] criticizes the operetta for its satirical superficiality and concludes that Britten needed to strike out on his own and write sincerely and from the heart. I agree with the conclusion, but I do think that Britten's own work in *Paul Bunyan* is utterly sincere and from the heart, some of it very successful. Britten always did his work, as Auden did not. It's easy to understand why Britten wanted to revive the opera.

What was needed, then, was not so much a change of direction: it was a divorce.

Britten accomplished a huge amount in this period, where the musical understanding of war is concerned. *Our Hunting Fathers* is a work of major insight into the sources of aggression against both animals and human beings. These insights are shared with Auden,

---

[42] Heather Wiebe, "Discovering America: From Paul Bunyan to Peter Grimes," *Cambridge Opera Journal* 27, No. 2 (2015): 129–53.

and Auden's psychological acuity left a lasting mark on Britten, who continued to focus throughout his career on the crowd's desire to destroy the outsider, inspired by a fear of something inside themselves. This insight would shortly be given brilliant expression in *Peter Grimes*. In *Sinfonia* and *Ballad*, he also developed a music of mourning for war's victims that would in some ways carry straight forward into the *War Requiem*.

There are two gaps, if we think of my Schopenhauerian challenge. First, the state is absent. Auden always had disdain for institutions, and this stopped Britten from depicting, or even thinking about, the institutional side of war-making. *Paul Bunyan* does make some facile gestures toward a decent state that would pursue peace, but the gestures don't amount to much. War will not be stopped, however, by the acts of romantic outsiders. Their cause involves not just the "pride" of individuals but also the power struggles of nations. Their solution, if there is one, also needs to involve nations and a reconciliation between nations. Auden's attitude becomes less political as time goes on, whereas Britten will attempt to grapple with public solutions, in all their ambivalence, in works as different as *Billy Budd* and *War Requiem*.

Second, the victims are seen only as corpses, and though *Ballad* dignifies them and suggests that their striving was for a worthwhile goal, it does not let us really see them or find beauty in their strivings. This part of Britten's imagination was shortly to be developed. Let us now turn, then, to the music of human love.

4

Britten and Pears: The Beauty and Nobility of Human Love

Spirto ben nato, in cui si specchia e vede
Nelle tuo belle membra oneste e care
Quante natura e 'l ciel tra no' puo' fare,
Quand'a null'altra suo bell'opra cede;
Spirto leggiadro, in cui si spera e crede
Dentro, come di fuor nel viso appare,
Amor, pietà, mercè, cose sì rare
Che mà furn'in beltà con tanta fede;
L'amor mi prende, e la beltà mi lega;
La pietà, la mercè con dolci sguardi
Ferma speranz'al cor par che ne doni.
Qual uso o qual governo al mondo niega,
Qual crudeltà per tempo, o qual più tardi,
C'a sì bel viso morte non perdoni?
—Michelangelo Buonarotti, Sonnet XXIV,[1] the last
sonnet in Britten's *Seven Sonnets of Michelangelo*,
Op. 22 (1940), written for Peter Pears

[1] Noble soul, in whose virtuous and dear limbs are reflected all that nature and heaven can achieve with us, the paragon of their works; graceful soul, within whom one hopes and believes Love, Compassion, and Mercy are dwelling, as they appear in your face; things so rare and never found in beauty so truly:

Love takes me captive, and Beauty binds me; Compassion and Mercy with sweet glances fill my heart with a strong hope.

What law or earthly government, what cruelty now or to come, could forbid Death to spare such a lovely face?

Translation by Elizabeth Mayer and Peter Pears (London: Boosey & Hawkes, 1943). I have substituted "virtuous" for "chaste," translating *oneste*, since the word *casto* is used

The Tenderness of Silent Minds. Martha C. Nussbaum, Oxford University Press.
© Oxford University Press 2024. DOI: 10.1093/oso/9780197568538.003.0004

> Music says "Love me". It does not say "Obey me"; it does not
> even say "This is true." Love me or Love with me. That is why the
> performer is the center of this act of Love: he is the instrument
> of it. His duty is to offer himself as a sacrifice to those who have
> ears to hear.
>
> —Peter Pears, "The Responsibility of the Singer"

British middle-class life, in Britten's time, did not look kindly on the desiring body—especially when the desires were those of an outsider minority. (Conventional desires are always easier to represent as morality or social duty rather than desire.) Already in "Rats" (see Chapter 3), a fear of something disorderly inside each person—Auden's "creatures of the night"—leads "our hunting fathers" to violence against both animals and outsider humans, who could be conveniently displayed as animals. The speaker expresses disgust and distaste for both vulnerability and sexuality, which is one form of our animal vulnerability.

For such fearful cultures, beauty is easier to love in a fictively disembodied form, though inescapably all beauty is bodily. (Even the chaste Aquinas defined beauty as "that which, being seen, pleases"—thus putting beauty in the realm of the body rather than the [invisible] soul.) But Schopenhauer's pessimism cannot be answered without displaying the human body and human love as beautiful and worthwhile (see Chapter 2). Through his thirty-nine year aesthetic and personal partnership with Peter Pears, Britten provided a powerful reply to this part of Schopenhauer's argument. Understanding the general nature of this reply is essential to understanding a crucial part of the *War Requiem*.

Shortly after Britten and Pears began their love affair while visiting in Grand Rapids, Michigan, Auden wrote a letter to Britten

---

for chastity elsewhere in the Sonnets. Perhaps Pears wanted to screen the sonnet's message somewhat from its original audience in 1940. I have also substituted Compassion for Pity, translating *pietà*, because "pity" now suggests condescension, which the Italian did not.

(intended to be read, as well, by Pears), warning Britten that he would not be able to fulfill his potential as an artist if he chose a stable domestic relationship:

> Wherever you go you are and probably always will be surrounded by people who adore you, nurse you, and praise everything that you do, e.g. Elisabeth, Peter (Please show this to P to whom all this is also addressed). Up to a certain point this is fine for you, but beware. You see, Benjy dear, you are always tempted to make things too easy for yourself in this way, i.e. to build yourself a warm nest of love. . . by playing the lovable talented little boy.

> If you are really to develop to your full stature, you will have, I think, to suffer, and make others suffer, in ways that are totally strange to you at present, and against every conscious value that you have. . . . [2]

With considerable condescension, Auden repeats a romantic cliché about the artist, as if all artists were the same and needed the same. In his own life, suffering came unbidden in the form of Chester Kallman's rejection of Auden's proposal of sexual fidelity, and his letter may express a "sour grapes" reaction. But Britten and Auden were always profoundly different. And though we cannot assess counterfactually how Britten's life would have unfolded without Pears, we can see that the non-Audenesque ingredients of their shared life permitted a great flourishing of creativity in both artists.

Britten ignored the warning. He chose stability and, eventually, middle-class British domestic love. Stability was a need of his creative process. He thrived on quiet, a degree of solitude, the beloved countryside of Suffolk, and a house that could keep his unconventional love from intrusive and destructive eyes. And he needed the emotional support and reassurance provided by a

---

[2] Quoted in Kildea (2013), p. 197.

stable quasi-marital relationship. So too did Pears. Through their choices, he and Pears were able to sustain a deep thirty-nine-year love, and one that was inseparable from the artistry of both men. Britten wrote nine song cycles and eleven opera roles for Pears, and they had a busy career as recitalists together, performing the song cycles (Britten was a superb pianist whose gifts as an accompanist are more fully recognized all the time) and also the works of Schumann and Schubert (*Winterreise* being a particular favorite). Pears, who loved travel as Britten often did not, also became his ambassador to many other countries, performing the opera roles all over the world.

As the world began to change, and after sex between men ceased, in 1967, to be a criminal offense, Britten and Pears wanted the world to know about their life together. In particular, they wanted the world to know that two men could love each other and sustain that love for many years, with both personal and artistic integrity, despite the world's hostility. Britten urged Donald Mitchell—one of the couple's few real friends, clear-eyed, insightful, and not self-seeking, whose attitudes seem undistorted by homophobic stereotypes—"to tell the truth about Peter and me."[3] Mitchell's pictorial biography, *Benjamin Britten: Pictures from a Life 1913–1976*,[4] documented the relationship and was really, as Pears said, "a life of the two of us."[5] Before Britten's death, too, the couple donated their letters—365 that survive (including telegrams and postcards)—to the museum at Aldeburgh and arranged for their publication. The resulting volume, *My Beloved Man: The Letters of Benjamin Britten and Peter Pears*,[6] is a remarkable portrait of their creative and personal partnership. As stage director Fiona Shaw says in her introduction to the book, "It is astonishing that these men created

[3] Mitchell and Reed, eds. (vol. 1, p. 56).
[4] Donald Mitchell and John Evans, *Benjamin Britten, 1913–1976: Pictures from a Life: A Pictorial Biography* (London: Faber & Faber, 1978).
[5] Quoted in Stroeher, Clark, and Brimmer (2016, Introduction, p. 16).
[6] Ibid. Letters will be cited by letter number rather than page number.

a totally realized domestic relationship that has remarkable contemporary immediacy during a period when it was illegal to love someone of your own sex. To me their lives seem an act of huge integrity." She observes that the lines sung by Collatinus and Lucretia in Britten's opera *The Rape of Lucretia* (which she directed), suited them perfectly, showing the composer's insight into "domestic love's fathomless depths": "O never again must we two dare to part / For we are of one another / And between us, there is one heart."

In this chapter I will examine the ideas of beauty and integrity that suffused this partnership and the works created with this love in mind, arguing that Britten implicitly replies to Schopenhauer's challenge: although beauty and human love are always beset by the world's aggression, they have worth and inner integrity and are, because embodied, therefore real and even immortal. I believe this idea is at the heart of the *War Requiem*. Again: I will not use the word *gay*, since both men disliked it.

Britten's Britain: From the Buggery Act to Decriminalization

Postwar Britain was among Europe's most repressive nations, where sex between men was concerned. France had decriminalized same-sex relationships in 1791, during the French Revolution, and France has remained a legally tolerant nation ever since. Germany had no laws against sodomy until 1871 (emulating Victorian Britain), although several individual states had previously had such laws; and even the new 1871 law, known as "Paragraph 175," was immediately opposed by the Social Democratic Party, which sought repeal. This campaign was supported by a wide range of prominent intellectuals, including Thomas Mann, Martin Buber, Rainer Maria Rilke, Herman Hesse, and many others (quite unlike public sentiments in Britain, as we'll shortly see). Paragraph 175 was strengthened by the Nazis and used to persecute men who had sex with men. After the war, however, it was rewritten as a simple age of consent law in East Germany in 1957 and in West Germany in 1969.

In Britain the Buggery Act, passed in 1533, made anal intercourse and intercourse between a human and a nonhuman animal punishable by death. The possessions of the convicted party were confiscated and went to the state. This law was replaced by a similar law in 1828, and "buggery" remained a capital offense until 1861. The law criminalized anal sex between males and females, as well as between males. Its original purpose was to penalize nonreproductive sexuality, but the focus on acts between males grew as time went on and anxiety about extramarital sex between males and females slightly lessened. (Distribution of contraceptive information, however, remained a crime, and philosopher John Stuart Mill went to jail for this crime as a young man.) Sex acts between women were never illegal in either Britain or Germany (in contrast to the United States). Britain's special anxiety about male–male sex probably derives from the prominence of many such men and the likely influence of their example.

In the early nineteenth century there were liberal voices, including the philosopher Jeremy Bentham, who wrote a series of works urging the decriminalization of male–male acts, very powerfully argued, with arguments courts still use today. But such was the climate in his era that Bentham chose not to publish these works in his lifetime, and they have been published only recently by the Bentham Project at the University of London.[7]

---

[7] The main work is *Not Paul, But Jesus*, published online in 2013 (Bentham, 1823/ 2013). Its first book, less controversial, was published during Bentham's lifetime under the pseudonym of Gamaliel Smith, and Smith constantly alludes to the excellent arguments produced by one Jeremy Bentham. In the full work, Bentham, in addition to arguing cogently for decriminalization, also claims that Jesus approved of male–male relationships and even had them himself.

There is no reason to think that Bentham had or wanted same-sex relationships. He was disappointed in love by a woman to whom he proposed marriage, and he chose a celibate life thereafter. But he loved to skewer irrational prejudices, especially those that oppressed.

As anxiety mounted during the increasingly repressive late Victorian era, the offense of sodomy (the more modern name for "buggery") was thought not to sweep widely enough, since not all male–male sex was anal, and evidence of anal penetration was difficult to produce. A new law, which would criminalize a much broader group of homosexual acts, was proposed by Henry Labouchere and passed by Parliament in 1885, as an amendment to a popular bill designed to protect women against trafficking by raising the age of consent from thirteen to sixteen. The Labouchere Amendment provided that (1) "[a]ny male person who, in public or in private, commits . . . any act of gross indecency with another male person, shall be guilty of a misdemeanor, and being convicted thereof, shall be liable . . . to be imprisoned for any term not exceeding two years with or without hard labor."[8] This law was understood to criminalize oral sex between males.

A veritable hysteria about male homosexuality then led to numerous arrests and convictions, including the famous conviction of Oscar Wilde. Wilde had foolishly brought a libel action against the Marquess of Queensberry (father of Wilde's lover, Lord Alfred Douglas), who had left a note at Wilde's club saying that Wilde was "posing as a sodomite" (only he could not spell the word, and wrote "somdomite"). After Queensberry won the libel action on grounds of justification, Wilde was prosecuted—under the Labouchere Amendment, not the sodomy law, because Wilde preferred oral sex, and there was no evidence that he had ever had anal intercourse with any of his contacts. A first trial ended in a hung jury, but the second led to a conviction and the maximum prison sentence. Wilde's health was broken, and he died in France in 1900, after his release from Reading Gaol, at the age of forty-six.

---

[8] The initial proposal was a one-year maximum, but legislators demanded a harsher penalty.

Wilde's sentencing provides a typical example of the public sentiments of the era. Mr. Justice Wills said:

> Oscar Wilde and Alfred Taylor, the crime of which you have been convicted is so bad that one has to put stern restraint upon one's self to prevent one's self from describing, in language which I would rather not use, the sentiments which must rise to the breast of every man of honour who has heard the details of these two terrible trials. . . . It is no use for me to address you. People who can do these things must be dead to all sense of shame, and one cannot hope to produce any effect upon them. It is the worst case I have ever tried.[9]

Although the Justice chose not to describe his "sentiments," his violent repudiation of the defendants made his disgust amply evident. Indeed, we might say that his whole speech (which was much longer than this) is more like vomiting than judicial argument. This judge had been on the bench for some time, dealing with homicides, rapes, and many other serious offenses causing harm to nonconsenting parties. What had Wilde done to merit the label "worst case"? He had had oral sex with a sequence of male prostitutes (only one nonprostitute, and this one was in his twenties and sought out Wilde eagerly, so there was no issue of "corruption of the young"). He treated all his partners with the utmost kindness and generosity, giving them expensive gifts—items, such as engraved silver cigarette cases, that later helped to convict him. The sex took place in seclusion, usually in posh hotels, so there was no issue of direct offense to onlookers. It seems simple lunacy to call this a "worst case." And yet that was the way Victorian Britain as a whole regarded it—not without enormous hypocrisy, since male–male sex acts, as well as sadistic beatings, were the staple of life in elite male "public schools."

[9] See H. Montgomery Hyde, *The Three Trials of Oscar Wilde* (New York: University Books, 1956), p. 339.

What became of men who wanted to avoid Wilde's fate? There were some courageous individuals who defied the law and got away with it, including John Addington Symonds, whose pamphlet "A Problem in Greek Ethics," correctly describing the sexual customs of ancient Athens, circulated underground.[10] Symonds gave a third-person case study of his life to sexologist Havelock Ellis,[11] declaring how greatly his health and happiness had improved once he decided to have sex with males. He concludes (in a manner that is highly significant for Britten's later choices):

> Although he always has before him the terror of discovery, he is convinced that his sexual dealings with men have been thoroughly wholesome to himself, largely increasing his physical, moral, and intellectual energy, and not injurious to others. As a man of letters he regrets that he has been shut out from that form of artistic expression which would express his own emotions. He has no sense whatever of moral wrong in his actions, and he regards the attitude of society towards those in his position as utterly unjust and founded on false principles.

It is especially significant that Symonds records a longing to give artistic expression to his desire. This Britten will boldly do, probably the first great artist in Britain since Shakespeare to celebrate a same-sex love in art.

Others, more fearful, got married to women and lived with men in fantasy. The philosopher Henry Sidgwick (1838–1900) has recently been shown to have had a same-sex sexual orientation, through biographer Bart Schultz's careful reading of his notebooks and diaries. But Sidgwick urged friends, including Symonds, not

---

[10] John Addington Symonds, *A Problem in Greek Ethics*. Privately printed (1883).
[11] Havelock Ellis, "Sexual Inversion," in *Studies in the Psychology of Sex* (London: University Press, 1900, vol. 2).

to risk arrest. He himself married a prominent woman, Eleanor, with whom he pursued the cause of women's higher education and other worthy projects. Together they founded Newnham College in Cambridge. Schultz has found evidence that Eleanor told friends that the marriage had never been consummated, and there is no reason to think Sidgwick had sex with men either.[12] Meanwhile, in his notebooks he imagines the men whom he wishes he could love, in an odd-numbered list, dated May 1867, including the following:

8. Their eyes are calm and they smile: their hands are quick and their fingers tremble.
9. The light of heaven enwraps them: their faces and their forms become harmonious to me with the harmony of the Universe.
10. The air of heaven is spread around them; their houses and books, their pictures and carpets make music to me as all things make music to God.
13. Some are women to me, and to some I am a woman.
14. Each day anew we are born, we meet and love, we embrace and are united for ever: with passion that wakes no longing, with fruition that brings no satiety.

Like Symonds, he imagines reciprocal love as well as sex. And, a typical Victorian, he imagines a Pre-Raphaelite type of domesticity, together with "houses and books," "pictures and carpets," from which, unlike Symonds, he saw himself as forever cut off.[13]

This, then, was the world into which Britten was born. In Britain, unlike Germany, no prominent intellectuals openly urged legal reform or even protested the cruel treatment of Oscar Wilde. "Our

---

[12] Bart Schultz, *Henry Sidgwick, Eye of the Universe: An Intellectual Biography* (Cambridge, UK: Cambridge University Press, 2004).

[13] This extract, dated May 1867, is addressed to Symonds, although there is no reason to think it was ever sent to him. See Schultz (2004). Sidgwick urged Symonds not to send compromising letters and to destroy any he had kept.

hunting fathers" hunted men down and subjected them to brutal penalties.

The two World Wars caused this sex panic to recede somewhat, as other, more urgent matters surged to the fore. But the Nazis' lethal persecution of male–male sex (the pink triangle as a brand of shame, internment in concentration camps, and many deaths) kept the issue before the British public and her artists, as we saw in Chapter 3. And right after the war, persecution in Britain reached a new height. A series of arrests and prosecutions of prominent men occurred, including the arrest of distinguished mathematician Alan Turing (1912–1954, thus born one year before Britten), whose codebreaking activities had been crucial to the war effort.[14] Given a choice between prison and chemical castration, he chose the latter, and shortly thereafter died of cyanide poisoning, very likely, though not certainly, a suicide.

In that same year the Wolfenden Commission was formed to investigate the possibility of legal change. The Commission submitted its report in 1957, recommending a complete decriminalization of male–male sex acts between consenting adults over 21. The Report evoked strong opposition. Conservative peer Lord Devlin gave a famous series of lectures published under the title of the first one, "The Enforcement of Morals" (1957), taking aim at John Stuart Mill's view that harm to others is a necessary condition of criminal regulability.[15] His argument rested on an idea of social solidarity. Societies will not make sacrifices for the common good, such as the acts that enabled Britain to win the war, Devlin argued, if they openly tolerate acts that disgust the average man, whom

[14] Turing's house had been burgled by someone whom his current male lover said he knew. In the course of the police investigation, Turing mentioned having a relationship with the lover and was immediately charged.

[15] Patrick Devlin, *The Enforcement of Morals* (Oxford, UK: Oxford University Press, 1965). One of the lectures later published in this small collection was delivered in 1960 at the University of Chicago Law School as the ninth Ernst Freund Lecture. For this debate see my Nussbaum, *From Disgust to Humanity: Sexual Orientation and Constitutional Law*. Inalienable Rights Series (New York: Oxford University Press, 2010).

Devlin (with a certain class condescension) called "the man on the Clapham omnibus."[16] Moreover, he argued, men who commit these acts, like alcoholics and drug addicts, cannot themselves contribute to a war effort.

The influential philosopher of law Herbert Hart (1907–1992) took up the defense of Mill's ideas. In lectures later published under the title *Law, Liberty, and Morality*,[17] he gave a devastating refutation of Devlin's arguments and a powerful defense of Mill's ideas (better than Mill had given them). Hart's prestige and the power of his arguments helped sway sentiment, and the ground was prepared for decriminalization, which eventually followed in 1967.

We now know that Hart was, so to speak, the Sidgwick of his era: a man strongly drawn to other men, who explored these emotions in his diaries but never had sex with a man.[18] Until his death, he remained married to his wife Jennifer, whom he loved, and with whom he had several children. The marriage, however, was not a happy one because after the initial exuberance of youth passed, he avoided sex with her, leading her to have at least one affair. Like Sidgwick, he explores his wishes for male–male happiness only in fantasy, particularly in one very moving diary passage describing his experience listening to Schubert's chamber music. Throughout his life he was prone to debilitating depression and anxiety.

Decriminalization did not happen easily, because no political leader wanted to propose such a controversial piece of legislation. Finally, a "Private Member's Bill" was introduced in the House of

---

[16] Clapham was a lower-class neighborhood, and no member of the upper or even high middle classes would ever take a bus to work.

[17] H.L.A. Hart, *Law, Liberty, and Morality*. Harry Camp Lectures at Stanford University (Stanford, CA: Stanford University Press, 1963).

[18] Nicola Lacey, *A Life of H.L.A. Hart: The Nightmare and the Noble Dream* (Oxford, UK: Oxford University Press, 2004), p. 203). Jennifer Hart gave Lacey complete access to her husband's diaries and permission to cite them in the book. (The Schubert passage is cited on p. 203.)

Commons by Leo Abse, an eccentric Welsh Jewish Labour Party MP who repeatedly championed antipuritanical laws (including divorce reform). He started to prepare the bill in 1962, but it was only with the Labour victory in 1966, together with the support of cabinet minister Roy Jenkins, that it finally passed, as the Sexual Offenses Act 1967. The corresponding bill in the House of Lords was championed by Lord Arran, whose brother had committed suicide, apparently on account of his same-sex orientation. (Arran's other great cause was a Protection of Badgers Act, which he succeeded in passing only in 1973. When asked why he had more trouble with badgers than with men who have sex with men, he replied, "There are not many badgers in the House of Lords."). In the parliamentary debate, Arran's rhetoric emphasized pity for these men and the need to recognize that they did not choose their way of life:[19]

How do they live? In shame if they restrain themselves; in fear if they practise their homosexuality. They are the odd men out: the ones with the limp. Can they help it? Are they deliberately homosexual? Will any man or woman in your Lordships' House tell us seriously that a man, out of perverseness—and I mean perverseness, and not perversion—purposely renounces the joys of love with the opposite sex, the joys of having a wife, the joys of having children? Is there a man in the world who would be, not so wicked, but so silly? As a Member of another place said in debate, "Look what they're missing." And is it even remotely possible that there could be half a million of such obstinate men in Britain alone?

With such friends, one might remark, what need of enemies? Even though Arran succeeded, there was nobody in the entire discussion

---

[19] 266 Parl Deb HL (5th ser.) (1965) col. 71-172 (UK), https://api.parliament.uk/histo ric-hansard/lords/1965/may/12/homosexual-offences. This includes the whole debate.

who expressed respect for the dignity of these men or the moral imperative of treating them as equals, nobody who represented their lives as worthy, beautiful, or good. Indeed there was constant reference to homosexuality as a "disease," and to the need for therapeutic treatment, despite general acknowledgment that none had as yet been found.

This was Britten's Britain. On one side, fear and shame; on the other, condescending pity. His choices seemed to involve, on the one hand, the tragedy of Turing, or at least the risk of that tragedy (Britten was once questioned by the police); on the other, the tragedy of Herbert Hart. What Britten and Pears accomplished, given this context, is extraordinary: they created dignity, success, respectability, stable love, and domesticity where no paradigm of any such relationship was known. If there was any sector of British society that came to their aid, it was the somewhat unlikely one of the Royal Family: Queen Elizabeth the wife of George VI, after 1952 known as the Queen Mother, befriended them for many years, as a lover of the arts and eventually a friend. Her daughter followed that lead, making Britten Baron of Aldeburgh before his death (Pears was a CBE), and, on Britten's death, addressing to Pears a letter of the type usually sent to a grieving spouse. (But in Chapter 6 we shall see that Britten cast aside his most important royal protector, the Earl of Harewood, the first president of the Aldeburgh Festival, when he mistreated a close female friend of Britten's, Marion Stein/Harewood/Thorpe.[20]) Their success against very long odds lies behind their gift of their letters to the nation, a nation that both men deeply loved.

---

[20] For a general account of royal family support for the LGBTQ community, see Frank Olito, "From Princess Diana to Prince Harry, Here Are 9 Times the Royal Family Showed Support for the LGBTQ Community." *Insider*, February 16, 2021, https://www.insider.com/royal-family-support-lgbtq-community-2019-6. The Queen posthumously pardoned Turing in 2013. And in 2016, just before the fiftieth anniversary of decriminalization, Parliament retroactively pardoned any man convicted of a consensual male–male sex act; the law was somewhat broadened in 2022.

Stereotypes

The world around Britten interpreted his life through a series of stereotypes about male–male love, which have only somewhat loosened their grip today. One I have already mentioned in Chapter 3: gay men are all tormented, to be pitied. Of course society did its best to arrange for this to be the case, but then it turned around and said: look, these people deserve to be kept apart as outcasts, because they are tortured souls. Even Lord Arran advanced a version of this cliché, though urging decriminalization. Not Britten and Pears: whatever the aggressions of society, the two men felt very little inner conflict or guilt about their sexuality. Pears reports that his feelings never seemed wrong. Britten took a little longer, but not much longer, and in their relationship a thought of its inherent wrongness does not appear even once, though a thought of danger from the world certainly does.[21]

A related social maneuver is to look at Britten's deeply insightful depictions of aggression and evil in his works and to conclude therefrom that he had a psychological deformation: "sublimated sadism" (Humphrey Carpenter) or "an abyss in his soul" (singer Robert Tear). People do not draw a similar conclusion about Shakespeare or Verdi. They give them credit for the tremendous power of their imaginations. No decent critic infers sadism in Shakespeare from the character of Iago, or in Verdi from the Grand Inquisitor. The

---

[21] Numerous friends thought that Britten felt guilt, though they tended to agree that Pears did not. But these seem likely to be projections of the ethos of the time: see Lord Arran's speech above. Pears firmly rejected the idea, after Britten's death, in a letter to author Michael Kennedy: "As to 'anguish through guilt'! Forget it! Ben never regarded his own passionate feelings for me or his earlier friends as anything but good, natural, and profoundly creative." Quoted in Carpenter (1992, p. 178). To which one of those "friends" replied to Carpenter (who advanced a related thesis, see below): "Of course Peter would say that." A ridiculous reply, since Pears never had an interest in whitewashing moments of conflict in the relationship, and if Britten had been tortured by guilt, who else would have known it better? Indeed, it is hard to imagine the relationship would have endured so relatively serenely in that case. Nor do the letters mention such an issue, though they mention other differences.

reason people treat Britten's work differently is, I think, that they come to it with a preconception that this artist is a damaged soul. No: Britten had reason to try to understand persecution and aggression, not because he was it but because he encountered it everywhere he went. Like Verdi, like Mahler, he grappled with evil in his own time, experienced its effects, and through an extension of the imagination managed to put it into his art.[22] Britten was not a perfect person, and many acquaintances whom he suddenly dropped felt they had reason to complain. But perhaps this way of dropping people insulated his art and its key relationship. (And maybe there were some who were self-seeking false friends who deserved to be dropped.) On the whole, I think Britten was as happy as recurrent physical illness and society's beastliness would permit him to be.

A second stereotype, or more a demand, is to pretend same-sex sex is not there and to insist that the parties not manifest it, so as not to make society uncomfortable. On the whole, no doubt partly out of fear of the law, but also out of personal taste and consideration for the feelings of others, Britten and Pears accepted this demand and refrained from any overt statement of their sexual relationship until, after Britten's death, Pears gradually began to speak of it—although erotic love was already plainly enough stated in the domain of song, though veiled by a foreign language. In their successive houses there were always separate bedrooms that visitors could be shown. Even Britten's devoted nurse, Rita Thompson, disliked any allusion to the fact that the two men had sex.

The flip side of the idea that male–male sex is not there is the idea that homosexual men are sex addicts, their lives utterly dominated by sex. Lord Devlin compared them to drug addicts and gave their addiction as a reason why they could not serve well in the military. Why would people think like this? Perhaps it is Lord Arran's

---

[22] Verdi was a leader of the Risorgimento, and his name was even used as an acronymic code by the Republicans: to say "Viva Verdi" was to wish for the reign of constitutional monarch Victor Emmanuel (Re D'Italia). Mahler was persecuted as a Jew throughout his career.

reason: that if you could control yourself you would not act like this. But there is also a prurient fascination with same-sex acts on the part of much of the public. Because *they* can't stop thinking about sex when they think of such men, the inference is made that those men themselves must be thinking of sex all the time.[23] Pears later expressed annoyance at this: just because two men look at one another admiringly, he complained, people assume they must be having sex. He felt that this was a grotesque image held up to young men with a same-sex orientation.[24] He wanted to display, by contrast, an image of restraint and stability. Nonetheless, one senses in what people write about them an undue amount of prurient curiosity about their sex lives, curiosity people would usually at least restrain when writing about a heterosexual marriage.[25] One of the most revealing comments one finds acquaintances making is that their life seemed "so ordinary"—as if they had expected some weird pathology.

---

[23] For a recent example of this prurience, see the following extract from Paul Cameron's pamphlet *Medical Consequences of Homosexuality* (Colorado Springs, CO: Family Research Institute, 1993), circulated by the Center for Family Values before the referendum on Amendment 2 in Colorado' The law was eventually overturned by the U.S. Supreme Court in *Romer v. Evans*, 116 S. Ct. 1620 (1996):

> The typical sexual practices of homosexuals are a medical horror story— imagine exchanging saliva, feces, semen, and/or blood with dozens of different men each year. Imagine drinking urine, ingesting feces and experiencing rectal trauma on a regular basis. Often these encounters occur while the participants are drunk, high, and/or in an orgy setting. Further, many of them occur in extremely unsanitary places (bathrooms, dirty peep shows), or because homosexuals travel so frequently, in other parts of the world.
>
> Every year, a quarter or more of homosexuals visit another country. Fresh American germs get taken to Europe, Africa, and Asia. And fresh pathogens from these continents come here. Foreign homosexuals regularly visit the U.S. and participate in this biological swapmeet (Cameron 1993).

[24] See Headington (1993, p. 289).

[25] There was also much prurient curiosity about other imagined sexual relationships of the two. About Pears, nothing is known, and that is what he wished, even after Britten's death. It is well known that Britten had a series of infatuations with teenage male singers, but it is also universally agreed that he never behaved improperly to any of them—this on the basis of each man's own later statements, as well as those of Britten's circle, for once not imputing stereotypical behavior where there was none. It is thought that occasionally these infatuations annoyed Pears, but not deeply.

Both the letters and Pears's later frank statements make it clear that their sexual relationship was strong and continuous. Pears volunteered that they had a "regular sex life" until Britten's final illness, and he mentioned that at that time Britten expressed guilt that he could no longer be a lover.[26] He also volunteered something one can also glean from the letters: that he played a more active and Britten a more passive role, although Britten always noted that in other areas of life he was "more masculine" than his partner.

Letters, Lives, and Beauty

There are not many letters for thirty-nine years—because they were together most of the time. The letters are from times when Pears was touring, either abroad or in different parts of Britain. They also used the telephone, but they often mention finding letters more intimate because with the phone there is usually someone else in the room, and there is often a bad connection. One letter from Britten traveled across the Atlantic unsealed, and Pears warns him not to do this again. So the world is being given an extraordinary privilege by being invited into their intimate space.

My first reaction on reading the letters was that they should serve as a model of how to sustain a long-term marriage. There are constant gestures of support and reassurance—and both men needed a lot of it. Pears had a lot of vocal problems, early on especially, and some of his trips are to study with well-known teachers. It paid off. He does his best singing in his fifties and sixties, and is first-rate right up until a stroke in 1980, shortly after his seventieth birthday. And the traits for which he is best known—warmth, impeccable diction, human presence, and textual sensitivity—grew and grew throughout his career. (The non-Britten role for which he is best known is as the Evangelist in Bach's *St. Matthew Passion*.) But like

[26] Headington (1993, p. 321).

most singers (since singers cannot hear themselves), he needed reassurance, and always got it. Britten, though enormously prolific, also had blocks and uncertainties. He also had physical ailments that impeded his creative life, including a long bout of bursitis that affected both his piano playing and his composing. Pears offers support in his turn. And the two also apologize constantly. It is obvious that their life was not always calm: acquaintances mention sharp remarks, and they too mention them in the letters. One is moody and snaps at the other, and so on. But they always apologize immediately. They also appear to share the burdens of household management.

Few straight marriages exhibit this continual reciprocal empathy. And, my second reaction, the thing that makes them utterly unique, is that they are both pursuing artistic careers at the highest level—without jealousy, without demands that one party cede his career to the other. I know of no straight marriage like this. Even when both are creative, it is so often the woman who is cast in the role of helpmate to the man. And if she does excel, there is anxiety lest she outshine him. It isn't just that they have no children, because plenty of straight couples don't have children. It is something in the social norms governing male–female relationships that impedes genuine equality. As J. S. Mill wrote, "the generality of the male sex cannot yet tolerate the idea of living with an equal."[27] (He came close—but only later in life, and only by telling the world that Harriet had contributed more to his work than the world could ever see.) I believe that the Britten-Pears relationship is marriage as it ought to be between two creative people—but cannot yet be between males and females in our society.

The letters are by turns tender, romantic, sensuous (Pears mostly, Britten is less explicit), jokey (again mostly Pears), daily, and

---

[27] John Stuart Mill, *The Subjection of Women*, 1st ed. (London: Longmans, Green, Reader & Dyer), edited by Susan Moller Okin (Indianapolis: Hackett Publishing Company, 1988 [1869, ch. 3]).

concerned with earnest matters of composition and performance, as well as discussions of literature and art (Pears read voluminously and became a keen collector), and assessments, not always kind, of the musical performances of others. Some are fairly long, but many very short, some just postcards (Pears: "I hope you will like a postcard from Bucharest. It is a charmless dump," 331[28]). They always express annoyance at separation and longing for togetherness. Some contain little drawings: Pears illustrates the initials BB and PP with a drawing of a bee (he often calls Britten "honey bee" or "honey B"), and a picture of a little man peeing. Many different pet names are used: "darling honey," "my own darling P," "my pussy-cat," "my boy," "my sweetest old pot of honey," "my darling Pyge" (180, Britten showing off his Greek![29]), and most extravagantly, from Pears, "my most beautiful of all little blue-grey, mouse-catching, pearly-bottomed, creamy-thighed, soft-waisted, mewing rat-pursuers" (11). Once again: the reader is not prying: Britten and Pears invited the world to read these words, learning that the sexuality of same-sex love is real, and at the same time part of a complex and long-lasting loving relationship—thus undermining several stereotypes at one time.

The letters concern matters high minded and utterly diurnal, passing from one to the other with the effortlessness of long-time daily life. One of my favorites, so very English, ends, "All my love, my sweet. Longing to see you. The house is upside-down with electricians rewiring us. The damp is still coming up, downstairs. We shan't be able to use that room for ages, I'm abit afraid. Hope the Rankl concerts go well. *Lots* of love, & get well *very* soon, Your devoted B."

In the Britten–Pears relationship, love and art, love and the sense of beauty, are everywhere intertwined to a remarkable extent. We

[28] These numbers refer to the numbering of the letters in Britten and Pears (2016), which is strictly chronological.

[29] *Pyge* is the ancient Greek word for buttocks.

can begin toward the end, eighteen months after Britten's heart surgery:[30]

> Sunday, Nov. 17th 1974
>
> My darling heart (perhaps an unfortunate phrase—but I can't use any other), I feel I must write a squiggle which I couldn't say on the telephone without bursting into those silly tears—I do love you so terribly, & not only glorious you, but your singing. I've just listened to a re-broadcast of Winter Words (something like Sept. '72) and honestly you are the greatest artist that ever was—every nuance, subtle & never over-done—those great words, so sad & wise, painted for one, that heavenly sound you make, full but always coloured for words & music. What have I done to deserve such an artist and *man* to write for? I had to switch off before the folk songs because I couldn't anything after—"how long, how long." How long?—only till Dec. 20th—I think I can *just* bear it
> But I love you,
> > I love you,
> > > I love you----B
>
> P. S. The Folk Song Suite ("Up she goes"?) is just finished— good I hope.

To which Pears sent this reply:

> My dearest darling,
> No one has ever had a lovelier letter than the one which came from you today—You say things which turn my heart over

---

[30] He was to die of congestive heart failure on December 4, 1976. Kildea's speculation that he had contracted syphilis from Pears (who may have had other relationships before theirs began) has been thoroughly refuted by medical specialists who say that before his surgery he was thoroughly screened for syphilis and tested negative. His heart was problematic since his childhood, and his symptoms had no relationship to those of syphilis. It is a phobic speculation, a blot in an otherwise fine biography.

with love and pride, and I love you for *every single word* you write. But you know, Love is blind—and what your dear eyes do not see is that it is *you* who have given *me* everything, right from the beginning, from yourself in Grand Rapids! through Grimes & Serenade & Michelangelo and Canticles—one thing after another, right up to this great Aschenbach —I am here as your mouthpiece and I live in your music—And I can never be thankful enough to you and to Fate for all the heavenly joy we have had together for 35 years.

My darling, I love you —P

The reader can't help being struck by the melding of aesthetic wonder and personal love. Britten loves the man *in* the voice, in its taste, its interpretive clarity, its sheer beauty. The work is the Thomas Hardy song cycle "Winter Words," written for Pears in 1953, in which the final poem, "Before Life and After," ends with "Ere nescience shall be reaffirmed/how long, how long"—alluding to the earth's transition from a time of human suffering to a time when all human happiness and unhappiness is erased—a dark thought, a Schopenhauerian thought, a thought of the erasure of all that matters to ignorant humans. But then Britten immediately turns the phrase around to express his longing for the return of Pears, totally inverting Hardy to assert the supreme meaningfulness of human love, even as death makes its looming presence felt. In Pears's voice he hears not "nescience" and the meaninglessness of effort, but beauty and meaning.

Pears's reply, too, celebrates the merger of life and art in the work, and he acknowledges that Britten's generosity went beyond his, in the power of the many creations he was lucky enough to have a role in. Their partnership was a life of joy, a position he reaffirmed frequently after Britten's death.

What the reader of these letters in general, and this one in particular, must conclude is that both men are profoundly un-Schopenhauerian. They see meaning, joy, and beauty in their life and love, and what Britten strives to create (even when his texts are pessimistic) are images of beauty and meaning. And there is something more to be said: although the text and even the music of *Winter Words* may represent bleakness, the music endows the tragedy of human life with beauty; thus, I believe, inverting Schopenhauer: by becoming art, the bleak becomes meaningful and beautiful, and so do the artists.

When we approach the *War Requiem*, then, ideas of the transformative power of art and the beauty of music must be always in our minds—not as removing life's tragedy, but as negating pessimism about it. And the solidity of love in his life nourished that antipessimism.

The Representation of Love, the Representation of Beauty

We could trace these themes all the way through Britten's works. But here I want only to look at three examples of music that Britten wrote for Pears, all of which look ahead to key moments in the *War Requiem*: "Being Beauteous" from *Illuminations* (Op. 18, 1939); "Spirto Ben Nato," the last sonnet in the sequence *Seven Sonnets of Michelangelo* (Op. 22, 1940); and "What if this present," a sonnet at the heart of the sequence *Holy Sonnets of John Donne* (Op. 35, 1945). *Illuminations*, settings of Rimbaud's prose-poems, was begun before Britten and Pears left England for the United States, and was finished there; it was not initially written for Pears to sing: his vocal development was just starting to peak, under the guidance of his new voice teacher, Clytie Mundy; but this song was dedicated to him. It was first performed by soprano Sophie Wyss, but Britten later preferred it to be sung by Pears.

"Being Beauteous": The Transformative Vision of Beauty

Devant une neige un Être de Beauté de haute taille. Des sifflements de mort et des cercles de musique sourde font monter, s'élargir et trembler comme un spectre ce corps adoré: des blessures écarlates et noires éclatent dans les chairs superbes. Les couleurs propres de la vie se foncent, dansant, et se dégagent autour de la Vision, sur le chantier. Et les frissons s'élèvent et grondent, et la saveur forcenée de ces effets se chargeant avec les sifflements mortels et les rauques musiques que le monde, loin derrière nous, lance sur notre mère de beauté – elle recule, elle se dresse. Oh! nos os son revêtus d'un nouveau corps amoureux.

*****

Ô la face cendrée, l'écusson de crin, les bras de cristal! Le cannon sur lequel je dois m'abbatre à travers la mêlée des arbres et de l'air léger.[31]

Rimbaud's prose-poem describes, I suggest, a transformative vision of bodily beauty by a pair of potential lovers—both the vision and the lovers being beset by hostility from the surrounding world—and then a somewhat anxious, but ultimately serene, yielding to sexual love. The characters are: first, a Beauteous Being, also called "our mother of beauty," tall, and wounded, showing

---

[31] Before a background of snow stands a tall Beauteous Being. Whisperings of death and circles of muffled music make this adored body rise up, expand, and tremble like an apparition. Scarlet and black gashes burst open in the magnificent flesh. The colors of ordinary life darken, dance, and break loose around this vision on its path. And the shudders rise and rumble, and the maniacal flavor of these effects—taking on the mortal whispers and the raucous music that the world, far behind us, hurls at our mother of beauty. She withdraws, she stands upright. O! our bones are reclothed in a new loving body.
*****
O the ashen face, the breastplate of hair, the arms of crystal. The cannon against which I must impale myself, amid the confusion of trees and the light breeze.

(I have made my own translation, consulting many others.)

gashes that reveal her flesh and blood—almost a Christ figure, the sword in her side. Then there are the "we," presumably lovers inspired by the vision of beauty, which causes a total transformation of their bodies into a "new loving body." And then, at the end of the poem (following a pause indicated in the text), one of the "we" makes a decision to yield to sexual penetration, which is described in anxious language: the penis is a "cannon" on which he allows himself to be "impaled." The other primary character in the poem is the world, which from the beginning is "whispering" in hostile ways, and with an unmusical music, described first as "hollow" and later as "raucous." The world's complaint becomes more aggressive, a maniacal shuddering and rumbling. The world is eventually "far behind" the lovers, but it keeps hurling its ugly noises at them nonetheless. The Beauteous Being withdraws. The lovers' bodies are transformed into a "new loving body." Eventually solitude is achieved, the lovers are moved by one another's bodies, described as beautiful. They then yield to passion, concealed by a covering of trees and "light air."

Unlike the subsequent song cycles, written for voice and piano so that the two could perform them together on tour, this cycle is scored for string orchestra.

The musical setting begins with an incantatory legato passage in C major in 12/8 rhythm, with repeated triplet chords in the strings, producing a shimmering background. The vocal line repeats one high note, then rises by a third—then descends, and returns again to the note, high E, to which it will return in subsequent visionary passages. The effect of being bewitched is created by means that are suggestive of Glass's minimalism, though obviously that would be anachronistic. (Both are influenced by Debussy.) The effect is of a charmed hypnotic state—followed by graceful light leaps to arrive at "ce corps adore." When the world enters, the tessitura is lower, the music staccato and harsh. The world's music is indeed "raucous," especially by contrast to what has preceded. As the world fades into the distance, harshness is banished, and hypnotic fascination returns. The shimmering C major triplets return, and there is the incantatory repetition of E, rising ultimately to G on "amoureux."

The music does not make a break as in the text, but continues on, as the "I" has a specific vision of the lover's face and chest hair, with two falling lines—and then an ecstatic repetition of the E-G sequence, but this time rising to G sharp, on the words "arms of crystal." (These are physical arms, —bras—not military arms.) Then the vision, sustained for nine eighth-notes, is followed by a fascinating suggestion of falling toward the other lover, as the "I" permits himself to be penetrated—anxiously at first, in marcato leaps with complex chromaticism on the words "impale myself"—but ending with a restful pianissimo closure in C major—middle C, so the intense high tessitura of the vision is abandoned, it seems, for a restful acceptance. The orchestra concludes with pulsing strings and then a shimmering high chord.

The dedication to Peter Pears, and the fact that after the premiere Britten wanted only Pears to sing it, invite us to search for a personal meaning. One can easily find it in Britten's decision to become sexually involved with Pears, and the lifelong erotic and artistic fascination that preceded and followed that decision. One should note the link between the vision of beauty and the wounded Christ, which will reappear at a crucial moment in the War Requiem (as well as in the Donne sonnets). The repose of the musical ending is rather foreign to the ethos of Rimbaud—just as the relationship it celebrates is a world apart from the fraught relationship of Rimbaud and Verlaine, which involved heavy drug and alcohol abuse, domestic violence (by Verlaine toward his wife and child), and ultimately attempted murder (as Verlaine shot Rimbaud in a jealous rage). The creativity of both poets was ruined by their relationship: Verlaine, after a stint in prison, sank into alcoholism (though not before producing some inferior volumes of poetry under the influence of his conversion to Catholicism), and Rimbaud gave up writing altogether to travel in Africa. Things would be very different for Britten and Pears, as they already seemed to know, and Auden to intuit, at this early time.

Spirto Ben Nato: Love's Commitment

The *Seven Sonnets of Michelangelo*, Op. 22, were completed in 1940 in Amityville, Long Island, although the first performance did not take place until 1942, when Britten and Pears were back in England. This became the most frequently performed of the Britten song cycles on their recital tours. Pears later commented, "They were the first of a whole row of works which he wrote for me. They have indeed on that account, as well as others, a very special meaning for me."[32] He also commented, in 1985, that Britten saw how much his voice had improved and wanted "to test me out," noting that the sonnets are "very complicated poems, very intense"—thus challenging not just the voice, but the pair's powers of coordinated interpretation.[33]

And indeed the pair developed a remarkable coordination and a virtual expressive unity from this point onward. Singer Dietrich Fischer-Dieskau called them the Dioscuri of "Heavenly Twins" (Castor and Pollux).[34] This idea of expressive and emotional unity, so central to the Sonnets, made Pears, a keen student of music history, comment that their work together reminded him of Schubert's observation that when he performed his own songs accompanying the singer Johann Michael Vogl, they seemed like one person. "I like to think that perhaps when I sang Ben's songs with him we also sounded like one person."[35]

The cycle was not, however, primarily a test; it had, as interpreters have felt ever since, the nature of a love letter. Britten himself

---

[32] Headington (1993, p. 99).
[33] Ibid.
[34] Ibid. (p. 314).
[35] Ibid. (1993, p. 315).

commented to a friend after the first performance at the Wigmore Hall: "I was rather nervous about presenting them. . . . It was rather like parading naked in public!"[36] However, Kildea's summary that the songs are "an impassioned love letter to Pears, ripe with unrestrained feelings and emotions,"[37] seems a little off: the sonnets, and their settings, are highly disciplined, complicated, intricate, and knotty. As Pears later wrote in his essay "Vocal Music," "they are highly concentrated and disciplined, and might not appear a suitable vehicle for varied lyricism. But in fact such a challenge always stimulates Britten."[38]

In an excellent study of Britten's use of the sonnet form to investigate love (both here and in the later John Donne sonnet sequence), Lloyd Whitesell argues that the sonnet is a form suited to an intricate dialectic involving "a progression of ideas" and that Britten found the form a musical challenge. Typically, his music did not simply imitate the poetic form with pause between octave and sestet. Usually, he would, in a through-composed manner, "desig[n] unique gestures of parallelism, development, and/or return for the individual features of each poem. This gives him the flexibility to mold the musical discourse to the twists and turns in the poetic argument."[39] In particular, the relationship between lyricism and declamation changes from song to song.

Illuminations was a work structured by Rimbaud, although Britten selected individual poems. *Seven Sonnets* is different. Out of the large number of sonnets Michelangelo wrote to the young nobleman Tommaso dei Cavalieri, Britten has selected just seven and ordered them thus: XVI, XXXI, XXX, LV, XXXVIII, XXXII,

---

[36] Ben Hogwood, "Listening to Britten—*Seven Sonnets of Michelangelo*, Op. 22." Good Morning Britten (blog), August 29, 2013. https://goodmorningbritten.wordpress.com/2013/08/29/listening-to-britten-seven-sonnets-of-michelangelo-op-22.

[37] Kildea (2013), p. 173.

[38] Peter Pears, "The Vocal Music," in *Benjamin Britten: A Commentary on His Works from a Group of Specialists*, edited by Donald Mitchell and Hans Keller (New York: Philosophical Library, 1952), 59–74.

[39] Whitesell (2013, p. 41).

and XXIV. We are then invited to look for an overall narrative arc to the sequence, as well as for obvious aesthetically pleasing effects of varied rhythm, pace, and tonality. We cannot interpret the final song without placing it, first, in the development of the sequence. Overall, the sequence focuses on the wonder of love, but also its difficulties. Along the way, there is much obscurity and many unanswered questions. Musically, there are often fundamental harmonic oppositions, such as C minor/major in Sonnet XXXI and B flat/ E in LV.

Sonnet XVI, primarily declamation, sets the stage, describing the difficulty of the artist who would attempt to depict the beloved, whose inner feelings are not fully knowable. It introduces the crucial theme of parallelism between inner and outer. In Sonnet XXXI the speaker's passion breaks out with rapid movement as he complains of his state, tossed about "between joy and grief." He concludes, however, that to be love's captive is his fate: "If to be happy I must be / conquered and held captive, no wonder then / that I, unarmed and alone, remain the prisoner of / a Cavalier in arms."

Captivity leads to rapturous illumination: "With your lovely eyes I see a sweet light / that yet with my blind ones I cannot see." Sonnet XXX, marked Andante tranquillo, has much similarity with the rapturous parts of "Being Beauteous." And it goes on to celebrate the spiritual unity of the lovers, developing further the imagery of light and darkness: "My will is in your will alone, / my thoughts are born in your heart, / my words are on your breath. / Alone, I am like the moon in the sky / which our eyes cannot see / save that part which the sun illumines." And the vocal line ends on "sole" on a long-sustained pianissimo high E.

From this immobile point of ravished clarity, however, the cycle descends again into difficulty. Sonnet LV, "*Poco presto ed agitato*," describes the artist's anguished reluctance to commit himself fully to love, though he states that he would like to do so, and though the sonnet moves toward lyrical tranquility at its close. Sonnet XXXVIII shows the lover despairing of a return of his love and wondering whether he could ever love again, "since with me you are not satis-fied." Sonnet XXXII, "Vivace," returns to passionate praise of what their love achieves and contains—but rapidly rushing ahead, very unsure, and always in the conditional mode: ". . . and if one spirit rules two hearts, / if in two bodies one soul is made eternal / raising both to heaven on the same wings; /. . . if in loving one another, forgetting oneself / with one pleasure and one delight there is such reward / that both wills strive for the same end; if thousands / and thousands do not make one hundredth part / to such a bond of love, to such constancy." And finally the line of doubt: "can, then, mere anger break and dissolve it?" The word *mere* seeks the answer "no." But the agitation of the music betrays residual uncertainty. So far, then, the cycle explores love's wonder but also, in a stylized way, the doubts and uncertainties that assail any such deep commitment.

When we arrive at Sonnet XXIV, after the tension and questioning of XXII, the impression is that of exiting from a dark maze into an open meadow filled with light. The key is the expan-sive and open key of D major, a favorite key of Britten's to address issues of love and peace (see Chapter 5). The piano part, stately, with solemn octaves, almost like a coronation of the lovers, begins alone, to be followed by the vocal line, soaring up to a high A, unaccompa-nied, in a rapturous praise of the spirit of his loved one, whose very limbs, both virtuous and beloved, show what perfection nature can achieve. This is the only time that the musical setting follows the strophic structure of the sonnet. It is the simplest setting in the cycle—as if, after all the difficulty and the vexed questions, it is all quite simple after all. You are both beautiful and good, and I love you. The piano takes over again, and then hands expression back to the voice, this time praising his lover's graceful spirit, which makes him believe that Love, Compassion, and Mercy dwell within, just as they are expressed in his face.

Piano and voice now join together: "Love takes me captive, and Beauty binds me. / Compassion and Mercy with sweet glances / fill my heart with a strong hope." Just as the piano and the vocal line now sound together, so the inside and the outside are now together. "Beauty binds me" uses a distinctive chromatic twisting shape common in the cycle, suggesting integration: strands that were heard separately are now, as Whitesell says, "bound together in the sestet."[40]

It must be said again: This ending is Britten's. The poems might have been arranged in many other orders, and other poems might have been selected. It is a totally anti-Schopenhauerian ending, affirming beauty, goodness, and meaning in a human love affair, and seeing the body as the fitting and symmetrical house of meaning and even of virtue. That is not to say that commitment and meaning entirely cancel angers and questions; that would be unrealistic in any relationship. But the dominant conclusion is intensely affirmative.

Overall, the sonnet sums up images from the whole cycle—inner/outer, character/body, captivity/commitment—suggesting that emotion and commitment are now fully integrated and trust has banished doubt.[41] The final tercet dares to ask whether there is any reason why this partnership could not be eternal.

At this point, after the singer has sung his final word, the piano goes on, pianissimo, in a kind of angelic conclusion, with rolled chords standing in for a harp, and ending on a very soft and distant D major chord. Whitesell finds this ending weak and unconvincing. I disagree. I think that Britten, conscious ever since childhood of impending mortality, is following the sonnet's suggestion that the love of the lovers—and the art that expresses it—may find its own way of conquering death—through human continuity, the only sort of immortality he ever believed in. The kind that both he and Pears have attained.

Whitesell suggests that the cycle is a "test" not only of Pears's voice but also of his emotional commitment. I see nothing in the

---

[40] See ibid., p. 56.
[41] See ibid., p. 57, who speaks of "a collaborative project, a shred destiny."

cycle to indicate this. It ends on a ringing, and fully mutual, note of affirmation. If it is a "test" of anyone, I believe that test is addressed to its audience: see who we really are, see what you don't typically see. See, if you can, the beauty that is exemplified here. That is a characteristic Britten–Pears gesture, as in the volume of letters, defying a world that sees only squalor and pathos in same-sex male lives to witness what has actually been realized in these two. More generally, it asks a post-Victorian audience to acknowledge that sexual love can also exemplify virtue, commitment, and beauty.

What If: Love's Power to Redeem

So far we have studied two affirmations of beauty (the first linking beauty to the body of Christ, the second linking bodily love to inner worth). Pitted against the world's hostility, beauty survives and even flourishes. But we have not yet turned to the horrors of war. I now examine Britten's *Holy Sonnets of John Donne*, Op. 35, written for Pears immediately after the war, and, specifically, right after Britten had been taken to Belsen to witness the horrors of that notorious concentration camp. The work had its premiere in November 1945.

Britten visited Belsen in the company of violinist Yehudi Menuhin, who was working with a Jewish organization operating under the aegis of the United Nations. Menuhin had volunteered to give concerts for the camp's survivors and local German civilians, playing the works of Mendelssohn, Beethoven, and Bach. Britten asked if he could replace the scheduled pianist.[42] The conditions, which have often been described in harrowing detail, were still awful when they arrived. As Menuhin recorded, "Men and women alike, our audience was dressed in army blankets. . . . [S]ince their rescue they had put a little flesh on their bones, but to our

---

[42] Kildea (2013, p. 254).

unaccustomed eyes they seemed desperately haggard, and many were still in hospital."[43]

Menuhin often described the experience, urging the world to confront the reality of the camp; but Britten remained locked in a shell-shocked silence. Once in the early 1960s, he did state to an interviewer, "We gave two or three short recitals a day. They couldn't take more. It was in many ways a terrifying experience."[44] One thing that is absolutely clear is that he and Pears never altered their pacifist stance, which they asserted repeatedly in program notes and other statements made after the visit. I shall delve into Britten's pacifism in Chapter 5, with much criticism. Britten did, however, turn to music to express his response to the horrors of war. Many thought that the experience shifted him from a theoretical pacifism to an active compassion—to what musicologist Justin Vickers calls a "desire to support life at all cost and to comfort those affected by the terrors of war."[45]

Donne's sonnets have death and loss as their theme—but, even more, the human responsibility for suffering and death. "I think the connexion between personal experience and my feelings about the poetry was a strong one," Britten later said. "It certainly characterized the music."[46] Britten completed the cycle in only a little over two weeks, part of the time sick in bed with a bad reaction to a typhoid shot. He dedicated it to Pears. As with the Michelangelo sonnets, Britten chose the material and arranged

[43] Ibid.

[44] Ibid., p. 255.

[45] Justin Vickers, "Benjamin Britten's Silent 'Epilogue' to 'The Holy Sonnets of John Donne.'" *The Musical Times* 156, No. 1933 (2015): 17–30. As this fascinating article shows, Britten had originally planned to conclude the cycle with a setting of parts of Donne's *Meditation*, including the famous lines, "any man's *death* diminishes *me*, / because I am involved in Mankinde; / And therefore never send to know / for whom the *bell* tolls; It tolls for *thee*." Speculations as to why the Epilogue was cut and only unfinished drafts survive are bound to be inconclusive. Mine would be that he had already communicated the message of universal compassion powerfully in his setting of "What if this present," in a more qualified, subtle, and interrogative form.

[46] Kildea (2013, p. 257).

the sequence—but Donne wrote only nineteen Holy Sonnets, and Britten set nine, so it is a much larger proportion of the material, and Britten included the most famous poems: "Oh my blacke soule," "Batter my heart, three-person'd God," "Thou hast made me," and ending with "Death be not proud." As with Michelangelo, the conclusion is a ringing affirmation, both verbal and musical, of the defeat of death. But the material inside the sequence is profoundly tortured and shows Britten confronting—as he had already in *Peter Grimes*—the terrible toll of human aggression, and expressing doubt in the goodness of the human soul. The sonnet form (as Whitesell again insists) is profoundly suited to this knotty questioning. The fact that the language of this cycle is English, the language that always elicited the best from both Britten and Pears (who was relatively comfortable in German but uncomfortable in French and Italian), makes these sonnets some of Britten's most powerful vocal works.

What is at stake in the sequence is still love—now, however, not love between two humans, but the love of humans for God and God for humans. Britten was not a conventional theist, but religious ideas had great meaning for him, and (as he said in his conscientious objector hearings) the life and teachings of Jesus in particular. Can the flawed human being find his or her way to the source of goodness that is Christ's life and teaching? And will his or her efforts be met with mercy, or with silence? Is there any hope of redemption, in the light of the horrors humans have created through war?

I want to examine just one sonnet, right in the middle of the sequence, the fifth of nine. It asks these questions with unusual power and uses the parallel between inner and outer beauty to give them a hopeful, albeit agonized, answer. It seems to me a crucial precursor of the Agnus Dei of the *War Requiem*.

> What if this present were the world's last night?
> Marke in my heart, O Soule, where thou dost dwell,
> The picture of Christ crucified, and tell

Whether that countenance can thee affright,
Teares in his eyes quench the amazing light,
Blood fills his frownes, which from his pierc'd head fell.
And can that tongue adjudge thee into hell,
Which pray'd forgivenesse for his foes fierce spight?
No, no; but as in my Idolatrie
I said to all my profane mistresses,
Beauty, of pity, foulenesse onely is
A sign of rigour: so I say to thee,
To wicked spirits are horrid shapes assign'd,
This beauteous forme assures a piteous minde.

The first line is set apart. The piano imitates trumpet fanfares, and with the dramatic declamation of the voice the whole, as Whitesell nicely says, "supplies a thrilling imaginative evocation of the day of judgment" (43). The vocal line continues in declamatory style throughout the octave, with no lyricism, over a dissonant accompaniment. There are sudden upward vocal leaps on "teares," "blood," and "forgiveness," as if to imitate the agony of Christ's physical suffering, which the speaker clearly has inside him as a vivid "picture."[47]

Doubt is forcefully dismissed at the opening of the sestet: "No, no." Then there is an abrupt shift to a quiet lyricism, as the speaker remembers loving words he said to his "profane mistresses," telling them that (their) beauty is a sign of compassion, whereas ugliness would have been a sign of harshness. The gentle music recalls a love lyric, as religious poetry often borrows the conventions of love poetry. The key parallel is between the speaker's (former) mistresses, whom he prized for their beauty, and Christ, whom he now calls a "beauteous forme." As critic Anne Ferry notes, the speaker's internal monologue is initially addressed only to himself, but is evidently meant to be overheard by Christ—whom he now addresses

[47] See Whitesell (2013, p. 43).

directly in "so I say to thee."[48] In effect, he is endeavoring to seduce Christ, using the trope he employed to seduce his mistresses. This rhetorical device engenders doubt in the listener. And yet, the evident capacity of music to evoke real tenderness and gentleness is nonetheless persuasive: there is something genuinely worthy and persuasive in this speaker, since he can fashion with his music the notes of real compassion. Will he win Christ's compassion? The soft downturn on "a piteous mind" suggests this as a distinct possibility—although the piano, with its soft continued trumpet-like reminders of the last judgment, leaves the listener profoundly uncertain.

Music's power to represent real beauty is, here, the "outer beauty" that, in the trope, is meant to signify inner worth. And is there no worth there, the song seems to ask? How can music create beauty, create, even, a picture of the body and blood of Christ, if the human soul is completely foul? While the speaker is using the inner-outer parallel to describe the relationship between Christ's beautiful body and his inner compassion, at the same time he suggests a parallel in his own heart: if humans can create compassionate music like this, can they be utterly unworthy of mercy? Or: Christ is here, in this music, and can this outward form of compassion not serve as proof of real active compassion in human life? It is a question, not an answer, but nonetheless a hopeful question.

By this time, Pears's mature voice was capable of greater expressive depth, and his performance of this song is among his finest. And Britten, as always, plays with a rare attunement, subtlety, and expressiveness. That too is part of the musical meaning: the bodily performance of compassion and human love is not only in the composition but also in its performance.

There are other works of Britten's that I might have used to study these themes: *Peter Grimes*, for its excoriation of the crowd's aggression against the outcast; and above all *Billy Budd*, for the image

---

[48] Quoted in ibid. (pp. 43–44).

of an innocent and beautiful Christlike figure brought to grief by human evil, and for the possibility of redemption through the influence of that sacrificed figure. But full interpretations of these operas lie well beyond the scope of this book. I think, however, that the works chosen in these two chapters give a sufficient background for approaching the *War Requiem*—a kind of repertory of characteristic Britten meditations on the causes of aggression and on the worth of human striving—if we add to these the theme I'll discuss in the following chapter: Britten's pacifism and some of its musical expressions.

5

Pacifisms and the Music of Peace

We have more control over our own characters than we have
over the external forms of society. So we must begin with ourselves, knowing that to the extent that we can win self-control
and strength in the qualities needed for the struggle, we will be
able to begin to modify society. . . . The responsibility thus rests
squarely on ourselves and our work begins there.
> —Richard B. Gregg, *The Power of Nonviolence* (1935)

Peace is not silent: it is the voice of love.
> —Britten, *Owen Wingrave* (1971), Owen's "peace" aria

Pacifism was a central part of the lives of both Britten and Pears,
from their days as conscientious objectors in World War II to
the end of their lives. It also poses a difficult challenge for people
responding to the *War Requiem*, since that work clearly grows out
of this long pacifist history, and yet is aimed at a far more inclusive
audience, most of whose members would have approved of violent
resistance against the Germans in World War II. Giving Britten a
commission to write a work commemorating the rededication of
Coventry Cathedral, bombed during World War II, was in many
ways surprising or even shocking, given his position. The shock is
compounded by his use of the poetry of Wilfred Owen about World
War I to commemorate World War II, a very different war, calling
for different sentiments and actions. And yet, as I shall argue, the
work transcends what I understand to be the grave errors of that
position, building on a common ground of reconciliation, rededication, and what I shall call "emotional pacifism"—rejection of

The Tenderness of Silent Minds. Martha C. Nussbaum, Oxford University Press.
© Oxford University Press 2024. DOI: 10.1093/oso/9780197568538.003.0005

retributive anger against enemies in favor of a spirit of love. It is that spirit of love that Britten obsessively pursues in numerous works related to the *War Requiem* and in that work itself.

Types of Pacifism: Britten, Pears, and Gandhi

"Pacifism" refers most familiarly to a position concerning action— a refusal to take part in acts of violence. I shall call this sort *action-pacifism*. In the thought of its major theoretical exponents, Gandhi above all, but also Martin Luther King Jr., it also refers, more deeply, to a position concerning an internal state of being—the refusal of retributive anger and the embrace of universal love and brotherhood. I shall call this *emotional pacifism*, and it is not only compatible with pacifism about actions, it is typically its source. The love in question is understood to be not romantic love, not friendly love, but an attitude that sees potential good in all people and aims at the preservation and enhancement of this precious potential. (Martin Luther King Jr. was particularly precise and eloquent in defining the type of love his movement sought and expressed.) Britten will develop the spirit of love in a highly individual way, connecting it to embrace of the body and even to a generalized quasi-erotic wonder at the beauty of bodies.

One can be a pacifist in the first sense, abhorring war and acts of physical violence, while still believing that retributive anger can be a creative force, and even that the criminal law should be developed in a retributive spirit. While in the end this position is not easy to justify theoretically, it is rather common. I believe it was the position of many people of my generation who opposed the Vietnam War and called themselves pacifists.

It is also possible to be a pacifist in the second sense, endorsing and cultivating in oneself a spirit of non-anger and love, while permitting violent actions in certain circumstances, particularly those of individual or communal self-defense. Such a person will abhor violent acts, but may still think them necessary at times to defend self or others. Martin Luther King Jr. held this position, although he opposed violent acts of self-defense in the civil rights movement for strategic reasons.[1] I shall call his approach one of *emotional pacifism and action-pacifism with exceptions.* Such exceptions may be either theoretical or pragmatic. King was an action-pacifist with theoretical exceptions that he forwent for pragmatic reasons. There may also be other varieties of what may be called *pragmatic pacifism*: looking to particular situations and asking, pragmatically, what approach will best achieve the legitimate end of protecting lives. Nelson Mandela, after initially trying nonviolence in both emotion and action, concluded that this approach was failing to advance his movement's legitimate cause of freedom from violent oppression, and turned to a limited use of violence (primarily against property), though never swerving from non-anger and a loving approach to enemies.[2] (It is not clear whether he also thought the exceptions theoretically justified as in *action-pacifism with theoretical exceptions.*) The pragmatic pacifist diverges from a total pacifism about actions, but is only a true pacifist, as most of the tradition defines pacifism, if *emotional pacifism*, a firm and exceptionless adherence to non-anger and love, is retained: such a person will not glory in the use of violence, and will use just enough to protect human lives, seeking reconciliation and an end to violence as soon as possible.

Gandhi was what I shall call a *total pacifist without exceptions*, whether theoretical or pragmatic, endorsing total pacifism in both action and the inner world with no exceptions at all. His mother's family were Jains, who endorse a very complete nonviolence in action, including toward all animals and some parts of the plant

---

[1] See Nussbaum, "From Anger to Love: Self-Purification and Political Resistance," in *To Shape a New World*, edited by Tommie Shelby and Brandon M. Terry (Cambridge, MA: Harvard University Press, 2018): 105–26.

[2] See Nussbaum, *Anger and Forgiveness: Resentment, Generosity, Justice* (New York: Oxford University Press., 2016), ch. 7.

world, and who ground that *ahimsa*, nonviolence, in a profound love of all living things. Gandhi rejected all forms of cooperation in all war efforts, including World War II. He cultivated and taught an inner spirit of non-anger and love. As part of his commitment to nonviolence, he totally rejected meat-eating and, increasingly as his life went on, the use of dairy products. Gandhi was a pragmatist in certain ways: he tolerated behavior in his followers that he rejected in himself. Thus Jawaharlal Nehru strongly supported military action against the Axis powers, feeling that the horrors of Nazism demanded urgent action. He thought that Gandhi's claim that Hitler could be converted to nonviolence by the power of love was utterly ridiculous, as indeed it was. Gandhi disagreed, but continued to work with Nehru. However, in the Indian independence movement itself, Gandhi insisted unequivocally on total nonviolence in actions (apart from meat-eating, as we shall shortly see), as a necessary condition for membership in his movement.[3]

Gandhi's position, though dogmatic, was not pragmatically absurd with respect to the British. The British, though beastly in many ways and violent when it suited them, were not unalterably wedded to remaining in India, and they also had their limits. General Reginald Dyer's massacre of innocent civilians at Jallianwala Bagh in 1919 had been harshly criticized in Parliament, so when Gandhi's peaceful marches were opposed by British troops, they restrained themselves to a degree, beating people up and imprisoning leaders, but not shooting people. Nor were the imprisoned leaders harshly treated. Nehru had loads of books, access to correspondence and writing materials, and even the Gandhian spinning wheel he requested in his cell. Meanwhile Gandhi, one of the greatest theatricalizers of justice the world has ever known, was more rarely imprisoned (basically, the British were afraid to court world opprobrium by doing

---

[3] During the Boer War, Gandhi did perform supportive service, founding and participating in the Natal Indian Ambulance Corps in 1899. But his pacifism developed and hardened as the years went on.

so), and he used nonviolent marches to draw the attention of the entire world to the dignity and restraint of Indian people, who had long been said (and by no less an authority on ethics than John Stuart Mill) to be children, incapable of reasoned self-government. Just as King knew that violence on the part of marchers for civil rights, even in self-defense, would be used to confirm all the worst stereotypes of Black people, so Gandhi knew the same about Indian violence: it would be used as proof of incapacity to self-govern.

He calculated correctly. Recently opened British archives show that the British were utterly flummoxed and mystified by this dignified behavior, and had no idea how to oppose it, whereas they knew well how to deal with force.[4] Nonviolence, then, was an apt pragmatic strategy to use with the British and could be endorsed by followers of Gandhi, like Nehru, who utterly rejected its use against Hitler, where it was utterly implausible. Gandhi was also a pragmatist about the dietary practices of others. Many of his leading followers continued to eat some meat, and most ate dairy products. Although he was obsessed with diet for himself, he abstained from preaching about diet to Nehru and other leaders of the independence movement. So we might say that in the end Gandhi was a *pragmatic dogmatic pacifist*.

Because Buddhism is another important source of pacifism in our world, it is also important to say that Buddhism, too, makes my distinction between emotional pacifism and pacifism about acts. Buddhist thinkers make emotional pacifism primary (Santideva's treatise on anger is one of the great works on this topic in any philosophical tradition), but take a variety of different positions, both pragmatic and theoretical, about the use of violence in action.[5]

---

[4] See Dennis Dalton, *Mahatma Gandhi: Nonviolent Power in Action*. Revised 3d edition (New York: Columbia University Press, 1993/2012).

[5] I owe thanks to Tom Ginsburg for discussion on this point. See Michael K. Jerryson and Mark Juergensmeyer, eds., *Buddhist Warfare* (Oxford, UK: Oxford University Press, 2010) and Michael K. Jerryson, *Buddhist Fury: Religion and Violence in Southern Thailand* (Oxford, UK: Oxford University Press, 2011).

Let me recapitulate: what does emotional pacifism entail? It is, after all, an unfamiliar concept. It requires trying with all one's might to extirpate hatred and retributive anger in oneself, so that one can approach others, always, with a spirit of love. The exemplars to bear in mind are Gandhi, Jesus, and (for those with a knowledge of Buddhism) the Buddha. King, who continually exhorted his followers to love their enemies, had to spend a lot of time explaining himself, even though they were familiar with the teachings of Jesus, because they really did not understand how they could possibly approach Southern bigots with love. He told them that loving your enemies doesn't mean that you need to like them, or agree with them; and of course it has nothing to do with romantic love. It means being oriented to them as to a person, a soul, with the potentiality for both good and evil, hence for change. One might think, here, of Jesus's parable of the Prodigal Son: his father embraces him with unconditional love even though he profoundly disapproves of his actions—which the father no doubt will subsequently criticize. The point is that the love is very basic and prior to the moral critique. Jesus and Gandhi want us to approach everyone in that spirit.[6]

The emotional pacifist risks being charged with cowardice. Both Gandhi and King sought to rebut that charge by showing the great risks pacifists run in a world of aggression. King's concept of "direct action" was the idea that protesters must put their very own bodies on the line, being ready to be beaten or jailed. Gandhi had already developed this idea—most memorably in the protest at the Dharasana Salt Works in 1930. All day long the protesters marched forward, four by four, only to be clubbed down by the British and taken off to be treated by supportive participants. The world was watching, and both the courage of the Indian men and the absurd thuggery of the British, who were trying to lay hands on an inner

---

[6] See Nussbaum (2016, ch. 3) on the Prodigal Son; on King, see Nussbaum (2018b).

source that they could not reach, became apparent to all, especially through Webb Miller's journalism.[7]

How did Britten orient himself in this world of different types of pacifism?[8] He had long had a profound abhorrence of violence in all its forms, both physical and emotional. In Chapter 3 I described the roots of this attitude in his school years, and it continued throughout his life. But in the run-up to World War II he became more aware of different theoretical sources of pacifism.[9] Ronald Duncan, with whom he collaborated on the "Pacifist March" (see Chapter 3), and who later supplied the (very bad) libretto to *The Rape of Lucretia*, was himself the author of a pamphlet entitled *The Complete Pacifist*.[10] But what he urged Britten to study was a more substantial book by Richard Gregg, *The Power of Non-Violence*.[11] In Duncan's *Working with Britten* he records that the Gregg book "influenced [Britten] considerably."[12] I have tracked down a copy of Duncan's pamphlet, now a rare item; but since it is indeed a pamphlet, some twenty-five pages long, with conclusions rather than arguments, I shall focus on Gregg in what follows.

Gregg's book is a first-rate example of public philosophy, written with conceptual and analytical clarity, well designed for nonacademic readers, yet profound and very serious. (I think it should be required of all undergraduates!) Gregg had spent years

---

[7] See Nussbaum (2016, ch. 7). Some nations have at times constructed analogues to "direct action" for conscientious objectors: activities that are not directly related to military activities but that incur real bodily risks, such as participating in medical experiments. (I owe this point to Lee Fennell.) Britain did not offer any such alternatives.

[8] Of course, not all of these examples were available to him in 1942, but his views remained utterly unchanged throughout his life.

[9] An influential pacifist work that Britten does not seem to refer to but might have known is Virginia Woolf's *Three Guineas* (London: Hogarth Press, 1938).

[10] Ronald Duncan, *The Complete Pacifist* (Leicester, UK: Leicester Cooperative Printing Society Ltd., 1937).

[11] Richard B. Gregg, *The Power of Nonviolence*. 2d rev. ed. (New York: Schocken Books (1935/1959).

[12] Carpenter (1992, p. 12). See Ronald Duncan, *Working with Britten: A Personal Memoir* (Welcombe, UK: Rebel Press, 1981).

with Gandhi, and it is Gandhi's version of nonviolence that he defends, though with none of its foreign terminology (*ahimsa*, *satyagraha*), and with one significant omission: though very clear about the importance of cleanliness in body and dress, Gregg is utterly silent about diet (as indeed was King), attempting to win over his British audience by not foregrounding a part of Gandhi's worldview that would seem to most readers unpleasant and foreign (although Britain had long had a strong vegetarian movement, from which Gandhi himself learned much during his years in London). The view defended is a total and unequivocal pacifism about both actions and emotions. Indeed, Gregg persuasively traces nonviolence to an inner disposition of love and a control over one's own aggression. Actions are mere symptoms: we must approach the root of the problem. Gregg makes no concessions at all to context and is determined to convince the reader that nonviolence is not only always superior theoretically but also always pragmatically feasible. Using historical examples (more and more of them as time goes on—the 1959 edition includes the Montgomery Bus boycott) and dwelling on how nonviolence actually works as a strategy, he encourages readers to suspend their skepticism and think it at least worth a try. His account of interpersonal dialogue is highly insightful and partly persuasive. Basically, he argues that opponents are used to force being met with force—but when they see the calm determined attitude of the nonviolent opponent, they are moved to wonder and introspection, and a relationship on an entirely new plane may be developed. The details of this idea are beautifully laid out, and in part persuasive.

One very important aspect of Gregg's analysis is his emphasis on the primacy of emotional pacifism—his idea being that inner anger and desire to defeat others is the origin of outer violence, and that a sufficient, possibly in the long run a necessary, way of curbing war is to delve into the inner world and change the emotions with which people confront one another, replacing aggressive competitiveness with generous love. King made this idea central to his movement, to great effect. And it is this aspect of Gregg's vision that seems to me especially important for Britten.

Not surprisingly, people who endorse aggressive and retributive anger like to portray emotional pacifism as a pathology, an unnatural way of being human. And, sure enough, just as people portrayed Britten's homosexuality as a pathology involving repressed sadism (see Chapter 4), so too they portrayed his pacifism as a disease. Thus, in a 1950 number of the journal *Music Survey* dedicated to Britten's music, musicologist Hans Keller pronounces: "Britten is a pacifist. It is an established fact that strong and heavily repressed sadism underlies pacifist attitudes."[13] And Carpenter gives Keller's view prominence in his biography of Britten because of its agreement with his own view of Britten's sexuality as grounded in repressed sadism. But Keller's absurd claim simply fails to take pacifism, and Britten, seriously.

We can see how well Gregg's analysis of emotional pacifism fits in with Britten's longstanding attitudes. Gregg's line of thinking developed Britten's attitudes further, in a direction that took him to the tribunals, and on to works of his maturity, including the *War Requiem* and *Owen Wingrave*. The personal example of Gandhi remained compelling for Britten, and he was shaken by Gandhi's assassination in 1948. He wrote to his publisher Ralph Hawkes, "The death of Gandhi has been a great shock to one of my strong convictions, & I am determined to commemorate this occasion in, possibly, some form of requiem, to his honor. When I shall complete this piece I cannot say." This may well have been the origin of the *War Requiem*. At any rate, when Britten was approached by the Coventry Arts Committee in 1958, he already had an outline ready.

As for Peter Pears: As a boy he quickly developed an aversion to violence, both physical and emotional. As with Britten, it began by seeing beatings at school—and, in his case, being made to beat younger boys. Even more painful was his memory of being made

---

[13] Quoted in Carpenter (1992, p. 315).

to box against another boy and humiliate him by defeat: "I was the winner and I felt absolutely terrible when it was over. I felt that I had really in some way committed a major sin in attacking this boy. . . . I was very profoundly, deeply shocked by a feeling that I had won and triumphed over another human being and reduced him to shame and pain and the rest of it. And I think it was probably that moment which said to me, 'I'm never going to fight. I am not going to take part in any war.' "[14]

As a boy Pears was a conventional Christian, but his family had Quaker roots. His great-great grandmother was the distinguished Quaker reformer Elizabeth Fry (1780–1845), who championed prison reform to improve the treatment of female inmates especially, and who also campaigned against the slave trade.[15] Pears remained in touch with Quakers throughout his life and introduced Britten to Quaker circles: they gave recitals at Friends' House. During his first hearing before the tribunal, Britten said, "I think with the Quakers I might find a spiritual home."[16] As Kildea remarks, Quakerism appealed to both men not only because of nonviolence but also because of Quakers' general antiauthoritarianism and trust in the conscience of the individual, as well as in a commitment to a culture of equal rights, including antislavery, women's rights, and the equal rights of Jews.[17]

Quakerism, however, was a wide tent. Although Quakers insisted on the divinity of Christ, they were tolerant of agnostics and even atheists. In his mature years, Pears and Britten were both religious in a general way but not theists, followers of Jesus but not church members. Britten, as we shall shortly see, denied conventional belief in God, and rejected the idea that pacifism had to rest on theism,

---

[14] Quoted in Headington, *Peter Pears* (1993, pp. 10–11); source not given but presumably an interview.

[15] Donald Mitchell, "Pears, Sir Peter Neville Luard (1910–1986), Singer." *Oxford Dictionary of National Biography*, September 2004.

[16] Kildea (2013, p. 205).

[17] Ibid.

but he accepted Jesus as a key moral exemplar. According to Pears, "He was religious in the general sense of acknowledging a power above greater than ourselves, but he wasn't a regular churchgoer."[18] He wrote a good deal for religious occasions, and said once to pianist Murray Perahia, "I'm not terribly religious in my ordinary life, but when it comes to my music I'm a very Christian composer."[19]

Like Britten, and no doubt a strong influence on Britten, Pears was a Gandhian, and affiliated with a number of pacifist groups worldwide, including the Fellowship of Reconciliation and the War Resisters League. These Gandhian views persisted through and after the war. In 1949 (thus after Britten's visit to Belsen), the two men gave a concert in Community Church Auditorium, which Donald Mitchell believes to be in the vicinity of New York (the program doesn't say). In the program they posted a statement of their pacifist principles, mentioning the example of Gandhi, and drawing attention to the way in which the existence of nuclear and biological weapons had made war even more irrational and destructive than it was before.[20] Later, their opposition to the Vietnam War was well known and was connected by many with *Owen Wingrave* (1971).

In one respect, both men diverged from Gandhi: both were keen meat-eaters throughout their lives. Steak tartare was a special favorite of Pears; and when once Pears cooked a curry that had no meat in it Britten complained.[21] But vegetarianism was no part of the Euro-American Gandhian movement. Neither Gregg nor King ever discusses it, and I am sure King judged that to do so would have weakened his movement. Britten and Pears did at any rate oppose fox-hunting and loved and cared for the animals they lived with. So far as I can see, they did not connect meat-eating with the pacifism they espoused, as would be natural given the British pacifist movement. A mysterious lacuna in this history is the unfinished

---

[18] Ibid. (p. 206).
[19] Ibid.
[20] The statement is reproduced in Mitchell (1999, p. 214).
[21] Headington (1993, p. 324).

opera of 1952, *Tyco the Vegan*, which Britten began to plan with South African novelist and poet William Plomer, who had apparently written a story with this title. It was to be a sci-fi opera for children, about some children who left earth and had to decide whether to return again. An unrevealing sketch of a Prologue survives, and one letter from Britten to Plomer discussing the children's choice and whether to include audience participation as with Tinkerbell in *Peter Pan*.[22] But we have no information about who Tyco was or why he was a vegan. The one known work where Plomer treats vegetarianism is a comic poem called "Satire," where the habits of people staying at a "vegetarian guesthouse" are gently mocked.[23] The tone of this poem rather tells against the opera's containing a serious discussion of veganism, or a critical reflection about Britten's habits. In any case the two dropped the project when they decided, instead, on the idea of writing the opera *Gloriana* for the coronation of Elizabeth II.

What should we make of this pacifism, which might be called *dogmatic pacifism* with no theoretical exceptions and no felt need for a pragmatic justification (less complete than Gandhi's on account of meat-eating but similar in spirit)? The first thing we must notice is that, like Gandhi and Gregg, Britten and Pears do not distinguish between emotional pacifism and pacifism about acts; they speak as if it is clear to them that the two entail one another. Thus they (and Gregg) make no room for a position such as that of King or Mandela, emotional pacifists, eschewing retributive anger, who nonetheless see a need for physical violence under certain circumstances. (The King–Mandela position is my position too, I should say, and I think it the most defensible position.) It would

---

[22] Lucy Walker,"Work of the Week 33. Tyco the Vegan," Britten Pears Arts (2021) https://brittenpearsarts.org/news/work-of-the-week-33-tyco-the-vegan. Plomer was an extremely interesting character, a novelist of note, a passionate opponent of apartheid, and a closeted gay man who pursued love affairs primarily in Japan.

[23] "In the vegetarian guesthouse, / All was frolic, feast, and fun; / Eager voices were enquiring, / 'Are the nettle cutlets done?'"

have been valuable to see how Gregg would have defended his own omission of that possibility. During World War II there were many people who were emotional pacifists but also believed that the threat to the world from a Hitler takeover must be resisted with force. Gregg presents no reply to them. The most we find is a very detailed and in part convincing account of how pacifists may by their dignity and respect for adversaries, gradually convert them. This is indeed plausible in many personal interactions, and even in public encounters with an adversary capable of being restrained, or at least contained, by law and principle, and in which the reaction of the general public is key to the pacifist's success—Gandhi in India, King in the United States. But it is not plausible in a confrontation with an autocratic national leader or leaders determined to crush other nations by massive force, such as the leaders of the Axis powers. As George Orwell said, in such dire circumstances, "Pacifism is objectively pro-Fascist. This is elementary common sense. If you hamper the war effort of one side you automatically help that of the other. Nor is there any real way of remaining outside such a war as the present one."[24]

Nor would Gregg be able to persuade the people of Ukraine today that nonviolence in response to Putin's imperialistic aggression was a wise or even a tenable strategy, however committed some of them might be to love and non-anger.

In short, the Gregg–Britten–Pears position has no room for the idea of a *just war* in defense of one's country and its values. In this respect the libretto of *Owen Wingrave* is disgracefully superficial, portraying the Wingraves as attached to an empty idea of glory, transmitted by sheer unthinking conformity. Only once is there even a brief mention of the sufferings of one's co-nationals. (Sir Philip once says, "What good are scruples . . .when the garrison's dying, women, children, gasping for food and water?") But for the most part Sir Philip talks about war as joyful and as bringing family

<hr />

[24] George Orwell, "Pacifism and the War." *Partisan Review* (August–September 1942).

glory. It is likely that Britten would have been a useless combat soldier, given his lifelong ill health; his heart defect would probably have prevented him from being given combat duty. But that is not what was at stake in the tribunals: for conscription included supportive civilian service, such as hospital duty. And even combat posts included a lot of intelligence work that took place far from actual combat and for which it seems that a high level of physical fitness was not insisted on. Pears seems to have been eligible for both types of service. It's easy to feel that they used their time more productively creating works of art—as Britten says in his statement to the tribunal; but many people in many lines of work might have made a similar plea. And as we approach the *War Requiem*, a work that uses poetry about World War I to comment on World War II, one feels the absence of any distinction between those two wars, or indeed between any war of national self-defense against imperialist aggression and a useless foray such as the Vietnam War. The furthest Britten ever went was to say that if Hitler came to power in Britain he would not cooperate with him; but he added (following Gandhi) that Hitler could be brought around by nonviolent resistance. And he did endorse Chamberlain's attempts to appease Hitler, supported the 1938 Munich agreement, and made no objection to the carving up of Czechoslovakia.[25] As I have said, he and Pears reiterated these positions often after the war.

To me, the position of Britten and Pears about World War II is deeply flawed and is itself a form of appeasement. They are in effect free riders on the courage and suffering of others. They do not want Hitler to take over Britain; they just want resistance, if any, to be done by others. (Gandhi was different, since he seems actually to have believed that it made no difference whether the Allies or the Axis powers won the war, a hideous position.) Even if we agree that the best long-term objective is to build a world of peace, refusing to aid in the fight against Hitler is horrible, and certainly

[25] Kildea (2013, p. 205).

retards that objective. British society was somewhat more friendly to pacifism than the United States ever has been, but the British also bore the costs of war far more than did the United States, being bombed on a nightly basis and risking invasion, and British people joined the war effort in far greater proportions than in the United States. Intellectuals and artists of all sorts got involved. Even Auden officially volunteered to return and serve, but was refused on grounds of his age (32); as mentioned in Chapter 3, he had already volunteered as an ambulance driver for the Nationalists in the Spanish Civil War, though Britten had tried to dissuade him.[26] Britten alludes to his creative projects. But lots of creative people put their creative projects on hold to help their nation survive. Just to cite cases I know personally: the philosophers R. M. Hare and Richard Wollheim were captured and spent time in prisoner-of-war camps (Wollheim briefly, in Germany, and then he escaped; Hare for three years in the notoriously brutal Japanese camps). Classical scholar Kenneth Dover was an officer in the Royal Artillery in Italy. Philosopher David Pears was accidentally gassed during gas-mask training in Oxford and spent the war in a sanitarium. Philosopher J. L. Austin was a leading officer in British intelligence, much decorated for his life-saving work on D Day intelligence. Classical scholar Hugh Lloyd-Jones became an officer in anti-Japanese intelligence in India and Burma, where philosopher Michael Dummett served under his command.[27] Writer Iris Murdoch worked with refugees under the United Nations Relief and Rehabilitation Agency. Robert Runcie, Archbishop of Canterbury from 1980 to 1991, served as a tank commander in the Scots Guards in Europe, eventually winning the Military Cross for two feats of bravery, saving comrades pinned under tanks. In May 1945 he was among

---

[26] Derek Cooke, *Gustav Mahler: An Introduction to His Music.* 2nd ed. (Cambridge, UK: Cambridge University Press, 1996, p. 12). Apparently, he never did drive an ambulance, but was put to work in the propaganda office.

[27] Dummett was later known for his tireless work against racism and in favor of changes in immigration policy.

the first British soldiers to enter the Bergen-Belsen camp. The great Roman historian Ronald Syme worked as a press attaché in the British embassies of Belgrade and Ankara, and his refusal to discuss the nature of his activity has led many to conclude that he was a British spy. Surely his great book *The Roman Revolution* is a passionately anti-fascist work, depicting the ascent of Augustus and his destruction of the Roman Republic as parallel to the ascent of Hitler and Mussolini, both being abetted by the passivity of those who might have resisted. This is just the tip of a very large iceberg—only some of the people I happen to know as teachers and colleagues.[28] Nor were these people gung-ho militarists: indeed, to anyone who knew them it may seem absurd that most of them served in the military at all.[29] ("He was a very gentle soldier," Runcie said to me of David Pears, and one could apply that description to others.) So Britten was pursuing his own creative work while many other gifted creative people served their country (frequently using their talents in languages, etc., in that service), thus contributing to a future not dominated by fascism.

Even more important, elite intellectual/artistic creativity is not a special excuse. Every Briton who served had his or her own way of being a creative individual—as a parent, a schoolteacher, a doctor, a bricklayer, a farmer. (Indeed. British law honored the creativity of farmers, giving Ronald Duncan a conscientious objector exemption because he was already serving as a farmer![30]) In short, the way

[28] The exception is Austin, whom I unfortunately never met, due to his premature death from Hodgkin's Disease in 1960, but I studied Aristotle with his wife Jean in a class she offered with David Pears.

[29] Nor were they all paragons of physical fitness; Dover reported feeling isolated in the corps by his "funnel chest," and it is difficult to imagine either Lloyd-Jones or Dummett surviving a normal basic training. A story Lloyd-Jones liked to tell with irony concerned a time when he was charged, as an officer, with lecturing the notoriously slovenly Dummett on the proper care of his uniform, introducing him to the shoe brush and the sewing kit. The fact that Lloyd-Jones saw this story as rather ridiculous says much about both men as unlikely soldiers.

[30] I have not been able to find out anything further about his farming activities or how legitimate his plea on that basis was.

in which *Owen Wingrave* holds national service up to ridicule is, to me, deeply offensive.

The best we can do on behalf of Britten and Pears in the 1940s is to recall that Britain has a longstanding tradition of respect for conscientious objectors (as does the United States), so long as the commitment to pacifism is total and not an objection to one particular war. At the founding of the United States, George Washington wrote a famous letter to the Quakers in 1789 saying:

> Your principles & conduct are well known to me—and it is doing the People called Quakers no more than Justice to say, that (except their declining to share with others the burthen of the common defence) there is no Denomination among us who are more exemplary and useful Citizens.
>
> I assure you very explicitly that in my opinion the Consciencious scruples of all men should be treated with great delicacy & tenderness, and it is my wish and desire that the Laws may always be as extensively accomodated to them, as a due regard to the Protection and essential Interests of the Nation may Justify, and permit.[31]

Washington's parenthesis ("except their declining") is a big exception, and no doubt was so to Washington himself. However, I am concerned here not with Washington's personal beliefs, but with his political stance. In his letter he recognized, and followed, an already longstanding tradition in recognizing, that there are sincere pacifists who are (basically) admirable citizens, and that a nation committed to liberty ought to respect their beliefs and not require them to perform military service. He left a loophole: accommodation might not always be possible. But the United States and Britain have always preferred accommodation to a harsh tyranny over conscientious scruples. We should certainly give Britten

---

[31] https://founders.archives.gov/documents/Washington/05-04-02-0188.

and Pears credit for passionate sincerity, and also for a visionary attachment to the goal of world peace, which the two men pursued in their musical lives throughout their lifetimes. And Pears, at least, had a longstanding affiliation with pacifist organizations that worked for world peace.

We should also recognize that both men were basically apolitical. Pears said that Britten "was never a member of any political party, other than the Peace Pledge Union," and that the same was true of him.[32] We should realize that for both men their political contribution was their artistic work, and Britten's works do make definite political statements. They constitute a major contribution to a future of peace and reconciliation.

Emotional Pacifism and the Stickiness of Retributive Anger

Britten's major contribution lies in the area of emotional pacifism, which, as I've said, is in principle compatible with service in a war of national defense, even though Britten thought it was not. Throughout his career he is preoccupied with mapping out, musically, the forces in human beings that work against peace, and also those that support peace. As Chapter 3 argued, Britten sees the roots of warlike aggression as not innate but socially learned, but learned on account of a very common human tendency to fear bodies and the vulnerability that being bodily entails. The remedy, insofar as there is one, lies in love of bodies and wonder at their beauty. This love he explores in many works, including those discussed in Chapter 4. Britten sees the love we need as not at all calm, and not "purified" from eroticism. It draws greatly on a powerful erotic love of another body, which inspires ecstatic wonder at that body's beauty and goodness. Moreover, with Donne, he thinks

[32] Carpenter (1992, p. 484).

that the love of Christ that might possibly redeem us is itself a love of Christ's beautiful body, which Donne insists on portraying as akin to the love that Donne used to have for his earthly mistresses. We shall see that Wilfred Owen, the poet Britten chose for a central role in the *War Requiem*, shares these preoccupations.

Another insight we will find in Britten is the enormous difficulty of getting rid of the desire to strike back. Nelson Mandela said that it took much of his time in prison (twenty-seven years) to uproot his desire for retribution against his opponents, reaching a point at which cooperation and sympathetic interaction came naturally to him. If this is true of that extraordinary leader, we can expect that most members of nonviolent movements will be less fully in control of themselves. The desire for retribution is powerful and probably in part inherited as part of our evolutionary equipment, though it is heightened by culture. Gandhi's followers lapsed during Partition, whenever he was not actually present, lashing out in hatred. Mandela's followers too kept seeking various forms of retribution against white South Africans, and Mandela had to intervene often to turn them around. If this is true even within committed nonviolent movements, what should we expect to find in war itself? Suppose a person follows the path that I deem most defensible, and joins up to defend his country. He then undertakes to kill combatants on the other side. While military instructors and theorists, from Seneca's *On Anger* to West Point of the present day (where I had the good fortune to lecture shortly after the Vietnam War), teach soldiers not to seek retribution, and not to hate the enemy, but to focus instead on defending what they love and protecting their comrades, it is difficult to maintain balance in the heat of battle, when you actually have to kill a human being. Hatred (often racialized) and bloodlust can easily bubble up to protect the psyche from collapse, leading, as Seneca already said, to gross crimes against humanity. So what are soldiers being asked to feel?

It is easy to answer this question when we are speaking about nonviolent protesters: they are to feel solidarity, a love of justice, and a love of their enemies. And they are also permitted to feel the type of nonretributive anger that I call Transition-Anger:[33] an anger whose entire content is, "This is outrageous. It must not happen again." This type of anger faces forward to create a better future, and is perfectly compatible with love of one's enemies. But in actual combat it seems difficult to maintain the distinction between Transition-Anger and retributive anger. The soldier is indeed seeking to create a better future, fighting the Nazis, say, to defend free Europe. But in the meantime he is asked to kill actual German soldiers. Given that all human beings contain the roots of retribution in themselves, and very few have mastered these desires as securely as Nelson Mandela, it is all too likely that the act of killing will be accompanied by retributive emotions. This is the weak point in my position. It is one thing to say, preserve emotional pacifism, but be willing to kill in defense of self and others. It is quite another thing to do it, while fighting in a war, however just. The very act one is asked to perform summons up the disruptive desires that even the best military training cannot entirely remove. In Part II we will see that Britten understands what I would call the "stickiness of retribution," and sees this as a profound problem for all who engage in war, and even for those who do not. We are all, so to speak, recovering retributivists (if we make an effort at all). The best environment for recovery is either a securely loving family or a securely loving nonviolent movement with a strong leader. The worst environment is probably war.

But let me turn, then, to the story of Britten's actual confrontation with the National Service tribunals.

The Tribunals in 1942

Despite being urged by the British Embassy in Washington to remain in the United States as "aesthetic ambassadors," Britten and

---

[33] Nussbaum (2016).

Pears ultimately decided to return to Britain, arriving there in 1942. (In a letter to Christopher Isherwood dated March 1942, Britten wrote, "I am more and more convinced . . . that I cannot kill," but also admits that "I am scared stiff of judges & all that."[34] The letter suggests a temperamental aversion to killing rather than a principled moral stance—at that time.) Both men applied for conscientious objector status.

Under the National Service (Armed Forces) Act 1939, conscientious objectors could cite either religious or political reasons.[35] There were four possible outcomes: unconditional exemption; conditional exemption; a direction to register for noncombatant service; and complete rejection. (Women were eligible for conscription starting in 1941, mostly for factory or munitions work, although they had an easier time with exemptions, especially if they had children.) There was an appeal process, but the decision of the appellate tribunal was final, and a would-be CO who defied it could be jailed—as composer Michael Tippett was: assigned duty as an air raid warden, he refused, and spent three months in Wormwood Scrubs Prison.[36]

Pears's hearing was initially scheduled for a time when he was touring with *Tales of Hoffman*, so he asked for and received a postponement.[37] At the eventual hearing in September 1942, he made a strong impression. He had been advised by Canon Stuart Morris, the General Secretary of the Peace Pledge Union, so he knew how to make his case. According to a fellow pacifist who attended the hearing, Pears was pressed hard to say whether he refused on principle or just found it inconvenient in light of his career. "I remember with what quiet conviction he answered those questions. His whole bearing and behaviour added weight to what he said, as

---

[34] Mervyn Cooke, *Britten: War Requiem*, Cambridge Music Handbooks (Cambridge, UK: Cambridge University Press, 1996, p. 16).

[35] See Kildea (2013, pp. 204–5) for this account of the process.

[36] Cooke (1996, pp. 14–15).

[37] Headington (1993, pp. 117–18).

one would imagine."[38] He was successful, receiving an unconditional exemption.

Britten had more difficulty at his hearing on May 28. Unlike
Pears he lacked a long record of membership in pacifist groups. He
submitted the following statement to the tribunal:

> Since I believe that there is in every man the spirit of God,
> I cannot destroy, and feel it my duty to avoid helping to destroy
> as far as I am able, human life, however strongly I may disapprove
> of the individual's actions or thoughts. The whole of my life has
> been devoted to acts of creation (being by profession a composer)
> and I cannot take part in acts of destruction. Moreover, I feel that
> the fascist attitude to life can only be overcome by passive resist-
> ance. If Hitler were in power here or this country had any similar
> form of government, I should feel it my duty to obstruct this re-
> gime in every non-violent way possible, and by complete non-
> cooperation. I believe sincerely that I can help my fellow human
> beings best, by continuing the work I am most qualified to do by
> the nature of my gifts and training, i.e. the creation or propaga-
> tion of music. [He mentions work he has been offered writing
> music for government projects.] I am however prepared, but feel
> completely unsuited by nature and training, to undertake other
> constructive civilian work provided that it is not connected with
> any of the armed forces.[39]

At the hearing, he too was advised by Morris, but his presentation
was less clear than Pears's had been, and made what Kildea calls "a
flaky impression." (After all, he was basically pointing to his own
elite creativity and putting himself in a special class.) He stated, "I
do not believe in the divinity of Christ, but I think his teaching is
sound and his example should be followed." He also mentioned

---

[38] Ibid., p. 118.
[39] Cooke (1996, pp. 15–16).

willingness to join the Royal Army Medical Corps and, as to pacifism, made no claim to longstanding pacifist beliefs, but simply said, "I think with the Quakers I might find a spiritual home." (As I've said, this is strictly false if it means that one can be a full member of a Quaker congregation while denying the divinity of Christ, but true in the sense that tolerant Quakers would be eager to include him and make common cause with him.) On June 3, he was put in the third category and ordered to perform noncombatant service.

Britten appealed in August, with the help of the BBC (they listed the various useful government projects for which Britten would be writing the music). He presented further letters of support from publisher Ralph Hawkes and Frank Bridges's widow, who testified to Britten's opposition to militarism as a boy. William Walton and Montagu Slater attended the hearing to lend support. This time he clarified his religious beliefs, saying that the local tribunal had misunderstood him: although he did not believe in Christ's divinity, "I don't seek as suggested to pick & choose from his teaching, but I regard the whole context of his teaching & example as the standard by which I must judge." He also clarified (or, rather, reversed) his position on noncombatant service, saying clearly that he could not participate in the medical corps, because that would be to participate in the war. He granted that "in total war, it is impossible to avoid all participation of an indirect kind but I believe that I must draw the line as far away from direct participation as possible."[40] On August 18 his appeal was accepted, and in May 1943 he was certified as a conscientious objector with no responsibility to perform noncombatant military service. Kildea notes that this status belonged to only 3000 people in Britain, which he estimates to be only 6 percent of the total number of conscientious objectors, though I am not sure where he gets that number.[41] Of Britten he

---

[40] See Kildea (2013, p. 205) and Cooke (1996, p. 16).
[41] Kildea (2013, p. 206). Britten was requested to give concerts for the Committee for the Encouragement of Music and Art (CEMA), which he had already volunteered to do.

very charitably concludes: "So he was free to get on with his work." Yes, and how many others were not!

People who knew and loved Britten do not say, even today, that he behaved like a spoiled child. His close friend Lennox Berkeley tried to object, saying "I've always been a pacifist at heart, how can one be anything else? But I think that if there ever was a case where force has got to be used, this is it."[42] Britten took the remark badly and wrote satirically about it to another friend; it contributed to ending their friendship.[43] Others simply stayed silent. I love Britten and Pears, but I do feel that Britten behaved in a self-serving way, since his statements at the first hearing make clear that at that time he was not a firmly principled Gandhian. In his tribunal experience, one sees more than a trace of that too-pampered boy mentioned in Auden's letter (see Chapter 3). I feel more sympathy with Pears, who was always absolutely consistent and who worked constructively for world peace with various pacifist organizations (something insisted on by Gregg, who says that the pacifist must not be passive). Both of them, however, continued to enjoy the fruits of violence committed by others, including later honors from the Crown.

Britten and Pears continued to have difficulties after the war arising from their pacifism, especially from the Federal Bureau of Investigation (FBI) in the United States. From 1942 on, the two men were watched, and by 1952 or so they were on an FBI list of "prohibited immigrants," meaning that every time they wished to enter the United States they had to apply for a visa on each occasion, have a formal interview, and then wait for the visa until the last minute, although it always arrived just in time. Britten remained on the list until his death; Pears finally was removed in 1983, thanks to the efforts of Donald Mitchell and friends in the United States. One comical touch, supplied by Mitchell, is a photo

---

[42] Letter quoted in Carpenter (1992, p. 137).
[43] The letter is quoted in Cooke (1996, p. 13).

of an FBI document about Britten released under the Freedom of Information Act (FOIA) to lawyers hired by Mitchell's American friends, allegedly containing the reasons for the prohibition: everything except Britten's name and the date has been blacked out![44] No doubt there would have been allusion to Britten's homosexuality as well as his pacifism. As Mitchell wryly notes, "There is certainly room for further dogged research in this area."[45]

Britten and Wilfred Owen

There is one more pacifist whom we must now consider: Wilfred Owen, whose poetry about the horror and the futility of war Britten selected to provide the text for key parts of the *War Requiem*. As we shall see, Owen was, like Britten, an emotional pacifist. But he was no dogmatist, and he appears to have made a judgment about the futility of World War I rather than believing that one should never participate in any war. Furthermore, despite all his profound objections to the war, he served honorably in it, and seems to have thought it important to be vulnerable in ways that others were vulnerable. In some ways, then, his position seems more defensible than Britten's. But, as we shall later see, it has two serious flaws that Britten will assiduously avoid.

Owen grew up in a middle-class English family in Shropshire.[46] His letters to his mother, to whom he remained extremely close throughout his short life, show him to be serious, protective of his younger siblings, and eager for education. By the age of eighteen

---

[44] See reproduction in Mitchell (1999, p. 215).

[45] Mitchell (1999, p. 216).

[46] Essential details are in Lewis's Introduction to the *Collected Poems*, and in Blunden's Memoir in the same volume. C. Day Lewis, "Introduction," in *The Collected Poems of Wilfred Owen*, by Wilfred Owen, edited by C. Day Lewis (London: Chatto and Windus, 1963, pp. 11–30). See also Edmund Blunden, "Appendix I Memoir, 1931, by Edmund Blunden," in *The Collected Poems of Wilfred Owen*, by Wilfred Owen, edited by C. Day Lewis (London: Chatto & Windus, 1931/1963, pp. 147–82).

he was firm in his commitment to poetry. In 1911 he entered the University of London, but was unable to pursue a degree because of a shortage of funds. So he became an assistant to a vicar in Oxfordshire, where his duties included visiting the poor and the sick. This experience, to which he reacted with what his editor C. Day Lewis plausibly calls "indignant compassion," made him begin to reject orthodox Christianity. He briefly became a tutor in a French family, and he was living in France, age twenty-one, when war broke out.

Early in the war, visits to hospitals in Bordeaux stimulated the concrete interest in what war does to the body that is such a central feature of Owen's poetry. He wrote home with vivid description of shin-bones and pus, in order, he says, "to educate you to the actualities of war." He soon decided to sign up, was accepted, and began training in June 1916 with the Manchester Rifles. Enthusiastic about flying, he briefly longed to transfer to the air force, but he was valued as an infantry offer, so his transfer request was denied. At the end of the year he was posted to France. Biographer Edmund Blunden quotes extensively from his letters of this period. He proved a courageous officer on the Somme sector of the Western front. But he suffered from what was then called "neurasthenia"—caused, he said, from "living too long by the *disiecta membra* of a friend"—so he was sent away from the front line—to Craiglockhart hospital, a mental institution (understood loosely)—where he met the older poet Siegfried Sassoon, who became a very important influence on his thoughts and his poetry. The men shared antiwar attitudes, and homosexuality was another bond between them in a repressive world. The two had a brief sexual relationship, passionate at least on Owen's side, and Sassoon helped him meet other gay men in London. The two continued to exchange letters that have now been published.[47]

---

[47] Rictor Norton, ed., *My Dear Boy: Gay Love Letters Through the Centuries* (San Francisco, CA: Leyland Publications, 1998a), printing extracts from a larger collection

By this time Owen's letters show the radical questioning of conventional Christianity that we know from the poetry, including his idea that Christ is a common soldier—as well as a tentative espousal of a pacifism that remained inconstant and unclear in scope. He returned to the front line, determined to put himself in a stronger position to speak in protest about the war. Always courageous in battle and a keen protector of the men in his command, he won the Military Cross in an action in October 1918. A month later, he was killed.

Owen, while holding World War I to be mostly pointless and wrongheaded, said that he, like Sassoon. was willing to fight in the name of what Sassoon called "defence and liberation," but not to further nationalist "aggression and conquest."[48] In June 1917, similarly, he speaks of his goal as the "extinction of militarism" (alluding to H. G. Wells's attack on "militant imperialism"), but also says, "I hate washy pacifists as temperamentally as I hate whiskied prussianists. Therefore I feel that I must first get some reputation of gallantry before I could successfully and usefully declare my principles." His stance was not constant: in May 1917 he had seemingly expressed a more comprehensive pacifism ("Be bullied, be outraged, be killed, but do not kill"). But as we can see, he veers back again after that to a more mixed stance.[49] And in August he even appears to depart from what I have called "emotional pacifism," saying, "thinking of the eyes I have seen sightless, and the bleeding lad's cheeks I have wiped, I say: Vengeance is mine, I, Owen, will

of gay love letters. Also, "You Have Fixed My Life: The Gay Love Letters of Wilfred Owen to Siegfried Sassoon." Excerpts from *My Dear Boy: Gay Love Letters through the Centuries*, edited by Rictor Norton. *Gay History and Literature* (1998b). See also Nigel Jones, "Anthem for Groomed Youth." *The Spectator* (January 6, 2018), which reviews biographies of Owen.

[48] Quotes from Sassoon's letter arranging for a question to be asked in the House of Commons, in Cooke (1996, p. 5). Sassoon also charged that "the war is being deliberately prolonged by those who have the power to end it," calling this a "deception." In a letter to his mother on August 15, 1917, Owen expresses approval of Sassoon's protest.

[49] Cooke (1996, pp. 4–5).

repay." No pacifist sentiments are found in letters during the last two months of fighting before his death.

What is absolutely clear and unequivocal, however we reconstruct Owen's views, is that Owen served, and not as a conscript. He made a decision to volunteer, and he did not think that this display of solidarity with other men was at odds with his principles. Indeed, he thought that it was crucial for any pacifist to show that he was not a coward.[50] Even had he not served, his objections would have been, like Sassoon's, specific to World War I, and not fully general.

Owen's poems, he announces in his Preface, are not "about deeds, or lands, or anything about glory, honour, might, majesty, dominion, or power, except War. . . . My subject is War, and the pity of War. The Poetry is in the pity. . . . All a poet can do today is warn. That is why the true Poets must be truthful."[51]

Above all, Owen warns by arousing compassion for the sufferings of bodies in war. Using the battering of consonants, the gaping of vowels, Owen's poetry finds many ways to chronicle the damage war inflicts upon the bodies of soldiers, and it is for ordinary soldiers, not for "heroes," that "pity" or compassion is aroused.[52] Other untruthful poets, the idea is, have represented war without the suffering, not showing the reader that they have often tended to romanticize them, preferring a false poetics of heroic and manly gallantry to the brute fact that "they are troops who fade, not flowers / For poets' tearful fooling."[53]

[50] Cooke (1996, p. 7).

[51] Wilford Owen, *The Collected Poems of Wilfred Owen*, edited by C. Day Lewis (London: Chatto & Windus, 1963).

[52] The word *pity* has now acquired nuances of condescension or superiority, so I prefer the word *compassion* (see Chapter 2), but in poetry *pity* is still widely used today in its original Greek-tragedy meaning, without any nuance of denigration—for example, by Seamus Heaney in *The Cure at Troy: A Version of Sophocles's Philoctetes* (New York: Noonday Press, 1995).

[53] Owen, "Insensibility." Fussell (1975, pp. 21–22) offers a marvelous commentary on Owen's poetry, juxtaposing it with the rhetoric of World War I recruitment posters, which never faced the body and always spoke in romantic abstractions such as "gallant lads," and used poetic euphemisms for bodily parts: blood is the "red wine of youth," and so on.

Owen shows the devastation war inflicts upon the male body with unparalleled immediacy, making the reader feel the battering and the gaping wounds through the music of his language. (Britten, having actual music to employ, goes much further.) But the battered bodies are not represented as ugly: the disgust that readers might feel for blood and gore is warded off, both by the power of compassion and by the sense of human beauty that the poetry creates. His anti-disgust project is thus very similar to Britten's, as is the way in which both men show the erotic loveliness of soldiers' flesh.

Like Britten, Owen was skeptical of traditional religion, though Jesus was a key ethical model. From early in his career he was especially skeptical of the forms of the traditional liturgy, which he saw as complacent and mechanical. In "Maundy Thursday" (1915) he writes:

> Above the crucifix I bent my head:
> The Christ was thin, and cold, and very dead:
> And yet I bowed, yea, kissed—my lips did cling
> (I kissed the warm live hand that held the thing.)

In a letter to his mother around the same time, he writes "none of your anglican simulacrums" and comments that the service leaves him older but otherwise unchanged.[54] Britten, similarly, sees meaning only in the living bodily reality of Christ, which he contrasts with dead tradition, a central structural feature of the *War Requiem*.

Owen, then, fits in well with Britten's overall project. Two glaring flaws, I believe, infect Owen's war poetry. The first is elitism, the second (less consistent) is misogyny. It is important to understand these because of the way in which Britten assiduously avoids both

---

[54] Cooke (1996, pp. 2–3).

errors by careful selection of poems, editing of those he does use, and in some cases rewriting.

Owen's poetry expresses the war experience of the British soldier. It lays claim at times to inclusiveness: "The Poetry is in the pity" ("Preface"). His famous phrase "the eternal reciprocity of tears" appears to embrace all soldiers and, indeed, those who mourned at home—and the reader as well. However, in many poems one encounters a problematic narrowing of vision. Owen's poetry insistently attacks obtuseness and lack of sympathy. But it is one thing to attack the obtuseness of leaders who have put the bodies of young men at risk without accepting accountability. It is quite another to suggest, as Owen surely does, that most of those young men are themselves rather commonplace mentally, and that true insight belongs to a poetic elite. "Insensibility" is in many respects a great poem, decrying the loss of imagination and feeling and praising "Whatever shares / The eternal reciprocity of tears." Some of the obtuse people whom the poem savagely excoriates are soldiers at home, apparently ignorant of the experience of men at the front. (Really?) But the first three stanzas concern soldiers at the front, as Owen inveighs against the "dullness" through which many protect themselves against the pain of combat. "Happy are those who lose imagination: / They have enough to carry with ammunition." And these half-dead people are contrasted with "We wise, who with a thought besmirch / Blood over all our soul." These lines provoke (in me) the reaction, How dare he! Some insulate themselves to bear the pain of war, some turn inward and write poetry. What right has the latter sort to look down on the former? Owen seems to think that poets are better than other people; and he may be connecting this superiority with homosexuality, since those obtuse types are just the sort to like conventional love objects. Nor is this an isolated case: "Strange Meeting" too expresses elitism, as in the lines, "Courage was mine, and I had mystery, / Wisdom was mine, and I had mastery."

These elitist sentiments are repeatedly uttered in his letters as well. On December 2, 1914, he wrote to his mother:

> The *Daily Mail* speaks very movingly about the "duties shirked" by English young men. I suffer a good deal of shame. But while those ten thousand lusty louts go on playing football I shall go on playing with my little axiom—that my life is worth more than my death to Englishmen.
>
> Do you know what would hold me together on a battlefield? The sense that I was perpetuating the language in which Keats and the rest of them wrote! I do not know in what else England is greatly superior, or dearer to me, than another land and people.[55]

On August 28 he had struck an even more ominous note, apparently sympathizing with eugenics. He said to his mother that "the guns will effect a little useful weeding," and that he minds the deaths of English soldiers less than those of soldiers from the continent "because the former are all Tommy Atkins, poor fellows, while the continental armies are inclusive of the finest brains and temperaments of the land."

Although I have suggested that Britten had an elitist attitude toward himself and his own military service, this was not a general feature of his approach to human beings in his musical works, and indeed this marked a difference between him and the always snooty Auden. He finds dignity and grace in simple working people in works from *Peter Grimes* to *Billy Budd* to *Albert Herring*. Indeed he never seems drawn to portrayals of elite experience—*Gloriana* being a special case, justified by the nature of the occasion.

A second flaw in Owen's poems is a marked tendency, while praising and eroticizing the daring of male bodies, to portray women as less compelling, less admirable. First of all, he completely

---

[55] See John Bell, *Wilfred Owen: Selected Letters* (Oxford, UK: Oxford University Press, 1985).

omits the roles women played at the front, as nurses, cooks, ambulance drivers, staffers, journalists, among other positions. Even on the home front women were not just sweethearts, sisters, and mothers, but were also munitions workers and played other dangerous and difficult roles. The women who do appear are sometimes objects of compassion, as they mourn the dead, but they are often portrayed as emotionally superficial: they tease and goad their lovers into combat ("to please his Meg / Aye, that was it, to please the giddy jilts / He asked to join," ["S. I. W."]); they fail to have compassion for veterans who return disabled ("All of them touch him like some queer disease./... To-night he noticed how the women's eyes / Passed from him to the strong men that were whole" ["Disabled"]).

Women, in virtue of their superficiality, fail to be erotically compelling, Thus "Greater Love," an ode to the bodily beauty of soldiers, denigrates heterosexual love and its female objects: "Red lips are not so red / As the stained stones kissed by the English dead," and so on. Similarly, in "Apologia Pro Poemate Meo," Owen writes: "I have made fellowships— / Untold of happy lovers in old song. / For love is not the binding of fair lips / With the soft silk of eyes that look and long." And in "Strange Meeting" the German soldier proclaims, "I went hunting wild /After the wildest beauty in the world, / Which lies not calm in eyes, or braided hair. . . . " Insistently, repeatedly, the female is soft, predictable, undaring, unexciting. Just *boring*, and a part of boring conventionality. No doubt these phrases record Owen's erotic experience, but they also unfortunately depict a particular sexuality as the deepest and best. "All women, without exception, *annoy* me," he wrote to his mother.[56]

These portrayals of women live side by side with the fact that Owen had enormous respect and love for his mother, and indeed for several other particular women mentioned in the letters. (But that is often true of prejudice: people exempt their close friends

---

[56] Lewis (1963, p. 18): "It is noticeable that, in his war poetry, Owen had no pity to spare for the suffering of bereaved women." This is exaggerated but contains much truth.

from their flawed generalizations.) Nor is his misogyny of the flagrant sort that we find in Sassoon's "Glory of Women."[57] It is a tendency, a set of omissions, a pattern of obliquely denigrating characterization. It still makes Owen's poetry a problematic source for texts addressing a general British public on themes of reconciliation and rebuilding. Britten never had a tendency to denigrate women in this way, so he had to work carefully.

One can avoid both of these flaws in Owen by choosing one's poems carefully and by deleting certain lines from those one chooses. And this is precisely what Britten does. He does not set "Insensibility," "Apologia Pro Poemate Meo," or "Greater Love." With "Strange Meeting" he judiciously edits, as we'll see, removing all the lines that suggest either misogyny or elitism. So far as I am aware, this aspect of Britten's creative rewriting has not been observed. Not only does Britten seem never to have felt contempt or hostility toward women, but he also understands that a project of postwar reconstruction must be truly inclusive and humble about the role of the artist.

The Sounds of Peace

Britten wrote works dealing with peace throughout his career, and I shall argue—following a valuable hint of Donald Mitchell's—that

---

[57] You love us when we're heroes, home on leave,
Or wounded in a mentionable place.
You worship decorations; you believe
That chivalry redeems the war's disgrace.
You make us shells. You listen with delight,
By tales of dirt and danger fondly thrilled.
You crown our distant ardours while we fight,
And mourn our laurelled memories when we're killed.
You can't believe that British troops "retire"
When hell's last horror breaks them, and they run,
Trampling the terrible corpses—blind with blood.
    O German mother dreaming by the fire,
    While you are knitting socks to send your son
    His face is trodden deeper in the mud.

the idea of peace summons up a distinctive sound-world, which we shall find in the *War Requiem*. First, however, here is a group of significant works, before and after *War Requiem*, in which peace is a central theme.[58]

The World of the Spirit (1938)

This is one of two radio cantatas Britten composed for the BBC, the other being the 1937 *The Company of Heaven*, a work about angels.[59] It is written for two speakers, soloists, chorus, and orchestra. Around the hymn *Veni Creator Spiritus* (Come, Creator Spirit)—suggested to Britten by his strong interest, at the time, in Mahler's Eighth Symphony—Britten and his librettist R. Ellis Roberts arranged a group of texts and narratives from the Bible, St. Francis, Empedocles, Tennyson, Wordsworth, Turgenev, Mary Duclaux, Emily Brontë, Henry Vaughan, and Gerard Manley Hopkins, an extract from a Catholic chaplain during World War I describing the heroic sacrifice of Rabbi Abraham Bloch, and A. Stanley's *The Testament of Man*, itself an anthology containing an extract from William Penn's Treaty with the Indians and a narrative of the death of Irish patriot James Connolly.

The cantata is perhaps too heterogeneous, both textually and musically, and the large role given to the speakers is distracting. But it does contain some wonderful stretches, in which Britten is exploring the sounds characteristic of peace. From the excellent Commentary by Donald Mitchell and Philip Reed,[60] I select the following extracts: "High strings provide a halo of sound"; "features

---

[58] I omit the three-minute film score for Paul Rotha's short film *Peace of Britain* (1936) and the *Pacifist March* (1936), written with Ronald Duncan for the Peace Pledge Union, oddly martial, discussed in Chapter 3.

[59] See Cooke (1996, p. 13) and Carpenter (1992, p. 118).

[60] Mitchell and Reed (1996), printed with the libretto in the Chandos recording of that year.

solos from pairs of flutes, oboes, bassoons, and clarinets, before ending in a luminous D major." Britten's choice of tonality (B flat) is an early example of his use of this key in the context of salvation and/or reconciliation (cf., for example, the epilogue of *Billy Budd* and the "Peace" aria from *Owen Wingrave*). The sense that peace is best characterized with sounds described as "ecstatic," "luminous," "radiant," and serene—Mitchell's later contention, to which I shall return—is something Britten is only broaching here and is already on the track of a musical idea to which he will return again and again.

Spring Symphony, Opus 44 (1949)

This important orchestral/choral work, one of Britten's most Mahleresque in its use of chorus and soloists within the confines of a symphony, as well as in its fertile use of the sounds and images of the countryside, is not often thought of as a pacifist work, but I contend that it is. Britten always associated emotional peace with being at home in the English countryside, where he found sources of personal and national regeneration. He originally thought of setting a Latin text, but he shifted to English poetry under the influence, he said, both of a rereading of a lot of English verse and "a particularly lovely spring day in east Suffolk." He put together an anthology ranging from the thirteenth to the twentieth centuries dealing, as he put it, "not only with the spring itself but with the progress of winter to spring and the reawakening of the earth and life which this means." The work, which had its premiere in 1949, is written for orchestra, both adult chorus and boy choir, and soprano, contralto, and tenor soloists. It is in the traditional four movements, but it also has a tonal arc leading from the B of the opening to the C major of the triumphant climax.[61]

---

[61] See Michael Kennedy, Notes to *"Benjamin Britten, Jennifer Vyvyan, Norma Procter, Peter Pears, Emanuel School Boys" Chorus, Chorus of the Royal Opera House,*

The first movement begins with icy winter and the unaccompanied chorus singing a prayer for spring's arrival. Soon we hear the call of the cuckoo ("The Merry Cuckoo") and then, in "Spring, the sweet spring," a variety of woodwind solos. The children's choir then whistles imitating the whistling of the working boy in "The Driving Boy."

The second, slow, movement focuses on what Britten called "the darker side of spring—the fading violets, rain, and night."[62] The central text, and in a way the emotional heart of the work, is Auden's poem "Out on the Lawn"—edited so as to keep references to war to a minimum and to focus on the joys of personal intimacy—"the tyrannies of love." War is far away, while the lovers, in the moonlight, enjoy "Our freedom in this English house, / our picnics in the sun." The poem is set as a contralto solo with wordless choral accompaniment. We are reminded that the body is not an abstraction but a daily reality and delight.

The scherzo comprises lively settings of three poems (ending with Blake's "Sound the flute") with various pairings of soloists and instruments: Britten pairs female voices with woodwinds, the male voice with brass, and children with strings, but all combine in the coda.

The Finale was described by Britten as "a Mayday festival, a kind of Bank Holiday." A flute begins the main theme, a waltz. The tenor, representing the Maylord, summons the people of London to the Mayday celebration: "London, to thee I do present the merry month of May"—as blasts from a tuned cowhorn answer his call. The chorus and soloists burst out with "Rejoice," and all take up the waltz theme. All forces eventually join in the joyful outburst—and

---

Covent Garden, Orchestra of the Royal Opera House, Covent Garden—Spring Symphony (London: Longmans, Green and Co., 1961), jacket notes for London recording of 1961 (Britten conducting the orchestra of the Royal Opera House, Pears as tenor soloist).

[62] This and subsequent Britten quotations from the jacket liner of the London original recording.

the children's chorus sings over them, in duple time, the thirteenth-century round "Sumer is icumen in."

It is a wonderful work and along with *Albert Herring* (see Chapter 6), the best representation of Britten's conception of a happy life. It is peace, but peace not as merely negative or an abstraction, but as active English life: both the city and the countryside, working people, children, cows, and local festive occasions. The Mayday that is gently satirized in *Albert Herring* is here simply celebrated, and we feel the relief of an entire nation, as Britain exits from war's icy winter and resumes normal bustling life. I feel that this work, though in many ways miles from the *War Requiem*, is its necessary complement. It shows what the project of the *War Requiem* is all about: to achieve a reconciliation that will make happy life possible. The sounds of peace are not just ethereal or ecstatic: they include the cowhorn, the songs of children, the passionate happiness of lovers.

Voices for Today, opus 75 (1965)

U Thant, Secretary-General of the United Nations (UN), invited Britten to write a work for the organization's twentieth anniversary. Thant, a devout Buddhist, had been active in Cold War mediation efforts, and no doubt found in Britten a kindred spirit. The work was premiered at the UN in 1965 and had concurrent performances in London and Paris. Although it is shortly after the *War Requiem*, it has close thematic connections. Its purpose is to envisage a world of reconciliation, a world beyond war.

The work is composed for adult choir, children's choir (boys' choir in the premiere), usually singing *a capella*, but with optional organ accompaniment. It lasts less than ten minutes. Its first section is a collection of sentences about peace assembled by Britten, Pears, and E. M. Forster, sung first by the adult choir, but eventually joined by the children's choir, at the point when several lines of the

Russian poet Yevtushenko say that you should not lie to the young, and then—the entrance of the children—"the young are people."

The second section is a setting of Virgil's Fourth Eclogue, in Latin, for adult choir, with wordless descant by the children's choir. The Fourth Eclogue predicts a future golden age for humanity, connecting this prophecy with the birth of a child. It has often been taken as a prediction of Christ's birth, but of course it isn't, since Virgil died in 19 BCE and the poem itself was written in 40 BCE. The poem is not about any specific person, nor was Virgil a proto-Christian. He may have been hoping for an end to the Civil Wars—which did occur in his lifetime, when the Emperor Augustus took over, introducing autocracy in place of the Roman Republic. Although Virgil has been thought highly favorable to Augustus in his later epic *Aeneid*, the ending of that work, in which Aeneas refuses mercy for his defeated opponent, yielding to a personal desire for revenge, gives rise to grave doubt, suggesting disillusionment: the promise that Rome will "spare the conquered and cast down the proud" has been undone by the spirit of revenge. But none of this should color our reading of the much earlier Eclogue, which is clearly looking forward to some wondrous golden age. In any case the Christian reading is plainly wrong.

Before section 1 and after each section, the chorus sings, "If you have ears to hear, then hear!"

I find this work a real failure in every respect. In musical terms, setting the texts for choruses renders them unintelligible; and although there is a certain amount of dreamy descanting, there are no new interesting musical ideas. The choice of texts in part 1 is, as many have said, much too heterogeneous, a ragbag of sentiments from all over, with no clear connection. They are meant to be voices from the past and present who can help us envisage a better future, and they range chronologically from Lao Tzu (b. 571 BCE), Sophocles (5th century BCE), and the Indian Emperor Ashoka (304–232 BCE) to two then-living figures, Yevtushenko and the Polish aphorist Jerzy Lec (1906–1966). Also included are

Jesus, Blake, Shelley, Tennyson, Hölderlin, William Penn, Camus, Melville, and the nineteenth-century Quaker politician John Bright. If the aim is to represent the diversity of humanity, the collection fails. It makes only two gestures toward the non-Euro-American world, China and India. There are no texts from Africa, and within Europe Britain is overrepresented. And, most stunningly, there are no texts by women, who have surely been associated with pacifism throughout history. Pears's own Quaker ancestor Elizabeth Fry might have been featured; or Emily Brontë, whom Britten uses elsewhere. And why not Vijaya Lakshmi Pandit, sister of Jawaharlal Nehru, who was the first female delegate at the United Nations from 1946 to 1968, and, in 1953, became the first female president of the UN General Assembly. And she was right there when Britten's work was performed. Why not Eleanor Roosevelt, who played a big role in the UN's creation? In short, the collection seems thrown together without much thought.

As for the Fourth Eclogue, whatever the complexity of Virgil's attitudes to Augustus, we cannot expect the audience to engage in subtle literary interpretation of a later text, and if people know Virgil at all, they would be likely to see him as an appeaser who sympathizes with the autocratic defeat of the Roman Republic and sees that sort of peace as a golden age. So it almost seems as if Britten, Pears, and Forster are saying, with their choice, that Neville Chamberlain was right and Churchill wrong—and of course Britten did think that Chamberlain was right, though whether he ever changed that view is unclear. What a spectacularly awful way to celebrate a peacekeeping body born out of the defeat of the Axis powers. Probably Forster (the most classically educated of the three librettists)—a liberal humanist who deplored the rise of the Axis powers—simply didn't think about Roman politics and chose the poem as a millennial vision. We should bear in mind, however, that Forster is best known, in this period, for the statement that he would rather betray his country than betray a friend, a Bloomsbury ethic that might itself be questioned. And why a work in Latin, the heritage of European elites, rather than some language more widely known within the UN? If Latin, why not an author such as Cicero, who gave his life for the Republic?

Owen Wingrave, opus 85 (1971)

I have already criticized the understanding of pacifism in this work, and I shall add no more, except that Britten said at the time that he was reacting to the Vietnam War (which of course raises anew all the questions I've already raised, since that was clearly not a war of national self-defense, and one might refuse service in that purposeless war without Gandhian pacifism). The opera does connect inner violence with outward violence in an interesting way, insisting on the need to reform the inner world as a prelude to the world of peace it envisages.

Although the work postdates the *War Requiem*, it does contain musical developments that are highly pertinent to that work. Let me turn to Owen's famous "Peace" aria, written in the key of B flat, which often has importance for Britten in connection to ideas of peace and reconciliation. Surrounded by the portraits of his military ancestors, Owen, having refused family pressure to join the family career, expresses his ideal:

> In Peace I have found my image,
> I have found myself.
> In peace I rejoice among men
> and yet walk alone,
> in peace I will guard this balance
> so that it is not broken.
>
> For peace is not lazy but vigilant,
> peace is not acquiescent but searching,
> peace is not weak but strong like a bird's wing

bearing its weight in the dazzling air.
Peace is not silent, it is the voice of love.

It is apropos of this aria that Donald Mitchell observes that it is part of a pattern in Britten.[63] He calls the aria "a radiant, ecstatic avowal which surely foresees a peace a good deal more profound than the absence of war. This, one feels, is the peace which is the result of inner reconciliation, of one man's victory over himself." He then suggests that this is part of "a consistent musical imagery . . . associated with the idea of pacification, of reconciliation." He compares the aria to Billy's aria in Act II of *Billy Budd*, using the words "radiant, ecstatic," of both. But in Owen's aria, he continues, there is a new development: the percussion instruments, previously associated with militarism, now (plus vibraphone, harp, and glockenspiel, and minus drums) are themselves transformed, providing "a shimmering radiance . . . surrounding and decorating the chordal affirmations of Owen's resolve."

"Radiant," "ecstatic," "luminous," "shimmering," "soaring," "a halo of sound," all these terms describe a cluster of musical ideas with which Britten approaches peace from 1936 onward. Musically, bells, harp, vibraphone, glockenspiel, high strings, woodwinds, the voices of children, sometimes the key of B flat major, sometimes D major—to which I would add the cowhorn of *Spring Symphony*, and that symphony's other sounds of the rural English countryside—all these are parts of what we could call the Peace Family, assembled in different combinations throughout Britten's career.

But there is one more element, and listening to baritone Benjamin Luxon, the original Owen, brings its absence vividly to mind: the tenor voice, indeed one particular tenor voice. The last Michelangelo sonnet, in the key of D, with its radiant soaring lines,

---

[63] Donald Mitchell, "'Owen Wingrave and the Sense of the Past: Some Reflections on Britten's Opera,' Liner Notes Accompanying the Complete Recording of the Opera Conducted by Britten" (1971). London Records, OSA 1291.

written for and inspired by Pears, is surely a part of the Peace Family (see Chapter 4). The role of Owen lacks something by being set for a baritone (as it had to be if Pears, by then too old to play Owen on television, was to sing Owen's older antagonist). I feel it falls a little flat and is well short of the demands of the ecstatic text. What Britten could have done with that aria were Pears its singer can only be imagined—but the *Seven Sonnets* give us an idea. Pears was Owen's inner spirit. In the *War Requiem*, a nontheatrical work, Britten is free to write for Pears the peace aria he is unable to give him in the later opera, and I shall argue that the Agnus Dei is that aria.

*****

This leads me to a conclusion not reached by Mitchell, but unsurprising, given the investigations of Chapter 3: *Peace is indeed the voice of love.* Just as war arises out of lack of harmony with one's own bodily being, so the victory over that body-shame, that inner reconciliation, lies at the heart of peace. Because love's object is beautiful, peace is not static: it moves to embrace the beloved body. Just as Christ is envisaged as physically beautiful, and lovable in a way analogous to the way Donne's mistresses are lovable, so peace is a movement toward a beloved other, not devoid of a very human eroticism, but an eroticism that transcends the particular and extends to a love of all humanity that is not static religious *agape*, but living human love—the love expressed in the slow movement of the *Spring Symphony*, with its wonder at the strength of daily human passion.

To sum up: Britten's political thoughts are profoundly inadequate to the world he and we are in. However, those flawed principles, fortunately, play a relatively minor role in the music. Far more salient in the music is his thought about emotional pacifism and the reform of the inner world, which one may accept without accepting Gandhian pacifism, but, rather, by joining them to an intermediate position such as that of King or Mandela. Since the *War Requiem* is not concerned with whether people should fight in World War II, but, rather, with the task ahead—that of building a future in which nations overcome the divisions and angers that lead to war—we may examine and ultimately embrace it wholeheartedly, while retaining the criticisms I have expressed in this chapter. Meanwhile, *Spring Symphony* reminds us of the point of peace: to live well together and be happy.

6

Reconciliation: Aldeburgh, Wolfenden, Coventry

To a happier year
— E. M. Forster (1879–1970), dedication to *Maurice*,
written 1913–1914, published posthumously in 1971[1]

Reconciliation, I shall argue, is a central theme of the *War Requiem* as it was of the Coventry rededication that was its occasion: reconciliation both between nations and within each nation, both the regeneration of war-torn nations through rebuilding and peace-making and the internal regeneration of nations by including outsiders whom they had previously excluded. In this chapter I examine the way in which these themes became central for Britten in the period leading up to the *War Requiem*, as he sought peace with a Britain that had oppressed and excluded homosexuals,[2] pacifists, and many others. Said Britten in 1964, "My music now has its roots in where I live and work. . . I am firmly rooted in this glorious

---

[1] E. M. Forster. *Maurice* (New York: W. W. Norton, 1971). *Maurice* is a novel about two young men who fall in love as students at Cambridge and, never consummating their relationship physically, go in opposite directions. One, aristocratic and with political ambitions, marries unhappily and represses his same-sex desires. Maurice, middle-class and without ambition, falls in love with a young working-class man and eventually has sex with him. The two men decide to live together, though this means life "outside class, without relations or money." Forster's Introduction says that the novel cannot be published at the time of writing because it has a happy ending and therefore can be construed to "recommend crime." Forster's sexual life was complex. Much of it took place outside Britain; but he also had a forty-year relationship with a British policeman, Bob Buckingham (1892–1975), whose wife allowed the affair. Forster died three years after same-sex acts were decriminalized.

[2] Once again, I avoid the word "gay" because Britten and Pears disliked it.

The Tenderness of Silent Minds. Martha C. Nussbaum, Oxford University Press.
© Oxford University Press 2024. DOI: 10.1093/oso/9780197568538.003.0006

county . . . I treasure these roots, my Suffolk roots."[3] Any reading of the *War Requiem* must include this desire for home and belonging.

First, I examine the founding of the Aldeburgh Festival, which from 1948 to the present day has made Aldeburgh the home of a musical feast that is at once high-level and homey, international yet rooted in the town and its environments. Then, returning to the theme of Chapter 4, I examine the way in which the struggle over homosexuality unfolded in the 1950s and early 1960s, as Britten gradually made his peace with the British public (not without the hostility of a rear-guard opposition in the music world itself)—in a way that returned to Britten's earlier ideas about the need for all people, whether same-sex or opposite-sex in orientation, to avoid bodily shame and disgust and the stigmatization of others on such grounds. Meanwhile, at the same time, the public prepared, with glacial slowness, to decriminalize same-sex relations. Finally, I'll examine the history of Coventry Cathedral and the commission that led to the work, showing that reconciliation was Provost Howard's chosen theme for the rededication and that he pointedly favored inclusion of controversial and stigmatized artists if they had distinguished contributions to make.

But first we must envisage the part of England that Britten loved, where he found his roots.

Britten's Suffolk Home

Aldeburgh, on the coast of the North Sea in Suffolk, strikes many visitors as wild and forbidding. To Britten, born in nearby Lowestoft, it was a beloved home and deeply intertwined with his musical life. The sounds and rhythms of the sea are heard in

---

[3] Speech on accepting the first Aspen Award in the Humanities, archived by the Britten-Pears Foundation and online at https://www.aspenmusicfestival.com/benja min-britten. The speech is full of fascinating reflections on the place of the artist in society and the duties of society to the artist.

many parts of his musical output—most famously in *Peter Grimes* and the "Four Sea Interludes" drawn from that score, but elsewhere too one can feel the surging and beating of the waves. Early morning swims in the cold sea water began his day for much of his life, and afternoon walks along the coast (after three or four hours of work in his study) were fertile periods when musical ideas germinated and musical problems were solved, since Britten was famous for not putting pencil to paper until late in the compositional process.

During most of the period I consider in this chapter, he and Pears lived in Crag House (4 Crabbe Street), right on the North Sea.[4] Of his move from Snape to Aldeburgh, he wrote to a friend, "you know how I am about the sea."[5] (He and Pears changed to the more secluded Red House in 1957, "alas, away from the sea, but, thankfully, away from the gaping faces & irritating publicity of that sea front.")[6] Britten always emphasized that he needed an exact and undisturbed routine of work. Composition, he insisted, was not passive waiting for inspiration, but a disciplined process. "I like working to an exact timetable," he said in a broadcast interview. "I often thank my stars that I had a rather conventional upbringing, that I went to a rather strict school, where one was made to work, and I can, without much difficulty, sit down at nine o'clock in the morning and work straight through the morning until lunchtime."[7] Afternoons, as mentioned, were for walks. His sister Beth said of the walks, "He walked far and fast [and] did much of the planning . . . and sometimes sang as he went." After that, she reports, another three hours of hard work in his study; "then dinner, perhaps a read or a game, and bed."[8]

---

[4] For wonderful photos from the time, see Mitchell and Evans (1978). Britten moved from Snape to Aldeburgh in 1947, purchasing Crag House.

[5] Carpenter (1992, p. 253), quoting a letter to Erwin Stein.

[6] Ibid., p. 377.

[7] Ibid., p. 200.

[8] Ibid.

But the sea was in his heart and his footsteps always. His letters to Pears are full of descriptions of the sea in its different moods, and the cold and often fierce ocean water seemed to him invigorating and essential. To Pears in September 1947, a little while after the pair had been traveling in Lucerne, "Eric [Crozier, the librettist of several Britten operas and at the time a close friend of Britten and Pears] came last night & it's lovely having him here. We've already bathed twice—cold sea, but wonderfully clean and refreshing after those stuffy Swiss lakes. . . . All my love, my dearest. Sing nicely. . . . Come here quick, because I think you'll like it."[9] Guests reported that those cold sea swims were virtually mandatory and that in weather when the sea was too rough, cold indoor baths were substituted. (Eric Crozier found this annoying, as if it were "a kind of moral code one had to obey." Pears, by contrast, was pleased, recalling: "I hadn't, until I met him, really realized what a charming occasion a cold bath is."[10]) Meanwhile Britten got the town to rename the street on which Crag House stood as Crabbe Street, after the poet George Crabbe (1734–1832)—born in Aldeburgh and one of its most famous residents—whose work inspired *Peter Grimes*.

The most glorious description of the Suffolk coast and Aldeburgh is Britten's music in *Peter Grimes*. If we want a literary description, there is one by novelist E. M. Forster (a lecturer at the first Aldeburgh Festival and later librettist, with Crozier, of Britten's *Billy Budd*, 1951), in an article he wrote about the first Festival. Forster's description is quoted by both Kildea and Carpenter.[11] But the best literary description I know is one in Wilkie Collins's novel *No Name* (1862). So I shall cite that one instead of Forster's. Collins visited the town in 1861 and decided to situate a crucial part of his novel's action there. His account, though a century earlier than Britten's time there, resonates with Britten's own ideas:

[9] Stroeher, Clark, and Brimmer (2016, p. 79).
[10] Carpenter (1992, p. 260).
[11] See Kildea (2013, pp. 316–17).

The most striking spectacle presented to a stranger by the shores of Suffolk is the extraordinary defenselessness of the land against the encroachments of the sea.

At Aldborough, as elsewhere on this coast, local traditions are, for the most part, traditions which have been literally drowned. The site of the old town, once a populous and thriving port, has almost entirely disappeared in the sea. The German Ocean has swallowed up streets, market-places, jetties, and public walks; and the merciless waters, consummating their work of devastation, closed, no longer than eighty years since, over the salt-master's cottage at Aldborough, now famous in memory only as the birthplace of the poet CRABBE.

Thrust back year after year by the advancing waves, the inhabitants have receded, in the present century, to the last morsel of land which is firm enough to be built on—a strip of ground hemmed in between a marsh on one side and the sea on the other. Here, trusting for their future security to certain sand-hills which the capricious waves have thrown up to encourage them, the people of Aldborough have boldly established their quaint little watering-place.[12]

The vulnerability of all human bodies and edifices, the relentless power of the sea, and yet the bold determination of the inhabitants—all this we hear, as well, in Britten's music. Collins's novel focuses on the stratagems of an outcast—a young woman, fittingly named Magdalen, left illegitimate by irrational quirks of British law—to regain her lost status.[13] Aldeburgh, with its wildness heightening the

---

[12] Wilkie Collins, *No Name*, edited by Mark Ford (New York: Penguin Books (1862/ 1994, The Fourth Scene). Aldborough was an alternative spelling of Aldeburgh.

[13] Magdalen and her sister were born to two parents who were unable to marry legally because the husband was still married to a woman committed to a mental institution in Canada, and he was unable to get a divorce. So the parents pretended to be married and lived a blameless middle-class life, securing the transmission of their estate to the daughters by an ironclad will. Then came the news that the woman had died; they rushed off to London and got legally married. At first they did not realize that this marriage

sense of the vulnerability of human projects, seemed to him a fitting stage on which Magdalen's strange drama could unfold. Much later it became the stage on which two modern legal outcasts would enact their plan of securing a home and a place in British music history and in the nation they both loved.

Aldeburgh: Founding the Festival

In 1947, Britten, Pears, and Eric Crozier founded the English Opera group, with painter and set designer John Piper, to promote performances of British works (primarily). The Board included music publisher Ralph Hawkes, émigré conductor and editor Erwin Stein, theater director Tyrone Guthrie, and art historian Sir Kenneth Clark.[14] The first prospectus announced:

> The time has come when England . . . can create its own operas. . . .
> We believe the best way to achieve the beginnings of a repertory
> of English operas is through the creation of a form of opera
> requiring small resources. [*The Rape of Lucretia* is discussed as
> the first example of this approach.] The success of this experiment
> has encouraged the . . . persons chiefly involved . . . to continue
> their work as a group by establishing . . . THE ENGLISH OPERA
> GROUP, incorporated on a non-profit-making basis. The Group

nullified the will in favor of the daughters, but when the family lawyer told them, they made an appointment to make a new will. However, by two separate mishaps, they both died before the new will could be made. The girls were therefore left illegitimate and stigmatized, and the estate went to a distant cousin, a cranky and egocentric invalid. Magdalen's Aldeborough scheme is to entice and marry the cousin, hoping to get the estate back on his soon-expected death. A highly skilled actress, she disguises herself successfully with the help of a traveling theater man, Captain Wragge. So even then, Aldeborough was the scene of an art "festival." (Collins is criticizing the provisions of the 1837 Wills Act, which clarified a looser common law situation by making it absolutely clear that the will of a man was revoked upon marriage.)

[14] Clark became "Sir" in 1938, when his knighthood was conferred, but he was not yet Baron Clark of Saltwood, as he became with a life peerage in 1969.

will give annual seasons of contemporary opera in English and suitable classical works including those of Purcell.[15]

The brochure announced Britten's *Albert Herring* (libretto by Crozier) as the Group's first project and made an appeal for 12,000 pounds, announcing that the first 2000 had already been donated by a "private subscriber." (The donors were Dorothy and Leonard Elmhirst, founders of Dartington Hall, the famous progressive arts-oriented school. They got some more money from the Arts Council, and appointed Anne Wood, who had worked with Pears at the BBC, as general manager. (This choice begins what I would call an Aldeburgh tradition of promoting women to high positions in opera administration, to be followed by similar choices in the Festival, as we shall see.) *Albert Herring* had its premiere at Glyndebourne in June 1947, with Britten taking up the unaccustomed role of conductor.

Albert Herring, one of the repertory's most endearing and musically rich comic operas, is a highly significant work in Britten's embrace of reconciliation with England and its exclusions, as I shall discuss in the following section. Although it had a mixed reception at its opening, it soon established itself in the repertory, and a demand for performances from other nations swelled. Britten, Pears, Crozier, and singer Nancy Evans (who would soon become Crozier's second wife) traveled together to performances in Amsterdam and the Hague, and were on their way by Rolls Royce to Lucerne (those "stuffy Swiss lakes") when, according to Crozier's memoir, Pears said, "Why not make our own festival? A modest festival with a few concerts given by friends? Why not have an Aldeburgh festival?" Or, in Pears's own version, "Why don't we have a festival in Aldeburgh? Why do we have to go abroad to Switzerland to perform *Albert Herring*? Why can't we perform it at

---

[15] Carpenter (1992, pp. 248–49).

Aldeburgh?"[16] That was the start of the Aldeburgh Festival, a hybrid arts festival that endures, and thrives, to this day.

Several key principles were established at the start. First, although Britten and Pears were to be key leaders of the Festival, and although performances of Britten's works would often take place there, the Festival would not be about them in the sense that the Bayreuth Festival is about Wagner. It would not be hagiographical or biographical, but would celebrate music from all over the world of Western classical music (and occasional Eastern departures[17]), with a focus on English music (including lesser-known and early English music—Britten especially revered Purcell) and on music by younger composers, as well as European music not so often heard in Britain (Russian music, for example). As we'll see, this led to an impressive record of performances of new works and to the establishment of fellowships and subsidies of various sorts, and later to a school for young musicians, now called the Britten Pears Young Artists Program.

From the beginning, Britten and Pears established the precedent that they would welcome visitors into their home in "open-house" style (Britten's sister Barbara doing the welcoming), and that they would take no remuneration for any concerts or performances they gave. They used their considerable power in the music world, not to make the Festival a monument to themselves, but to lure the best artists and composers to participate, and to urge all participants to foreground the works of young composers. Eventually, there were composers in residence and a composer competition. By 1982, the Festival had performed new works by seventy-five composers, including thirteen new operas.

---

[16] Ibid., p. 252.

[17] Britten was far more open than most composers of his era to learning from other cultures. His travels in Asia, especially Bali, led to creative imitations of Asian gamelans using Western instruments (xylophone, glockenspiel, orchestral percussion, in several of his works, as well as to the creation of a ballet, *The Prince of the Pagodas*, inspired in part by Asian folklore.

Bayreuth and Salzburg, the two comparisons frequently made, utterly lack this fostering intent.

The fostering occurred not only at the elite artistic level, but also at the level of local amateur performance. Britten is famous for composing a great deal for amateurs, especially amateur choral groups, both adult and children's. He began this outreach to the community with the very first festival, where his cantata *Saint Nicolas* (Op. 42) was created for and performed by local amateur musicians, both choral singers and string players, assisted by a professional tenor soloist (Pears), a professional string quintet to lead the other strings, and professional percussionists.

Second, it was not simply a music festival: visual art was a part of it from the very beginning, as were lectures, poetry readings, and theatrical performances. Pears had become a keen art collector and was always an ambitious reader of literature. Both men were allied with painter and set designer John Piper through the English Opera Group, and, with Crozier, they were connected to E. M. Forster, by that time world-famous for novels such as *A Passage to India* and *Howards End*, and soon to begin work on the libretto for Billy Budd. The idea of the festival was from its inception multidisciplinary. This makes it very different not only from Bayreuth but also to some extent from the Salzburg Festival, which includes some theatrical performances and the occasional lecture, but no visual art or poetry readings.

Third, the Festival was designed to suit its home: it would be low-key, modest (from the first year the budget was relatively small, and it has always been balanced), homey (the Open House), and designed to make use of local buildings—the Aldeburgh Jubilee Hall, the nearby Church of St. Peter and St Paul—thus showing visitors the attractions of this Suffolk town. When, later, a larger venue seemed needed for both concerts and operas, the organizers converted a brewery in nearby Snape, Snape Maltings, with the original malthouse equipment still visible. (Opened by Queen Elizabeth in 1967, it burned down, but was rebuilt and

reopened by the Queen in 1970.) Of course international glit-
terati came eventually, but the surroundings remained low-key
and the Festival was intended to foreground, not to overwhelm,
the town.

At the beginning, the directors were just the founding three;
then, when Crozier dropped out in 1955, just Britten and Pears in
that year, and then Imogen Holst joined the team, and remained a
director, for a while the sole director, until her retirement at the age
of seventy in 1977. Holst, the daughter of composer Gustav Holst,
was a composer and music historian; she was Britten's assistant
for a while in the 1950s, and left diaries that are crucial sources for
his compositional life. Equally important, she is probably the first
woman to direct a major arts festival in Britain, so Pears and Britten
made a very important progressive statement by foregrounding
her. After Britten's death, many international musicians joined the
team at various times. The Festival had no performances in only
two years, 2020 and 2021, for obvious reasons, but returned with a
doubly long festival in 2022.

Let us return, however, to the first Festival, in 1948.[18] The first
season set the tone for what was to come: low-key, interdiscipli-
nary, the attraction being the quality of the artists who came to
present their work. There were lectures by art historian Sir Kenneth
Clark on Constable and Gainsborough; by theater director Tyrone
Guthrie on contemporary theater; by music administrator Steuart
Wilson on the future of music in England;[19] by South African writer
William Plomer[20] on Edward Fitzgerald; and by E. M. Forster on
Crabbe and *Peter Grimes*, and what he would have written were he
the librettist. (Fortunately, he was not![21]) There was an exhibit of

[18] See Mitchell and Evans (1978) for reproductions of programs and advertisements.
[19] Note that Wilson shortly after this joined the antihomosexuality movement in the
music world, though it is unclear what his views were at this date.
[20] On Plomer's collaborations with Britten, see Chapter 5.
[21] "I should certainly have starred the murdered apprentices. I should have introduced
their ghosts in the last scene, rising out of the estuary, on either side of the vengeful
greybeard, blood and fire would have been thrown in the tenor's face, hell would have

Constable and Gainsborough paintings, and modern paintings of Suffolk. There were performances of Britten's newest opera *Albert Herring* and the first performance of the new cantata *Saint Nicolas*. Britten and Pears gave the second performance of Britten's Canticle 1 (see the following section) as part of a recital of English music from Elizabethan times to the present. There were a piano recital by Noel Mewton-Wood and a concert by the Zorian quartet including works by Tippett and Bridge, with Britten at the piano. Performances of music and drama for children were announced, though I can find no information about their nature. National critics were not invited, although they were later welcomed when they did begin to come in Year 2 (all but one, Frank Howes, whom Britten detested).

Administratively, the Festival had most of the local luminaries on its Executive Committee, with the Countess of Cranbrook as the Committee's chair. But the more weighty job of president of the Festival was held by George Lascelles, Seventh Earl of Harewood (1923–2011), a member of the Royal Family—cousin of Elizabeth and Margaret, the elder son of the sixth Earl of Harewood and Princess Mary, Princess Royal, the only daughter of King George V and Queen Mary. At his birth Harewood was sixth in line of succession to the throne. But to Britten and Pears he was a close friend and a major force in the opera world. He was director of the Royal Opera House (1951–1953; 1969–1972); chairman of the board of the English National Opera (1972–1985), managing director of English National Opera North (1978–1981), and Governor of the BBC (1985–1987). Not a pacifist, he was a prisoner of war in Colditz; Hitler had signed his death sentence in 1945, but the sentence was not carried out. He founded the magazine *Opera*, edited *Kobbe's Opera Book*, and started a record label dedicated to rerecording historic performances. He was a close friend of Maria Callas.

---

opened, and on a mixture of *Don Juan* and the *Freischütz* I should have lowered my final curtain." One hopes this is meant to be a joke, but humor in Forster is an uncertain and elusive quality.

Britten and Pears knew Harewood[22] from the opera world, and Britten introduced him to his future wife, Britten's great and lifelong friend, the concert pianist Marion Stein, whom Britten had known since she was a teenager, through her father. Harewood and Marion met at the first Aldeburgh Festival and married the following year. For their wedding, Britten composed an anthem, "Amo Ergo Sum." (Because Marion was of Jewish origin, Queen Elizabeth, the wife of George VI, initially opposed the marriage but relented.) The friendship with Harewood was further cemented by this marriage, and the four were fond of traveling together around Europe.[23] This marriage and its unhappy end will concern me in the following section. But at the start of the Festival, Britten and Pears had the auspicious backing of a major member of the Royal Family who was also a passionate opera devotee, and who through marriage became a close personal friend. This certainly would have helped to cast a protective mantle of respectability over the enterprise.

The Wolfenden Commission: Prelude to the End of Outlaw Status

Here, then, are two outlaws, pacifists and same-sex lovers, welcoming the world, literally, into their home. (Sometimes the room with the large double bed was shown to friendly visitors[24] as theirs, but sometimes a single-bedded top floor room was shown as Peter's room—which it also was, since Pears felt he needed a place where he could practice without disturbing Ben—so eventually Britten told Crozier, who often used the little room, that it was

---

[22] Harewood insisted on the pronunciation Har-wood; but the eighth Earl has recently changed the pronunciation to Hare-wood, because he found that nobody was using the original pronunciation, and taxi drivers often misunderstood him.

[23] See Kildea (2013, p. 362).

[24] For example, Michael Tippett and William Walton's wife Susana, Carpenter (1992, p. 248).

no longer available.) When a photographer from the *Ladies Journal* took a picture of the double bed for a story on Britten in 1948, it remained unpublished.

This postwar period saw an increase in prosecutions for homosexual conduct, as Chapter 4 detailed. The recommendations of the Wolfenden Commission took ten years to become legislation. Leading politicians, prominently including Lord Devlin, defended the status quo. Devlin's argument that men who had sex with men would prove incapable of defending their nation in a future war may have seemed particularly relevant to Britten and Pears, well-known pacifists.

There was, furthermore, an antihomosexuality movement within the music world itself, specifically targeting Britten and Pears. In the late 1940s, a cabal of composers took shape, led by the eminent William Walton, knighted in 1951. According to composer Michael Tippett[25] (not part of the group), they went drinking together and "nursed absurd fantasies about a homosexual conspiracy in music, led by Britten and Pears."[26] When Britten was offered the music directorship of Covent Garden, Walton's widely reported response was, "There are enough buggers in the place already, it's time it is stopped." Walton remained envious of Britten throughout his life. But in the early 1950s his sentiments spread to others not in competition with Britten. In July 1955, Sir Steuart Wilson, a former member of the Arts Council—who had accepted Britten's invitation to lecture at the first Aldeburgh Festival—announced in the press a campaign to rid the music world of homosexuals. "The influence of perverts in the world of music has grown beyond all measure. If it is not curbed soon, Covent Garden and other precious musical heritages could suffer irreparable harm."[27] A minor composer,

---

[25] On Tippett's pacifism and imprisonment, see Chapter 5.

[26] Quoted in Kildea (2013, p. 376).

[27] It is possible that Wilson resented working as deputy general administrator at the Royal Opera House (ROH) under general administrator David Webster, who lived with a same-sex companion. Wilson resigned from the ROH in 1955, shortly before launching his crusade.

Walford Haydn, asked to comment, opined: "Homosexuals are damaging music and all the other arts."[28] He followed this pronouncement with accusations of grooming the young and of favoritism in hiring. And these sentiments fit well with the period's crescendo of public animosity in the light of the revealed treason of Kim Philby, Guy Burgess, and Donald Maclean—never mind that only Burgess was homosexual, though Maclean may have had some affairs with men among his many affairs with women. (Nobody at the time suggested that being a promiscuous heterosexual, as Philby and Maclean both were, was a correlate of treason.[29])

How did Britten and Pears survive? Genius and creative attainment were obviously insufficient: Turing saved the whole nation, but that was not enough to save him. Turing's error was to admit openly to the police that he was having an affair with a man—in the course of explaining how he obtained information about a person whom he suspected of burgling his house. Britten and Pears certainly did nothing this careless, and they lived with utmost respectability—and yet they did not conceal their relationship, and as time went on they acknowledged it more and more, as we'll see. Connections with royalty probably helped to insulate them: not just Harewood, but Queen Mary (later the Queen Mother) too, and eventually Elizabeth, became patrons, and Britten was commissioned to write an opera for Elizabeth's coronation. Still, in the late 1940s and 1950s, royal patronage was volatile, and Harewood was the only solid ally and friend they had in royal circles.

It is in this context that we must consider Britten's famous break with Harewood, and his request that Harewood resign from the directorship of Aldeburgh. Harewood, starting in 1959, had been

---

[28] Kildea (2013, p. 376).
[29] The same scare existed in the United States: the famous "Lavender Scare." The ostensible rationale for the connection to treason was the vulnerability of homosexuals to blackmail. But of course that was a danger only as long as same-sex relations were illegal. Furthermore, in social terms, heterosexual adultery could, and often did, give rise to blackmail.

carrying on an affair with a violinist, Joanna Tuckwell, and had a child with her. Finally, he divorced Marion in 1967. In 1965, when the affair was clearly known, Britten broke all ties with him. Odd things are said about this break. Carpenter reports with evident approval the view of a "friend" who imputed the break to Britten's personal shame about his own sexual life and a fear of any scandal touching himself: if there were a scandal, of whatever sort, he would surely be dragged into it. It seems strange that the infidelity of a well-known heterosexual would be taken as a reflection on the life of Britten and Pears, and of course the idea that Britten was ashamed of their relationship is belied by hundreds of letters and statements and is solely in the mind of the "friend" and the homophobic public. But more to the point: he and Carpenter seem to have forgotten entirely about Marion, Britten's close friend long before she met Harewood, and a close friend until the very end of Britten's life. Kildea describes her as a "gentle, conciliatory figure, passionate about music,"[30] and so she seems to have remained. Clearly, she was suffering through her husband's very public desertion, and it seems equally clear that Britten, forced to choose, chose her—showing respect for a woman and not shame at himself. And it was a somewhat risky act, before decriminalization, to forfeit the protection that royalty offered for the sake of a friend. We do know that the friendship between Britten and Marion endured and was a source of support to both.

And no doubt Marion needed his support, as long as he could give it. She did not love wisely. In 1973 she became the second wife of prominent politician Jeremy Thorpe, who is now known to have been bisexual and to have had a lengthy and fraught relationship with a drifter named Norman Scott who kept blackmailing him— until, it is believed, Thorpe concocted an outlandish plot to murder Scott. The plot was executed with such incompetence that only a Great Dane was actually killed, and Thorpe stood trial in 1978

---

[30] Kildea (2013, p. 361).

for conspiracy to murder Scott. He was implausibly acquitted, but was ruined anyway and lost his political career. These events, the subject of the excellent mini-series *A Very English Scandal* (2018), starring Hugh Grant as Thorpe and Ben Whishaw as Scott, show Marion standing by her husband in and out of the courtroom, with great loyalty, and they remained together until both died in 2014. We will never know what Britten would have made of that scandal, and we certainly do not know what Marion knew or did not know about her second husband's life, nor whether he was ever unfaithful to her, though it is likely that he did conspire to murder Scott. But in any case, she loved him and was loyal to him. And in the break with Harewood, Britten was loyal to her.

The first Festival was held well before any of these events unfolded, and Harewood was still capable of protecting Britten then—if he ever was (his capacity to protect anyone seems questionable). At the Festival itself, Britten and Pears made two musical choices that in retrospect seem incredibly bold. The first was to make the new *Canticle I* a centerpiece of the recital he and Pears gave. Written for a memorial concert in 1947 for Dick Sheppard, vicar of St. Martin in the Fields and one of the founders of the Peace Pledge Union, this seven-minute work for tenor and piano was being given only its second performance. The text is by Francis Quarles (1592–1644). According to the official account given by the Britten-Pears Library, "Although ostensibly a text celebrating the poet's ecstatic communion with God, Britten clearly meant the work also to be interpreted as a declaration of the personal and professional relationship that now existed between himself and Pears." Even had that official account not existed, who could doubt the meaning of the words in the Aldeburgh context?

> Ev'n like two little bank-divided brooks,
> That wash the pebbles with their wanton streams,
> And having rang'd and search'd a thousand nooks,

Meet both at length at silver-breasted Thames,
Where in a greater current they conjoin:
So I my best-beloved's am; so he is mine.
Ev'n so we met; and after long pursuit,
Ev'n so we joyn'd; we both became entire;
No need for either to renew a suit,
For I was flax and he was flames of fire:
Our firm-united souls did more than twine;
So I my best-beloved's am; so he is mine.
If all those glitt'ring Monarchs that command
The servile quarters of this earthly ball,
Should tender, in exchange, their shares of land,
I would not change my fortunes for them all:
Their wealth is but a counter to my coin:
The world's but theirs; but my beloved's mine.
Nor Time, nor Place, nor Chance, nor Death can bow
My least desires unto the least remove;
He's firmly mine by oath; I his by vow;
He's mine by faith; and I am his by love;
He's mine by water; I am his by wine,
Thus I my best-beloved's am; thus he is mine.
He is my Altar; I, his Holy Place;
I am his guest; and he, my living food;
I'm his by penitence; he mine by grace;
I'm his by purchase; he is mine, by blood;
He's my supporting elm; and I his vine;
Thus I my best beloved's am; thus he is mine.
He gives me wealth; I give him all my vows:
I give him songs; he gives me length of days;
With wreaths of grace he crowns my longing brows,
And I his temples with a crown of Praise,
Which he accepts: an everlasting sign,
That I my best-beloved's am; that he is mine.

Musically, the work is in B flat major, one of the two key signatures Britten employs for thoughts of peace (the more tranquil and even playful one, compared to the declaratory D major). As in the final Michelangelo sonnet, the vocal line is virtually unaccompanied, naked: here the piano swirls and twirls around it, creating sounds of water and greenery to decorate and complement the more dramatic sounds of the voice. (The contrast is highly suggestive of the contrast suggested in the letters between the playful pussycat Britten and the more "masculine" Pears.) By the end, the voice and piano are playing back and forth in responding gestures. If the final Michelangelo sonnet declares love's commitment after anxiety, Canticle I does something far riskier: it shows love's happiness, playful sensuality, and secure mutuality. (Forster said that the reason he could not publish *Maurice* when he wrote it was that the pair end happily.) And it is all in English, with no fig leaf for the potentially embarrassed public.

The other statement Britten and Pears made at the first Festival was to choose *Albert Herring* as its operatic centerpiece. In this case I must make an exception to my general principle of not discussing major Britten operas in this book, though I shall not engage in detailed musical analysis. The opera was, of course, new, a good reason to present it. But it was also all about a small Suffolk town, its sexual prejudices and repressions, and their joyful overcoming by a formerly repressed young man—a rather risky topic in the circumstances. And yet *Albert Herring* is so endearing, so gentle in its satire, that it won and still wins the day.

The setting is Loxford, a fictional market town in east Suffolk, in 1900.[31] Albert Herring, a young grocer, lives under his mother's domination, unable to enjoy a sexual life out of sheer fear of her disapproval—though he envies the happiness of the young couple

[31] The original source from which the libretto was drawn is *Le Rosier de Madame Husson* (1888) by de Maupassant, so it was Britten and Crozier who transposed it to Suffolk, making the self-reference emphatic.

Sid and Nancy, whose displays of affection show him how re-
warding sexual life can be. Meanwhile, the town has the task of
choosing a May Queen. Led by the formidable Lady Billows, they
deliberate, considering a whole list of young women. They sternly
find fault with the sexual conduct of all of them: nobody is pure
enough for the job. Then someone suggests Albert. All agree that
he meets the purity test, and he is crowned May King. At the ceremony he is tricked by Sid into getting drunk and goes on an ex-
tended spree. Fearing that he is dead, his family and friends start
grieving for him, showing real emotion. But he returns, none the
worse for his experiences, which clearly include more drinking,
brawling, and some type of unspecified sexual activity. Albert feels
liberated from his mother's heavy hand and announces newfound
freedom and happiness.

This satire on British sexual mores is neither caustic nor dev-
astatingly negative. It is actually loving, and it ends in reconciliation. The opera's emotional center is Nancy, both sexual and moral,
who doesn't like the way her lover has tricked Albert, and has genuine sympathy for him. At the end, the town welcomes Albert, and
relaxes its stern demands. It is perfectly clear that all sexual activity
has come under suspicion, so in a sense it doesn't really matter
whether Albert's debut is heterosexual or homosexual. The libretto
gives no clue, though in one recent production the director has
Albert pull some women's underclothes out of his pocket, and no
doubt this is what most of the audience would have imagined, and
would imagine even today, since in 1900, the opera's dramatic date,
a gay coming-out was not in the cards. But Peter Pears is playing the
role, so the question is gently raised. (Pears disliked playing heterosexual love scenes: the role of Essex in *Gloriana* was not a favorite.)
And the whole plot is so suggestive of Britten's own life and his own
move away from prissy purity (and his mother's very strong influence) that it can certainly be read as a gentle self-satire. In a recent
marvelous production by the Chicago Opera Theater, as Albert
returns to work at the very end and says to Lady Billows, "Let me

get on, for I'm all behind," the hero smiles subversively, tapping his backside.

Instead of avoiding all questions about the relationship between his sexual life with Pears and society's norms, in short, Britten and Pears foregrounded these questions—with humor and with an inclusive message: No matter what Albert's sexuality is, audiences should agree that repression is damaging and that the whole town can live in peace together by relaxing its severity. The most interesting thing about the ending is that the audience is told nothing about Albert's orientation. The work's message is that all Alberts are entitled to seek happiness and to live at peace with their Suffolk neighbors. All of this is done in some of Britten's most inventive and delightful music. Britten and Pears were never narrowly focused on the plight of same-sex lovers. (Don't forget that long list of women who are rejected for alleged impurity at the opera's start.) They were concerned with shame about the body and sexual repression more generally, as damaging to women and men, whatever their orientation. Nothing in Britten, I believe, is "all about" homosexuality. He is concerned with human embodiment, human sexuality, and human freedom, all very badly treated in the England of his time.

The opera ranks with the comic masterpieces of Rossini and even Mozart, and the only reasons it is rather rarely done by U.S. opera companies are that it is so extremely English and that it is a chamber opera, unsuited to a larger house. But because it is a good work for younger artists it is often done by universities and conservatories, as well as by smaller chamber-size opera companies, for example, the Chicago Opera Theater, which performed it in January 2023. Significantly, it was a striking success even at the height of persecution, receiving its American premiere at Tanglewood in 1949 and its Australian premiere on Australian television in 1959. Britten led performances in Copenhagen and Oslo in 1949, touring with the English Opera Group. Somewhat astonishingly, it was a hit in the Soviet Union in 1983, promoted by

Sviatoslav Richter, a friend of Britten's, who called it "the greatest comic opera of the century."[32]

In both *Canticle I* and *Albert Herring*, then, Britten and Pears announce their wish to be reintegrated into a renewed British society on their own terms, which is to say terms of both liberty and dignity—and an equal freedom for others who have been repressed, prominently including women. They contribute to that renewal and integration through the inventive playfulness of Britten's music and Pears's performances, which are themselves gestures of loving membership in the nation and region.

In short: Britten and Pears survived the repression of the 1950s with courage, by foregrounding their love, choosing friendship with a woman over royal protection, advancing the careers of women in the arts (especially Imogen Holst)—and, at the same time, giving back to the region they loved, both by creating the Festival itself and by creating both a work for local musicians (*Saint Nicolas*) and a great comic work about the region and its mores (*Albert Herring*) to stand beside the tragic masterpiece (*Peter Grimes*) that Britten had already created.

Coventry: Reconciliation and Rededication

Coventry Cathedral situates itself at the juncture of Europe's violent past and its as yet uncertain future. Destroyed in a single night of bombing on November 14, 1940, the first sustained air attack on a British city, it became a symbol of the war's threat to British traditions and values, but also of their resilience.[33] On Christmas

---

[32] Personal diary, published in Bruno Monsaingeon, *Sviatoslav Richter: Notebooks and Conversations*, translated by Stewart Spencer (London: Faber & Faber, 2001 p. 292).

[33] See the searing account of that night in Provost Richard Howard's wonderful book on the entire sequence of events: Richard Howard, *Ruined and Rebuilt: The Story of Coventry Cathedral 1939–1962* (Coventry, UK: Coventry Cathedral, 1962).

1940, the BBC chose the ruins as the site of its Empire broadcast, to demonstrate Britain's courage and continuity.

During the 1940s and 1950s, the city was rebuilt, but the reconstruction of the Cathedral, "designed as a demonstration of local and national recovery from the war,"[34] was not complete until 1962. (The Queen had laid the foundation stone in March 1956.) From the beginning of the planned restoration, Provost Howard and his committee adopted three principles. First, they chose to emphasize the idea of resurrection and of a better world that might follow the world that created World War II. Second, they decided to have transparent public discussion of all their decisions but, at the same time, to follow their own judgments of artistic excellence, even when the artists' ideas proved controversial. Third, they decided that the new Cathedral would be a place dedicated to ideas of reconciliation—later spelled out as those of Reconciliation Between Nations, Reconciliation Between Separated Churches, Reconciliation Between Classes in Industry, and Reconciliation of Man With God. (In all of the talk of Church Unity that suffuses Howard's book, the unity in question is only Christian unity. There is no discussion of how Jews, Muslims, and others would relate to the Cathedral, although the choice of Jacob Epstein as a key artist makes a bold move in that direction.) Howard was in active conversation with prelates in Germany in particular, and German churches made significant contributions to the new project.

To plan the restoration, as Howard's book narrates it, a Committee was formed. After a lengthy competition with many submissions, Sir Basil Spence was chosen as the chief architect. Although his design underwent later modifications, it is essentially what one sees today. Daringly modern, the plan also incorporates remnants from the old Cathedral—the charred cross from the altar and a cross of burned nails, made from three nails from the roof

---

[34] Wiebe (2012, p. 192).

truss of the old Cathedral, as relics, images of sacrifice, reminding the visitor of the past, but pointing ahead to a soaring future with aesthetic images of fertility and peace. A second cross of nails was donated to Kaiser Wilhelm Memorial Church in Berlin, which was destroyed by Allied bombing and is also preserved as a ruined memorial alongside a newer building. Subsequently, other such crosses of nails were given to other visitors. Reconciliation with Russia was emphasized by placing a copy of the Stalingrad Madonna in both the Coventry and Berlin cathedrals. Thus Britten's idea of having the three vocal soloists in the *Requiem* represent the three formerly antagonistic nations was already implicit in the plans surrounding the Cathedral's rebuilding.

Spence's architectural plan gave rise to heated public debate, but given the uniform support from architectural experts, it was eventually accepted. The Committee, on which Howard's voice had a large influence, then went on to select other artists, this time without competitive submissions. Public concern deepened when Roman Catholic artist Graham Sutherland—controversial in many cases (Lady Churchill not only abhorred his portrait of her husband but actually destroyed it!)—created a vision of Christ presiding over the four Beasts of the Book of Revelation that showed Christ with a very human face (based in fact on the face of a friend of the artist). That controversy persists today, although it has diminished and the tapestry is widely admired. Britten's friend and associate, painter John Piper, was chosen to design the Baptistry window. Although his entirely abstract composition was surprising, the sheer beauty of his use of color won people over. The most controversial choice also turned out to be the one whose work won instant and lasting acclaim. Jacob Epstein was a controversial figure throughout his career, both in his life (having children with several other women while remaining married to his wife) and in his work, which used nudity and was often even charged with indecency. His sculpture for Oscar Wilde's tomb in Paris was for a while veiled by the French police, and the nude figure's testicles were removed by vandals. So although Epstein did not have affairs with men, he prominently spoke up for those who did, and treated Wilde as a martyr. Furthermore, of course, he was Jewish, and the idea that Jews are hypersexual and hyperanimal was very prevalent at the time. Howard did not include Jews in his plans for interreligious unity, but when it came to artistic excellence he tells us that he boldly chose the artist he thought the best. Howard describes how he first had to win over the Committee to this choice, and then to convince Epstein, by then over seventy, to undertake the job of creating a huge bronze sculpture for the Cathedral's façade. In one of his very last works before his death of a heart attack in 1959, Epstein created St. Michael and the Devil, the towering figure of the angel trampling underfoot a very human-looking devil—to remind us, said Howard, of the human roots of all evil.

All of this was discussed widely in the press, so Britten would have known of the Committee's choices and their desire for excellence despite controversy, including controversy about sexuality and even homosexuality. He would consequently have been reassured that his controversial views and life were not disqualifying.

The theme of remembrance-with-reconciliation was emphasized by the architects and formed the centerpiece of the rededication service. The visitor is enjoined not simply to mourn, but, remembering the past, to get on with building the future. Sacrifice must be followed by redemption—of English traditions, and, beyond that, of a European peace. To this day, services of reconciliation are held daily. The Cathedral's current website states:

> Coventry Cathedral is . . . one of the world's oldest religious-based centres for reconciliation. . . . [Following the destruction of the Cathedral in 1940] Provost Dick Howard made a commitment to not seek revenge, but to strive for forgiveness and reconciliation with those responsible. During the BBC radio broadcast from the cathedral ruins on Christmas Day 1940 he declared that when the

war was over we should work with those who had been enemies "to build a kinder, more Christ-child-like world."[35]

Howard (1884–1981) had been able to save only a few artifacts from the smoking ruins (the relics that now appear in the restored Cathedral); the next day, he wrote the words "Father Forgive" on the smoke-blackened wall of the sanctuary—deliberately omitting the word "them," and thus emphasizing that we all need forgiveness.[36] (Today, the Cathedral's reconciliation ministry, the Community of the Cross of Nails, engages in conflict resolution all over the world.) Although Howard retired in 1958, he was no doubt present at the 1962 rededication.

The Commission and the Creation of the *War Requiem*

The idea of a festival to celebrate the rededication was originally brought to the Cathedral Committee by two local business leaders in 1956.[37] The idea, as developed by the committee, was that the entire diocese would celebrate and that this celebration would "reach every section of the people and every furthest place in the diocese, so that all should have an opportunity of making their contribution."[38] (The Diocese of Coventry includes Coventry and Warwickshire, both in the East Coast.)

At this point the Cathedral Committee set up a Festival Committee consisting of twenty-four subcommittees to plan the Festival, one being the Arts Committee. At this point Howard's

---

[35] https://www.coventrycathedral.org.uk/reconciliation/reconciliation-ministry. It is interesting that the website I cite here (2023) has been edited in many small ways and is different from the version I first accessed in 2018, though not in any major respect.

[36] One can see this in the photo that is the frontispiece to Howard's book.

[37] Howard (1962, p. 177).

[38] Ibid. (pp. 177–78).

book leaves off, but there is a very thorough account of ensuing events in Michael Foster's *"The Idea Was Good": The Story of Benjamin Britten's War Requiem*, published for the fiftieth anniversary of the premiere, in 2012.[39] Howard was apparently not directly involved in the Festival planning, and there is no internal record of the deliberations of the Arts Committee. (If there had been, Foster's officially sanctioned and very careful book would have reported them.) Clearly, the committee decided that they wanted to commission a large musical work. Since ideas of resurrection and reconciliation were at the heart of Howard's vision, it is no surprise that the committee designing the Festival to rededicate the Cathedral turned to Britten. Many works were performed at the Festival, but his was the only invitation issued directly by the Festival Committee.[40]

We do not know what other composers were considered, if any. What they needed, clearly, was a person on board with the theme of reconciliation, someone first-rate, someone adept at writing Anglican liturgical works, someone basically friendly to the type of Christian teaching championed by the Coventry clergy, with its Jesus-oriented emphasis on peace and mercy, and someone whose name would be a big draw—also, not incidentally, someone known for keeping to deadlines and delivering promised work. Ralph Vaughan Williams had already written a major oratorio on the topic of war and peace in 1936 (*Dona Nobis Pacem*); he was in his eighties and died in 1958. William Walton had written a major oratorio, *Belshazzar's Feast* (1931), but he was a slow and laborious worker, not good with deadlines—quite apart from his unpleasant attacks on other composers, if the committee was aware of them. He had no connection with Christian liturgical music. Michael Tippett was certainly a strong candidate, and *A Child of our Time*

[39] Michael Foster, *"The Idea Was Good": The Story of Benjamin Britten's War Requiem* (Coventry, UK: Coventry Cathedral Books, 2012).

[40] Wiebe (2012, p. 195).

(performed 1944) is a fine oratorio. He too, however, worked very slowly, and by 1958 time was running short. (And if the committee was worried about sexual orientation, he was also homosexual.)

Britten outclassed both Walton and Tippett, both in esteem and in popular success, after the acclaim given both *Peter Grimes* and *Billy Budd*. He was amazingly prolific, and he liked to write for amateur choral performance, often in an Anglican idiom (whereas the other two were purely secular). He was always thoroughly professional, turning in scores on time. That trait was crucial: Britten, using a large amateur chorus drawn from surrounding towns, completed the score of the *War Requiem* a full year in advance, in May 1961, so that they could begin rehearsing. Indeed, all those people who go on about Britten being "troubled" and "pathological" seem not to understand the kind of healthy living, discipline, and hard work required to carry on a prolific career of artistic creation for forty years! Although not a theist, Britten was in his music, in his own words, "a very Christian composer" (see Chapter 5). By this he clearly did not mean that he was putting on an act: though not a theist, he was a follower of the teachings of Jesus throughout his life. Finally, Britten had made a gift to the nation of a major music festival, which drew people to the Midlands (albeit a different part of the Midlands) and showed the composer's rootedness and lasting love of the land. In that sense he had become a major public figure, making contributions that went beyond the purely musical. He had excellent connections with first-rate singers and orchestras, and people wanted to work with him. So it seems to me that there should have been no serious debate about whom to invite. In any case, they invited Britten.

The chair of the Arts Committee (who later became chair of the entire Festival Committee) was a longstanding acquaintance of Britten's, John Lowe (1906–1996).[41] Lowe, a radio producer, administrator, and occasional conductor, had been conductor of the

---

[41] Foster (2012, pp. 136–77).

Cambridge Philharmonic Chorus in the mid-1940s, where one of his most successful performances had been Bach's *B Minor Mass*, with Kathleen Ferrier and Peter Pears as soloists. So his acquaintance with Britten dates at least from then. He then went on to be a music producer at the BBC Third Programme, and eventually head of BBC Midland Region Music and the BBC Midland Chorus— hence his connection to Coventry. His first known direct contact with Britten was in 1945, when he invited him to contribute a musical theme to be the basis of an on-air improvisation by organist Marcel Dupré. In 1947 he instituted a series of song recitals on the Third Programme, requesting the producer to include "plenty of Pears plus Britten wherever possible, and Ferrier." (Pears is sometimes underrated today, thought of as simply an adjunct of Britten. It is useful to observe that Lowe ranks him alongside Ferrier, one of the greatest contraltos who ever lived, and one of the most distinguished British singers ever.[42]) Later, in his Midlands capacity, Lowe conducted broadcast performances of two of Britten's works: "Five Flower Songs" in 1951 and the Choral Dances from Gloriana in 1954. Lowe, then, liked working with both Pears and Britten, and had done so successfully for many years. As a radio producer, he knew the esteem in which the public held Britten. As a choral conductor, he knew how prolifically and well Britten wrote for choral performance.

Britten was approached through Lowe on October 7, 1958.[43] The letter of invitation stated: "The new work they seek could be full length or a substantial 30/40 minutes one: its libretto could be sacred or secular. . . . The committee would be very pleased if this great occasion could help bring forth an important new work from you . . . they would be v. pleased if you would conduct it."[44]

---

[42] Tragically, Ferrier died of breast cancer at the age of forty-one, in 1953.

[43] Philip Reed, "Britten in the Cinema: Coal Face," in *The Cambridge Companion to Benjamin Britten*, edited by Mervyn Cooke. Cambridge Companions to Music (Cambridge, UK: Cambridge University Press, 1999), p. 21.

[44] Kildea (2013, p. 453); Cooke (1996, p. 21).

Britten replied by return mail:

Would you please tell the Arts Committee at Coventry how touched I was by their kind invitation to write something for the consecration of the new Cathedral in 1962. I should very much like to undertake this—one of the reasons, I must confess, being the, for once, reasonable date attached. Seriously, I should be very honoured to be connected with such a significant and moving occasion, and shall do my best to turn out something worthy of it.[45]

Formal contractual arrangements did not begin until the summer of 1960, when a representative of the festival contacted Britten's publisher, Boosey and Hawkes. The correspondence shows that the Festival representatives had initially construed Britten's enthusiasm to suggest that he did not require any payment for his work. Britten wrote to clarify, saying "My feeling is that to commission a work of this size is a serious matter, they must be prepared to pay for it just as they have had to pay the workmen to build the Cathedral."[46] If they did not offer a "reasonable commission," then they "must take their chance as to whether the work will be ready on time or not." The publisher's representative pointed out that Britten had already declined three other commissions for the Festival. Eventually, after Britten and Pears visited Coventry in September 1960, the Festival committee offered a thousand pounds as a commissioning fee, which they said should include the necessary performance fees as well. (Considering the eminence of the performers, this was an incredibly low offer!) The contract was eventually signed in November. It stipulated that the work would occupy a full evening. Britten would be paid half up front and half after the first performance. The Festival claimed the right to one further performance

---

[45] Cooke (1996, p. 21).
[46] Carpenter (1992, p. 395); Cooke (1996, p. 22).

and stipulated that no other performances of the work would be given until after June 30, 1962.[47]

Britten's pacifist views and his life with Pears were known to all. He would reasonably think that he was invited as the person he was and that his plan of setting Owen's poems—he had already been working on Owen, and his Nocturne includes a setting of "The Kind Ghosts"—was in the spirit of the Festival. By this time he was also prominent in the Campaign for Nuclear Disarmament (CND), a group that advocated unilateral nuclear disarmament. Again, this would have been known to all and was not seen as disqualifying, as it probably would have been in the United States. The overall aims of the Coventry restoration and Provost Howard (succeeded in 1958 by Provost Harold Williams) were his aims also.

John Lowe, now promoted to director of the Festival, drafted a press release about the work-in-progress that mentioned the use of Owen's poems. Britten asked him please to hold back that part until formal arrangements had been concluded with the Owen estate and his publishers. This happened eventually, in 1961.

The work then began. Britten stayed in Aldeburgh—as he put it "quietly??? working." To his publisher he described himself as "going into Purdah now," to get on with the large work. During this period he was also writing a cello sonata for Mstislav Rostropovich and a setting of the *Jubilate Deo* for the Duke of Edinburgh. By May 1961 he was able to describe concretely to Lowe the large resources he would need: as large a chorus as possible, and a large orchestra, including "triple woodwinds and a nice assortment of brass for the *Tuba Mirum* (possibly as many as fourteen)." He insisted on specific spatial requirements: the chamber orchestra would be directly in front of the conductor with the two male soloists. For the boys' choir he requested a remote position, preferably near the organ console, since they sing only with the organ.[48]

[47] Cooke (1996, p. 22).
[48] Cooke (1996, p. 24).

By late 1961, he had decided that the work's title should be *War Requiem*.

Next came casting. Lowe had engaged the City of Birmingham Symphony Orchestra, surely with Britten's approval. In February 1961 Lowe suggested the Melos Ensemble as the chamber orchestra. It was understood throughout that both the main chorus and the boys' choir were to be amateurs from the region (the adults were drawn from several choruses in the Midlands). Pears plainly would be the tenor soloist. Pears suggested Dietrich Fischer-Dieskau (1925–2012) as the baritone, both for musical reasons and for reasons of nationality. (Fischer-Dieskau, one of the greatest singers of the century, excelled in the interpretation of poetic texts and had an unsurpassed capacity to build musical drama through verbal articulation.) Britten wrote to Fischer-Dieskau in February 1961, urging him to accept. "These magnificent poems, full of the hate of destruction, are a kind of commentary on the Mass. . . . They will need singing with the utmost beauty, intensity, and sincerity."

Fischer-Dieskau happily agreed. It is worth bearing in mind that the singer had been conscripted into the Wehrmacht in 1943 and was sent to the Russian Front as a horse tender; later he became a Grenadier in Italy, where he was captured by the Americans in 1945 and spent two years as an American prisoner of war, singing lieder to homesick German troops.[49] His family home was destroyed during the war. He also had a brother, with both physical and cognitive disabilities, who was sent by the Nazis to an institution and starved to death.[50] So he had seen the destruction of war first-hand and had every reason to join Britten's project. A further reason, as he mentions in his autobiography, was that he had been offered the role of Billy in the first German production of *Billy Budd*, but had to decline because of overbooking, so he was very eager to have another chance to sing the music of a composer he admired, and

---

[49] See Lewis (2012); his obituary appeared in the *New York Times*, May 18, 2012.
[50] Ibid.

Britten's letter, which he quotes In full in the memoir, easily won him over.[51] (Had he declined, Britten's second choice was the distinguished operatic baritone and lieder singer Hermann Prey.)

Next came the task of finding a suitable soprano soloist. Lowe had suggested Elizabeth Schwarzkopf—astonishingly, given her Nazi Party membership, although perhaps Lowe simply did not know of this. Britten was more interested in the Russian soprano Galina Vishnevskaya, whose powerful and intense dramatic soprano he greatly admired and whom he had gotten to know through her husband, Rostropovich, by now Britten's close friend. But when Vishnevskaya approached Mme. [Yekaterina] Furtseva of the Soviet Ministry of Culture for permission, she was curtly denied: "But how can you, a Soviet woman, stand next to a German and an Englishman and perform a political work?"[52] Lowe's invitation was simply turned down without any reason given. Britten made a further plea to the Ministry of Culture, but to no avail. Vishnevskaya kept hoping the Soviet ministry would change its mind, but she was then abruptly summoned back to Moscow to appear in a television show.[53] At the premiere, therefore, her role was on short notice taken by English soprano Heather Harper. (Vishnevskaya did, however, perform in the first recording.)

The next question involved who would conduct at the premiere. All along the Committee had hoped that it would be Britten, but the composer was never comfortable leading a large orchestra, as he told them at the start. As the premiere drew closer, Britten had recently had minor surgery and felt that he simply could not perform the whole job. So the larger task of directing the main orchestra was assigned to Meredith Davies (1922–2005), a respected interpreter of Britten's music who had already been training the chorus, while

---

[51] Dietrich Fischer-Dieskau, *Reverberations: The Memoirs of Dietrich Fischer-Dieskau*, translated by Ruth Hein (New York: Fromm International Publishing Corporation, 1989, p. 256).

[52] Kildea (2013, p. 456).

[53] Cooke (1996, p. 27).

Britten conducted the chamber orchestra. Davies also conducted the soprano and the chorus, Britten the tenor and baritone soloists. Britten henceforth followed this split arrangement in performances of the work, except for one performance in 1963 and for the 1963 Decca recording.[54]

The arts festival lasted two weeks and included many performances of drama and music. Few highlighted the theme of reconciliation: that was left to Britten. On May 25, 1962, in the presence of the Queen, the new Cathedral was officially consecrated. On May 30, *War Requiem* had its premiere.

The opening had its share of obstacles, despite Britten's best-laid plans. Harper had only ten days to learn her part. Britten was promised outstanding acoustics (and indeed Howard believed that they were outstanding, and devotes an entire chapter of his book to this point), but Britten, having initially believed him, found the conditions "appalling," the acoustics "lunatic." The Cathedral staff were waging "really Trollopian clerical battles, but with modern weapons." Builders made constant noise, authorities refused permission for a tiered platform in front of the altar for orchestra and chorus, and the entire chorus threatened to walk out if an attempt were made to reduce their numbers to save space.[55] Fischer-Dieskau found Coventry cold and rainy, and was appalled by the hotel, where "wind blew through the tiny rooms, meals ordered from room service failed to arrive, and the nonfunctioning electric sockets could be made to work only after endless efforts by workmen dripping with perspiration." The Cathedral greeted him with "penetrating cold," which "defied all description," and when he begged for some heat for the sake of health, the custodian laughed and said, "'Just practice hard, that'll make you warm.'"[56] And yet: there was Britten's music, for which he records enthusiastic

[54] Ibid. (pp. 27–28).
[55] Carpenter (1992, p. 407).
[56] Fischer-Dieskau (1989, pp. 256–57).

admiration, as he does for Pears. During the first performance, he records, he felt emotionally undone: "Dead friends and past suffering arose in my mind."[57]

Despite all obstacles, then, the performance took place, and the work was widely, almost universally, acclaimed. It has taken its place ever since as a twentieth-century masterpiece. The pride Coventry Cathedral takes in it can be seen from their sponsorship of the Foster book, which is sold in the Cathedral bookshop.

The work is dedicated to four friends of either Britten or Pears, three of whom—Roger Burney, David Gill, and Michael Halliday—died in the war. The fourth, Piers Dunkerly (who took part in the Normandy landings and was taken prisoner at that time), died by suicide in 1959, during a period of depression.

After the work's dedication is an epigraph—Owen's own:

> My subject is War and the pity of War.
> The Poetry is in the pity . . .
> All a poet can do today is warn.

In the late 1960s, Britten said to Sidney Nolan, apropos of the *War Requiem*, that it was a work of "reparation of the world": "an attempt to modify or to adjust the wrongs of the world or the pain of the world with some dream, with some aesthetic kind of object." To his sister Barbara, he said, "I hope it'll make people think a little."[58]

*****

Now we must ask how the *War Requiem* works and what it says. I have spent a great deal of time on prior works of Britten and on the history of his complicated interactions with British society. Now it is time to examine key questions raised in the musicological literature about the *War Requiem*, to see what answers are tentatively

---

[57] Ibid. (p. 258).
[58] Kildea (2013, p. 453).

suggested by this history. Many of these questions are ill-framed in terms of what I have argued so far, so pointing this out now will give me a clear field to approach the work on my own terms, with clearer and better-defined questions.

1. **Does Britten, in the *War Requiem*, unqualifiedly reject established British society and organized religion?** By now we can see that the answer to this question is very likely to be "no." In the material I have examined, Britten has profound criticisms to make, both of society and of organized religion, and he does not waver from those criticisms. But the attitude he takes in the postwar period is one of a kind of loving but stern internal criticism, combined with a desire for reconciliation. The reconciliation must not be any old truce: it must be on the grounds of freedom, justice, and love of peace that he sets forth. But he certainly holds open the possibility that a reconciliation may be achieved, and he repeatedly invites his society to join him in seeking one. These ideas must be tested when we examine the work itself.

    As for organized religion, it is not a single thing, as musicologists tend to forget. Britten repeatedly gave unambiguous endorsement to the teaching of Jesus. Organized religion is sometimes at odds with those teachings, particularly when it endorses retributive anger and depicts God in delighting in retributive violence. So we can expect Britten to dissect the liturgy, not to give it a thumbs up or thumbs down as a whole. But he is in at least partial sympathy with Christianity, and it is that type of Christianity that was exemplified by the Anglican clergy of Coventry.

    Even should there be aspects of traditional Christianity worth endorsing, however, there is a further question to pose: Should people rely on divine intervention to help them deal with war and the aggression that inspires it? It seems, so far, very likely that Britten's answer to this question will be "no."

2. **Is the *War Requiem* a public or a private work?** This question makes little sense as such. War is always both public and private, concerning the fates of nations and the most profound sufferings of individuals. Even the grief brought by war is both public and private. Troops play a public role, but each soldier is an individual with personal thoughts and emotions. And the commemoration of war dead is in one sense a public act, but it also gives expression to deep personal griefs. The best war memorials have always known how to fuse the public with the private. Take Maya Lin's Vietnam Veterans Memorial, where the presence of more than 58,000 names of individual participants on the black granite wall is a great part of its stunning achievement, beckoning to visitors to decorate it, as people do, with personal photos and other mementos, thus making their private grief part of a public narrative.

Surely, Britten's work is written for a public occasion, and, as a Requiem Mass, it links itself to a long shared tradition of choral masses and of rituals aimed at building, as Wiebe says, "a sense of community and shared memory." And unless we should view the Mass itself as a whole as representing aspects of society that Britten utterly rejects, a view I believe insufficiently sensitive to the different strands within the liturgy, we must see his enterprise as linking his attempt to the parts of this tradition he endorses—while, at the same time, avoiding the sanctification of violent death in a way consistent with Britten's critical project. In the process, it also clearly concerns emotions of grief, hope, and aggression that are inside each person—if that is what is meant by the term *private*—but that are hardly secret.[59] Indeed the work aims to draw public attention to them. Britten understood that war is in this way

---

[59] Thus Michael Kennedy's "dealing with dark and secret places of the heart, with the private rather than the public," concerning the Owen poems, seems misjudged (Kennedy, 1981, p. 225). There is nothing secret about wounds and blood, and Britten's whole project is to make it impossible to ignore these facts.

inevitably both "public" and "private," concerned with a shared event that touches the depths of the self. If the question means that the two male soloists representing soldiers are the work's "private" dimension and that this is more important than its "public" aspects, it is wrong on both counts. Being a soldier is a public position. The two soloists are not two unique individuals expressing hidden and uniquely personal emotions; they are the British soldier (and, at times, the German soldier). And this aspect of the work, while it complicates, qualifies, and questions the Mass, does not, I shall suggest, reject it wholesale.

More generally: while Auden in his later years turned away from engagement with public affairs and meanings, Britten did not. As Wiebe again rightly says: the *War Requiem*'s challenge was to "maintain war's immediacy and personal reality, . . . to preserve the realness of its violence . . . while simultaneously enfolding that trauma into a larger sense of continuity and community."[60]

3. **Does Britten, in the *War Requiem*, turn away from his unqualified pacifism about both emotions and actions, in favor of a position more conciliatory to the use of force?** This question remains to be examined in the context of the work as a whole, but it would be very surprising if the answer were "yes." At the time, Britten and Pears were members of several pacifist organizations, including the Campaign for Nuclear Disarmament—campaigning for unilateral disarmament as an approach to the Cold War. Later works such as *Voices for Today* and *Owen Wingrave* contain an unqualified pacifist message, and we know that the Vietnam War only intensified Britten's opposition to military solutions. (Once again I protest: if he thought the foolish and venal Vietnam War showed us anything pertinent to the justification of World War II, he

---

[60] Wiebe (2012, pp. 196–98).

made a huge mistake.) The only space I can imagine in this consistent history would be one in which Britten might insist that emotional pacifism should be the most important focus of our attention—and that if this emotional change were once accepted as a central social aim, the question of violent actions would no longer be on the table. On these propositions he might possibly make common cause with those (for example, King, Mandela) who agree with him about emotional pacifism but feel that, given that this peace-loving disposition has not yet been victorious over aggression, people of peace may occasionally need to use force in defense of self and others. We shall see whether the work contains any gestures of friendship toward those who hold this position.

4. **Is the *War Requiem* in a significant sense "about" Britten's homosexuality?** The moment this question is asked it must itself be questioned. British society treated homosexuality as a psychological problem, separating it from straight sexuality, which is assumed to be unproblematic. For Britten, that bifurcation is itself the problem. Ever since *Our Hunting Fathers*, he is concerned with the ways in which dominant groups, fearing their own bodies and their unruly desires, project images of filth and disease onto others whom they then exclude, driving the alleged "rats" out of the house. The "rats" targeted by body-shame and body-hatred are not just homosexuals; in that work they included Jews, pacifists, and very likely women. But in any case the problem lies not in those persecuted as rats, but with the persecutors. So it is very likely that a work by Britten might be "about" homosexuality in the sense that this is an instance of the persecution of outsiders by people who hate and fear themselves. But the onus of criticism is on those whose unresolved fears generate violence. Furthermore, Britten makes it abundantly clear, in *Albert Herring* and elsewhere, that any lasting solution to social issues of fear-driven shame must be fully general. Albert

gets the right to his sexual life, whatever it is, and we are deliberately not told what it is. And so too do all those women whom puritanism has driven out of the "May Queen" competition. No meaningful work dealing with sexual shame could be "about homosexuality" without being, at least as much, "about heterosexuality" and, more generally, "about" the bodily desires of women and men. Indeed, the outsider, whom persecution has given a Du Boisean "double vision," may even lead the way to a healthier life for all.

A further point should be repeated. One aspect of the public phobia about homosexual men that annoyed Britten and Pears the most was the idea that their lives were all about sex (see Chapter 4). The two always sought to show their sexuality as one part of a full life in which steadfast love was the dominant architectonic sentiment, and in which sexuality was mentioned side by side with work, housekeeping, travel, food, swimming, getting rid of mold in the basement, entertaining friends, and so forth—all the things that straight society found it so hard to ascribe to homosexual men.

In short: If the question were, "Is the *War Requiem* about the sources of aggression and violence in the psyche, and the connection of violence with bodily shame?" the answer is very likely to be "yes." If the question were, "Is the *War Requiem* about embodied love and its beauty?" its answer might again have an affirmative answer. But the question as it is so often posed presupposes that homosexuality is a psychological problem, and that is not a view Britten and Pears ever held. It is this questioner who needs treatment.

A related insight in the earlier works was that aggression is often born of a frantic desire to show invulnerability and masculine toughness, imperviousness to pain. This is really an aspect of body-flight and body-hatred. Britten's work is indubitably about vulnerability and the need to confront it, as a necessary condition of any progress beyond war. Again, this involves a critique of dominant modes of masculinity that could possibly be easier for the outsider to make, but this makes the work more "about" what we might call mainstream masculinity than about homosexuality.

5. **Is the *War Requiem* an optimistic or a pessimistic work?** This question is so far too crude to be answered. What are some better questions in this general vicinity? One might be the following: Does the work look forward with hope to a time without wars, or does it suggest that the causes of war are unlikely to be completely removed from the human psyche and therefore from society? But even should we answer this question in the way that we might call "pessimistic," a further question remains: Does the work suggest that, even without a total and permanent end to all wars and their causes in the human psyche, nations and their individual citizens might make incremental progress toward a world in which it is at least more likely that peace will prevail? And: even should the progress of nations be uncertain, can we see some beauty in the human being, both body and soul, that can give us hope for our lives and their worth? These questions, I believe, are the really interesting ones to pose about the work.

PART II

WAR REQUIEM

Overall Ethos and Dialogic Structure

The musical world of the *War Requiem* is one in which war's chaos and savagery dominate, and yet human beings retain a longing for some type of regeneration and reconciliation and for a better future.[1] The text of the Requiem Mass (sung by the two choirs, an adult choir and a boys' choir) provides the work with its formal frame and makes an orthodox and monumental statement, while the Owen poems, sung by the tenor and baritone soloists, supply a skeptical and tragic human intervention, intimate[2] rather than monumental, accompanied by a chamber orchestra. These interventions, as Donald Mitchell says, "continually interrupt—better, disrupt— the majestic flow and momentum of the Requiem"; they "provide a caustic commentary on the 'values' with which unthinking tradition blandly and blindly, and above all solemnly, associates the grand old, age old, Latin text."[3] However, I shall argue that Mitchell's verdict is too simple: the interventions, I shall argue, do not negate

---

[1] In this section, and in the readings of "At a Calvary" and "Strange Meeting," I draw on my article "Mercy in Music," in *The Oxford Handbook of Western Music and Philosophy*, edited by Tomás McAuley, Nanette Nielsen, Jerrold Levinson, and Ariana Phillips-Hutton (Oxford, UK: Oxford University Press, 2018, pp. 803–22). However, I now interpret the work differently in some crucial respects. I remain grateful to the editors for superb comments.

[2] But not "private"; see the end of Chapter 6. The soloists speak of suffering that ought to be part of public deliberation.

[3] Mitchell (1999, p. 207).

tradition. Instead, as I'll try to show, they call for the replacement of a religious tradition that is all too often obtuse and merely traditional with the living, generous, spirit of Christ's body and blood.

Indeed, I think that it is better to think in terms of a dialogue with the traditional Mass rather than a sardonic commentary. Tradition, in Britten's view, needs stern critique, and aspects that prove obtuse or empty will need replacement. Above all, tradition needs to be completed by the real experiences of soldiers and to rethink itself in the light of these experiences. But it is better to think of the songs as posing questions that tradition must answer if it is to become more adequate to guide people moving forward.

The poem settings are a commentary but not a detached commentary. They are inhabited. They *embody* the experience of soldiers. Deliberately positioned in front of the choirs and the main orchestra, close to the audience, they make us see and feel the soldiers, both as they are battered by cannons and pierced by shells, and as they long for a better world beyond war. They make central the fact that war's toll is on the human body and that the body, so often treated obtusely or even contemptuously by the culture of "our hunting fathers," is the site of our humanity, its triumphs and its losses, its suffering and its dignity.

A Journey of Emotion and Reflection

Britten, like Owen, sought to inspire real thought about what war is and does, how it arises, and how societies might combat those causes in the future, pursuing peace and cooperation. This thought must be suffused by emotions if it is really to change people. As we have seen, however, Britten understands that emotions already embody forms of thought and that a composer, working with emotional materials of rhythm, dynamics, orchestration, and melody, can weave these materials into a complex argument, plotting an experiential path for the listener that contains both emotion and reflection, working closely together.

Listeners can take different paths through the work, and there are also different ways of understanding its overall architecture and movement. In this Part, I offer my own reconstruction of what might be called the journey of one imagined listener. attentive to the work's nuances and also to its relationship to the surrounding culture. This is not to say that other listeners, fully attentive, might not take other journeys, particularly as time goes on and the cultural surroundings change. But I shall recommend at least one prominent path through the work, and one that I believe was structured by Britten himself. Here I briefly announce the argument that I shall unfold in what follows.

As Schopenhauer said (see Chapter 2), we go to a musical work with our own urgent practical questions about life's meaning. And yet, in the encounter with the work, we become detached to a certain extent from our egos. Our most pressing personal concerns are typically submerged as we consider general questions affecting an entire society. So I would maintain that the *War Requiem* poses this question: what should today's societies think about war, particularly as we face forward toward an uncertain future?

The work begins with generalized mourning for those who have died in war. At first the mourning is traditional and conventional— not hollow or false, but also inadequate to take the full measure of war's toll. Then the tenor and baritone soloists, set in front of the chorus and the main orchestra, address the audience with greater immediacy. In a setting of Owen's "Anthem for Doomed Youth," they make clear to the listener the real human cost of war, its waste of young lives. Those who wait at home are also affected: and these survivors are urged to reflect, not with militarism or heedless pride, but with "the tenderness of silent minds"—a willingness to open oneself to real thought. What has brought about this pain? And what could conceivably end it?

The long *Dies Irae* movement deepens the confrontation with self and society, as Britten embarks on a critique of Western societies' deep-rooted tendencies to retributive anger and violence. Here, I shall argue, the liturgy itself becomes (on the whole) the antagonist, as we understand that inherited images of God as a God of vengeance and war have sowed seeds in our personalities that are difficult to uproot. (Britten shows this by musical means, as we shall see.) We see the terrible sadness of young soldiers, about to lose their lives ("Bugles sang"), and we also see their manic bravado ("The Next War")—and understand their plight as linked to cultural valorization of aggressive militarism. At the same time, parts of the tradition contain ingredients of a solution, in the life of Jesus, loving and peaceful.

The work's critique of retributivism now deepens, as Britten artfully shows us how, even in trying to end wars, people too easily become dominated by retributive emotion and aggression. The seeds of war are so deep in the personality that emotional pacifism seems a distant goal ("On Seeing a Piece of Heavy Artillery Brought into Action"). This troubling thought, however—a thought conveyed through artful musical devices—is to some extent counterbalanced by a tender awareness of the worth of the young soldiers who have died ("Futility"), and of the mission of Jesus ("pie Jesu") to human beings.

Disturbing thoughts about the tenacity of aggression are further deepened in the Offertorium, as the wanton violence of human beings, both emotional and physical, proves deaf even to angelic voices urging peace and mercy ("The Parable of the Old Man and the Young").

In the ensuing Sanctus, while the liturgy praises God in a distant and distanced way, Owen's poem "The End" brings listeners to the lowest point of the work, an almost Schopenhauerian moment of futility and despair.

But Britten pulls us back from the abyss. In a movement that I consider the heart of the work, the Agnus Dei, he manifests the beauty of human beings, human embodiment, and human love, through meditating, along with Owen's "At a Calvary on the Ancre," on Christ's fully human sacrifice and its meaning for human beings.

But if Schopenhauer's pessimism is rebutted and we grant that human lives have worth, this tells us little about societies. At various points in the work, Britten has indicated paths of reconciliation between tradition and the needs of the future, and between the pacifist critic and his society. What, however, does the work say about the future of Europe? Can nations come together to forge a future without rancor? The last movement of the work, Libera Me, is preoccupied with this question, as Owen's poem "Strange Meeting" shows a possible reconciliation between former enemies—but only after death. The poem and the ensuing interweaving of soloists with the two choruses meditate in an uncertain and ambivalent way about the likelihood of future peace, as the work ends.

That is the path that I shall trace through the work, presenting each step with detailed musical and cultural arguments.

Now, however, we must back up to lay some necessary groundwork.

Plan and Musical Resources

The *War Requiem* is unique among Requiem masses—and in a sense in the entire history of Western orchestral/choral literature—for the complexity of its musical structure. There are two orchestras: a large symphony orchestra and a chamber orchestra; two choirs: a large adult choir (at the premiere, amateurs from the surrounding area), a boys' choir;[4] and three soloists: soprano, tenor, and baritone.

---

[4] The term *boychoir* is also used in speaking about the work, but Britten's score reads "boys' choir." In some performances (for example a 2022 performance by the Boston Symphony Orchestra), a mixed-sex youth choir is used rather than a boys' choir. Since the United States does not have Britain's tradition of boys' choirs, the requisite musical excellence can often best be found that way.

Britten drew attention to the spatial arrangements he wanted: the chamber orchestra would be in front of the conductor (at the premiere there were two conductors, so the chamber orchestra was behind Britten, who conducted them, but in front of Davies, who conducted the main orchestra), along with the two male soloists. The soprano was to be behind the main orchestra, along with the adult choir. (Vishnevskaya was not pleased with this placement, which she initially considered a relegation, but her role in the work is definitely with the adult choir and the main orchestra.[5])

The boys' choir, Britten insisted, should occupy a remote position: "The boys, however, I would like to have placed at a distance, they perform throughout only with the organ, so it would be good if they were near the organ console. I realize there is no gallery in Coventry, but I am sure some remote position can be found for them."[6] It is worth noting that Britten typically wanted his boys' choirs to sound earthy and not ethereal. Thus Britten rejected the standard English boys' choir sound, which he thought too pure and disembodied, preferring a warmer, earthier, "impure" sound, complete with breaks and scratches, that he felt was more familiar in German boys' choirs.[7] Wiebe persuasively reads this as a rejection of a prettified Victorian Christianity in favor of a Christianity of this world. Remote placement, then, does not mean remote sound. For the premiere Britten's favorite boys' choir was unavailable, but the conductor of the choir that eventually performed reassured Britten that the boys "do not train as 'hooty-fluty,' but use the boy's whole voice."[8]

---

[5] On her initial dissatisfaction, see John Culshaw, *Putting the Record Straight: The Autobiography of John Culshaw* (New York: Viking Press, 1982, p. 312).

[6] Letter to John Lowe, May 12, 1961, quoted in Cooke (1996, p. 24). Britten finished a full score by Christmas 1961, which he thought essential so that the large amateur choir would have enough time to rehearse.

[7] Wiebe (2012, ch. 2). Britten even forced the withdrawal of a recording of *Ceremony of Carols* with the wrong boys' sound.

[8] Wiebe (2012, p. 61).

The orchestral resources are large. The score[9] specifies, for the main orchestra:

3 Flutes (Fl. III doubling Piccolo)
3 Oboes
English Horn
3 Clarinets (Cl. III doubling Cl. In Eb and Bass Cl.)
2 Bassoons
Double Bassoon
6 Horns in F
4 Trumpets in C
3 Trombones
Tuba
Pianoforte
Organ (or Harmonium): here Britten notes that given the
    desired remoteness a portable organ might be best for the
    boys, though a grand organ plays with the orchestra in the
    last movement.
Timpani
Percussion (4 players): 2 Side Drums, Tenor Drum, Bass Drum,
    Tambourine, Triangle, Cymbals, Castanets, Whip, Chinese
    Blocks, Gong, Bells (C and F#), Vibraphone, Glockenspiel,
    Antique Cymbals (C and F#)
Strings

For the Chamber Orchestra, Britten specifies:
Flute (doubling Piccolo)
Oboe (doubling English Horn)
Clarinet (in Bb and A)
Bassoon
Horn in F
Percussion (Timpani, Side Drum, Bass Drum, Cymbal, Gong)

---

[9] Britten and Owen (1962).

Harp
Two Violins, Viola, Violoncello, Double Bass

Britten's attention to the Percussion and his inclusion of tuned percussion instruments (a favorite choice of his) stand out, as well as the focus on the C-F# tritone, even in the selection of orchestral resources.

The Choice of Owen

In the early 1960s Owen was not very well known, and one might wonder why he was chosen to provide the additional texts for the *War Requiem*.[10] After all, he was a poet writing about World War I, and the Coventry event focuses on World War II. The most obvious answer is that Owen is a great poet who expressed in wonderful poetry sentiments about the horrors of war that were dear to Britten's heart. His purpose in the *War Requiem* was less to look backward than to create an arresting warning for the future, and for this Owen seemed the obvious choice. Britten called him "by far our greatest war poet, and one of the most original and touching poets of this century."[11] He read Owen seriously and passionately, and had already set "The Kind Ghosts" in his 1958 song cycle "Nocturnes." And in a 1958 BBC broadcast, "Personal Choice," that asked people to choose a favorite text, Britten chose "Strange Meeting," which will play a key role in the *War Requiem*. During this period, he was also reading Owen's letters, fascinated by Owen's life.

In Chapter 5 I discussed at length the similarities and differences between the two men: Britten's pacifism is far more global than Owen's, which seems to have allowed for differences among wars. Owen also enlisted, while Britten refused even supportive civil

---

[10] See Foster (2012, ch. 3) for a good discussion of this question.
[11] Quoted in Kildea (2003) and in Foster (2012, p. 44).

service. But Owen's work has streaks of elitism and misogyny that Britten rightly rejects, both in his selection of poems and in his careful editing of those he does select. Clearly, Britten thought that there were elements in Owen that he did not support, but that these could be avoided or pruned away.

There were some worthy poets who wrote about World War II, in particular Keith Douglas (1920–1944), who was killed during the D-Day invasion of Normandy. But although Douglas is much admired for his vivid depiction of war's horrors, he did not convey Owen's clear antiwar warning for the future, nor has his poetry continued to inspire over the years, as Owen's definitely has.

Another point in favor of the choice of Owen is that he is a very musical poet, using sound effects to batter the reader with the acoustics of war. As we shall see, Britten responds to the challenge of setting these sonic disruptions against the background of the traditional Mass.

The Tritone

The C-F# tritone is a major structural feature of the work, figuring even in Britten's specification of the tuning of the bells. This interval, traditionally found discordant and ominous, is used throughout the work—especially in *Requiem Aeternum*, Agnus Dei, and Libera Me—to create an impression of unresolved tension and anxiety. Almost identical passages in which the tritone is voiced by unaccompanied chorus are placed at the ending of those three movements, thus at the beginning, middle, and ending of the work.[12] Sometimes the tritone is resolved—and we shall have to

[12] See Dennis Shrock, *Choral Monuments: Studies of Eleven Choral Masterworks* (New York: Oxford University Press, 2018, pp. 401–2); Peter Evans, *The Music of Benjamin Britten* (Minneapolis: University of Minnesota Press, 1979), p. 36, observes that Britten uses the tritone to create tension in other works as well.

observe this closely, asking whether, so to speak, the anxiety is resolved into hope, indifference, or despair.[13]

Influences

Britten's main musical influences in this work are Gustav Mahler (1860–1911), whom he loved throughout his career, and Giuseppe Verdi (1813–1901), whom he also loved and whose *Requiem* (1874) is an example he follows in some respects in composing his own.

Mahler is, along with Britten, one of the great musical excavators of the human heart. He said in a letter to his friend Max Marschalk that his musical imagination took its start "at the point where the *dark* feelings hold sway, at the door which leads into the 'other world'—the world in which things are no longer separated by space and time."[14] In Chapter 3 I have shown how often Britten's music about war and aggression makes reference to Mahler's funeral marches, and, in Chapter 2 I have noted how deeply Britten as a listener responded to Mahler's expressions of grief and pain. Mahler shares with Britten a keen sense of the fragility of human projects—and yet of the power of human love, which endures despite their fragility. The two men share an anti-Schopenhauerian take on human suffering and frailty.

Another bond is love of the human voice. Mahler was a conductor of opera for most of his career—such a good one, in operas ranging from Mozart to Verdi to Wagner, that he was greatly admired despite the vitriolic anti-Semitism that the Viennese opera

---

[13] See Graham Elliott, *Benjamin Britten: The Spiritual Dimension. Oxford Studies in British Church Music* (New York: Oxford University Press, 2006, pp. 140–43).

[14] Letter to Marschalk, March 26, 1896, in Gustav Mahler, *Selected Letters of Gustav Mahler*, edited by Alma Mahler and Knud Martner (New York: Farrar, Straus, & Giroux, 1979, pp. 178–79); this segment of the letter is also cited in Cooke (1988), and I here follow Cooke's translation rather than that of Wilkins and Kaiser in the Mahler/Martner volume. See the detailed discussions of Mahler in Nussbaum (2001, ch. 5, ch. 14).

world always directed at him. He never wrote an opera, very likely because, as a Jew, he would be unlikely to get an opera produced. (Opera, we must bear in mind, is a very expensive medium, requiring someone's willingness to pay the costs. Britten was an outsider in some ways, but a privileged insider in others.) Mahler did, however, draw on the expressive capacities of the voice in many of his symphonies (2, 3, 4, 8, and *Das Lied von der Erde*), which use either chorus or soloists or both.[15]

Britten knew all of Mahler's symphonies and song cycles, but three stand out as possible specific influences: the Eighth Symphony (often called Symphony of a Thousand), which uses a vast chorus and numerous soloists and sets the text of the last scene of Goethe's *Faust*, as well as the hymn Veni Creator Spiritus; the Second or "Resurrection" Symphony, which uses chorus and two soloists, soprano and alto, setting one text from the folk-poem collection *Des Knaben Wunderhorn* and a poem about human resurrection by Friedrich Klopstock with verses added by the composer; and *Das Lied von der Erde*, a orchestral song cycle not among the numbered symphonies, which uses two soloists, a tenor and either an alto or a baritone, who sing poems by a variety of Chinese poets. The Eighth Symphony suggests itself on account of its vast resources, its use of both religious and nonreligious texts, its choice of a hymn that Britten elsewhere uses (see Chapter 5), and its theme of overcoming death and evil through love. The Second Symphony shares with Britten the theme of regeneration or resurrection, and it also suggests, I believe, that social regeneration takes place not through conventional religious uplift, but through the daring of the loving artist, who goes his own way, undeterred by social forces of hostility and exclusion—a very Brittenesque thought.[16] Furthermore, its use of the two soloists

---

[15] Britten conducted the Mahler Fourth at Orford Church on July 6, 1961, and thus was actively engaged with Mahler while drafting the *War Requiem*: see Stephen Downes, *The Enforcement of Morals* (Oxford, UK: Oxford University Press, 2013), pp. 79–80).

[16] See Nussbaum (2001, ch. 14).

conveys a sense of intimate presence, against the orchestral background. *Das Lied von der Erde* was, we know, loved by Britten for its searing expression of human loss and pain (see Chapter 2). Its connection to Mahler's own discovery of a fatal heart defect is an uncanny tie to Britten's own history, and the work as a whole grapples with mortality in a far less optimistic spirit than the other two works, though a kind of resignation is apparently achieved at the end.

We obviously do not need to choose among these three. Britten knew them all and was his own person. But I feel that the most often discussed "influence," the Eighth, is the least congenial to Britten's spirit, since it presents a simple, conventionally religious story of salvation—in the process describing the body and sexuality as things from which human beings need to be saved. (I have always thought the ending of *Faust* quite unworthy of Goethe, that magnificent humanist and daring lover, and I find the Eighth pallid and conventional compared to most of Mahler's work.) The Second gives a much more interesting and Brittenesque account of what resurrection might be: embodied love and creativity triumphing over ossified conventions.[17] *Das Lied* calls into question whether any such triumph over death could ever be achieved. Both of these thoughts are, I think, in the *War Requiem*, and we must continually ask which thought gains the upper hand.

Verdi is another composer whom Britten loved and admired. Particular favorite operas were *Aida* and *Falstaff*.[18] His is an influence of a different sort: for he also composed a *Requiem* that has both structural and expressive kinship with Britten's. The movements of the *War Requiem* are divided just as they are in Verdi, and not as in Mozart, who allocates separate movements to the different parts of the *Dies Irae*. In many parts of Britten's

---

[17] Ibid.
[18] See Gilles Couderc, "The *War Requiem*: Britten's Wilfred Owen Opera," *Arts of War and Peace* 1, No. 1 (2013): 12.

work, particularly the *Dies Irae*, the Agnus Dei, and the Libera Me, there are musical references to or at least affinities with the Verdi *Requiem*, which I shall describe in their places.[19] Verdi's *Requiem* is also a Requiem Mass by an unbeliever: it was written to commemorate the humanist writer Alessandro Manzoni, a fellow liberal and a supporter, with Verdi, of Italian unification—a cause opposed by the Catholic Church and especially Pope Pius IX, whom Verdi regarded as his archenemy. Like Britten's, Verdi's *Requiem* has often been thought too secular and "operatic" for performance in a devotional context. Verdi's *Requiem*, like Britten's, is written from the point of view of a humanism opposed to religious tyranny that nonetheless sees some worth in some religious traditions. It also has a sense of drama that is indeed "operatic," and in this Britten certainly follows Verdi's lead.

Verdi is far more worldly than Mahler, who delves into the heart but has little interest in politics. And while not a pacifist in terms of actions, Verdi exhibits a general political spirit that can, I believe, be described as emotionally pacifistic, or at any rate as favoring the triumph of love and brotherhood over hatred, fear, and retribution. In *Don Carlos* he depicts with devastating musical insight the role of the Church in tyrannizing over both political and emotional freedom. And his great comic opera *Falstaff* has, it seems to me, considerable kinship with *Albert Herring*, in its gently humorous acceptance of middle-class life, with all its absurdities and excesses, and yet its capacity for forgiving love. In that very different way Verdi, too, is a fellow spirit of Britten's, though, unlike Britten, with a robustly joyful temperament. These spiritual affinities are, to me, more interesting than specific musical ones, which will be noted from time to time.

Sometimes these musical continuities (I'd rather call them that than musical debts) have been seen as a weakness in the

---

[19] See Cooke (1996, p. 54) and Malcolm Boyd, "Britten, Verdi and the Requiem," *Tempo*, no. 86 (1968): 2–6; a shorter version as an appendix in Foster (2012, pp. 132–33).

work.[20] But how can that be a plausible position? As Britten put it: "I think that I would be a fool if I didn't take notice of how Mozart, Verdi, Dvorak—whoever you like to name—had written their Masses. . . . If I have not absorbed that, that's too bad. But that's because I'm not a good enough composer, it's not because I'm wrong."[21] In short: to be a continuer of these great composers, one cannot be a robotlike hack; one must be a worthy artist. Britten's work invites these comparisons only because of its independent musical and dramatic force. Furthermore, part of the *War Requiem*'s design is to display and show respect for tradition and continuity. The continuities are most prominent in the choral and orchestral settings of the Requiem Mass, the part of the work that evokes tradition—not in the Owen poems, which challenge tradition and create a dialogue with it. Thus the people who look for characteristic Brittenesque idiosyncrasy in the part of the work that sets the Requiem Mass are looking in the wrong place. Britten's setting of the Mass is of course original in its own way; but if it lacks some traits that Britten's admirers cherish in him, it is because Britten has set things up that way, constructing a dialogue between critical questioning and tradition—in which tradition is not entirely bad and dead, but the source of human community and richness, if it can only be adequately liberated from the weight of what is dead or obtuse within it.

One more point should now be made. Britten, like Verdi, loved the public and loved to write for the public. He wrote numerous works for amateur performance and even for musical instruction (the wonderful "The Young Person's Guide to the Orchestra"). And of course the *War Requiem* was written for a huge public occasion. If it were going to change people as Britten hoped, it would have

---

[20] See, for example, Kennedy (1981, p. 228): "The resemblances [to Verdi] . . . are disturbing, the orchestra writing much more obvious and conventional." He adds that this was probably deliberate on Britten's part, but counts it as a weakness nonetheless.

[21] Carpenter (1992, pp. 409–10).

to meet them where they were, and move them, using the dramatic resources Britten knew so well how to command in the opera house. Musicologists who choose to write on Britten may not always share Britten's respect for popular audiences and their tastes.[22] The musical continuity that some critics deem lacking in idiosyncratic originality may be exactly what opens the work to the ears of the public. If the work had been a song cycle of Owen poems, it could have commanded only a far narrower audience, and the job of making people really think about war would not have been accomplished.

What follows will be a reading of the work's central themes, not a complete musical commentary—Cooke has done that extremely well. I will focus on some sections in more detail than others, searching for the central themes and structures that will help us chart the journey of thought and emotion that Britten arranges for his audience.

1. *Requiem Aeternum*[23]

CHORUS

| Requiem aeternum dona eis, Domine; | Lord, grant them eternal rest; |
| et lux perpetua luceat eis. | and let the perpetual light shine upon them. |

BOYS' CHOIR

Te decet hymnus, Deus in Sion:	Thou shalt have praise in Zion, o God:
et tibi reddetur votum in Jerusalem;	and homage shall be paid to Thee in Jerusalem;
exaudi orationem meam,	hear my prayer,
ad te omnis caro veniet.	all flesh shall come before Thee.

---

[22] Outside the conventional category of "classical music," Britten's knowledge and tastes were uneven. He loved English folk tunes, and his settings of these are among his most successful compositions for piano and voice. He also had great curiosity about Asian music. But as to jazz, swing, and rock, the story is far less clear, although *Paul Bunyan* made some efforts to incorporate a jazz idiom. Today it is difficult to speak of his work as reaching a "popular" audience. In 1962, classical music and opera were still mainstream tastes.

[23] My typography and spacing (including the indentation of the Owen poem) follow those of the score, except that I have added, to the right of the Latin, the English translations given in the liner of the original recording, assuming that these had Britten's approval.

TENOR SOLO

What passing-bells for these who die as cattle?[24]
Only the monstrous anger of the guns.
Only the stuttering rifles' rapid rattle
can patter out their hasty orisons.
no mockeries now for them from prayers or bells,
nor any voice of mourning save the choirs,—
the shrill, demented choirs of wailing shells;
and bugles, calling for them from sad shires.
What candles may be held to speed them all?

Not in the hands of boys, but in their eyes
shall shine the holy glimmer of good-byes.
The pallor of girls' brows shall be their pall;
their flowers the tenderness of silent minds,
and each slow dusk a drawing-down of blinds.[25]

CHORUS

Kyrie eleison.	Lord, have mercy upon us.
Christe eleison.	Christ, have mercy upon us.
Kyrie eleison.	Lord, have mercy upon us.

The *Requiem Aeternum* begins with the adult choir singing the words of the traditional Mass: hesitantly, with struggle, as if trying to rise lifting a large weight. This effect is far from conventional. Most Requiem masses convey communal sorrow, but it is, so to speak, sanctified sorrow, directed at death, seen as a necessary part of life. Here we have the sense of an entire community put under enormous pressure—not by an expected and sanctified part of life but by a non-necessary and all-too-human incursion into life's fabric. Throughout, the choir's statements are distant and ghostly, expressive of both anxiety and exhaustion—fragments of a culture that is in disarray after great suffering.

---

[24] The poem is Owen's "Anthem for Doomed Youth," here quoted in full.

[25] This poem was worked and reworked by Owen; *Collected Poems* presents three complete drafts (one, on p. 185, being a photograph of the first draft in Owen's hand), and numerous variants. Britten for the most part uses the CP text; but in the next to last line he chooses the variant "silent minds" over "patient minds," a significant choice to be further discussed. See Owen (1963, p. 185).

The tolling bells sound the ominous C-F# tritone that returns throughout the movement.[26]

The boys' choir now enters in a brisk tempo, and with a chromatic twelve-tone sequence, seemingly striking a reassuring note of unburdened innocence and cheer—but very far away. War has put childhood, innocence, and cheer on hold, or at least has relegated them to a great distance.

The tenor now begins the Owen poem, with the chamber orchestra, in a section marked "Very quick and agitated." From the very first words, the voice addresses the audience with an immediacy and realism that contrasts markedly with the uneasy ghosts of the traditional text. It is an abrupt, jolting intervention, the tenor's entrance accompanied by what Cooke vividly calls "a nervously brittle harp tremolo on the same pitches [as the choral tritone]."[27] As Wiebe nicely puts it, "The worldly experience of war arrives as if conjured from the space of the bells' tritone, like a film close-up revealing the nature of this disruption."[28] This, the setting seems to say, is what war really is. This is a real person, experiencing those shocks. Britten's scoring creates a variety of effects, "wailing" (flutes and clarinets) banging, together with horn fanfares, all of which intensify Owen's verbal effects, putting us in the middle of battle, with its chaotic and inharmonious noises.

The opening lines of the poem seem to speak directly to the bells of the traditional requiem, objecting to them: for surely the "passing bells" are those that we have just heard, sounding the ominous tritone. The poem says that these bells are inappropriate for "these who die as cattle." The tenor line rises to G flat on "as" and then abruptly descends with a marked *sforzando* from F to G flat below, emphasizing the way the soldier is marked as lowly, mere

---

[26] See Wiebe (2012, pp. 206–12), an excellent reading of this section. She points out, rightly, that it is not correct to say that the choir is simply uttering traditional platitudes: the setting expresses anxiety.

[27] Cooke (1996, p. 61).

[28] Wiebe (2012, p. 208).

animal fodder for war's cannons. This critique is followed by a similar abrupt descent on "prayers or bells," linking the defective way of seeing soldiers to traditional religious mourning, now seen as insufficient, mere mockeries. Instead, the poem continues, the "music" of war to accompany these deaths must be only the "monstrous anger of the guns," the "stuttering rifles' rapid rattle," and these onomatopoetic phrases are made yet more vivid by musical whistling and rattling. And on "Nor any voice of mourning save the choirs, / The shrill, demented choirs of wailing shells," the tenor line imitates the sounds of battle, especially in the chromatic melisma on "wail-."

There is sharp protest here, but it is important to say precisely what it is and is not. I believe it is clear that the community of sincere and burdened mourners are not being repudiated as obtuse traditionalists, far less as ugly warmongers. Rather, the point is that, in the light of the real experience of war, all musical expressions of mourning are eclipsed by the unmusical reality of war itself, which, it is suggested, the community of mourners has not yet fully faced. Just as, in Mozart's "Non più andrai" (see Chapter 2), the sounds of music do not belong at the battlefront—only banging and whistling—so too, here, the very idea of music is so far from the horrible experience of war that it seems like a mockery of what the soldiers are enduring. That is not to say that the community is evil or clueless in its mourning. Instead, their understanding needs to be enlarged to accommodate a horrible experience that, so far, lies at a great distance from them. And, as we hear, that horrible experience can be at least approached in the music of mourning—of Britten's daring and highly original kind.[29]

I must pause at the words "like cattle," which is so emphasized in the musical setting. Owen clearly thought, and often said, that

---

[29] For a related conclusion about this movement, see Shrock (2017, p. 422).

World War I was pointless and that it did treat young men's bodies as mere cannon fodder. That would be an absurd characterization of Allied soldiers at the front in World War II. Most of them surely did not think that they were being sent off to die "like cattle." They thought, correctly, that they were being sent off to fight for freedom and democracy against one of the most evil autocrats in history and that their sacrifice was noble. Just as today's Ukrainian soldiers are not mere cattle (indeed, I note that even cattle are not "mere" cattle, but sentient beings with a life of their own), but proud and heroic patriots sacrificing for a just cause, so here. Owen's poem creates an off-stage villain, the warmonger state, who has no place among the Allies in World War II. Britten's blind spot about just war is exactly here, in his willingness to use these lines without critical thought. His important musical-dramatic point in this song, about the horror and enormous suffering of war, transcends this difficulty, but it is no mere quibble, given that such attitudes lie deep in Britten's life and beliefs.

With "What candles may be held to speed them all?" (marked *forte*, with a *sforzando* on "all," the tenor line rising melismatically from D flat to (high) G flat, and descending, as before, to the F an octave lower), there is a sharp change of thought and tone. The shift is from past to future: from the terrible experience of the soldiers who have died to the question before the community: how *shall* we honor them? If traditional mourning is insufficient, given the ugliness of what they experienced, what is there left to say, or to sing? Britten's music, which makes the listener really face the ugliness of war—in a detached way that invites real thought rather than causing revulsion or evasion—is a beginning of his answer.

The war noises now cease. The musical world grows quiet, deliberative. With the line "Not in the hands of boys, but in their eyes," the music soars upward against a very thin accompaniment, introducing the theme of the value of the lives that war threatens—and that same musical treatment is given to "the pallor of girls' brows shall be their pall," suggesting the equal worth and equal vulnerability of the female lives at home, an insight of Britten's and not (or not clearly) Owen's. The vocal line recalls phrases from the boys' choir, thus suggesting that the community includes young and innocent lives, now burdened with mourning. The music then turns deliberative and inward, as the line "Their flowers the tenderness of silent minds" descends from the heights as if thought is turning in on itself. Britten preferred "silent" to various other Owen attempts, including "comrades," which would have made the tenderness belong only to soldiers. Here, it plainly belongs to everyone, and especially, on each performance occasion, to the audience, which is literally sitting in silence. The audience is the deliberative repository of the poem's message, which is one of mourning, condemnation of war's horrors, and the need to deliberate about a better future. The movement broaches that possibility—only to fade away, with (*pp*) "and each slow dusk a drawing down of blinds."

A challenge has been put before the community: not simply to mourn in the traditional way, but really to face the horror of war, which must mean concerted and wholehearted efforts to avoid future wars.

The chorus now reenters, pianissimo, ghostly, fading away to *pppp*, singing the traditional Kyrie eleison, Christe eleison, Kyrie eleison, sounding the ominous tritone, an effect to be repeated at crucial moments in the work, suggesting, in its frequent association with the word *requiem*, that any repose that humans may achieve is likely to be unstable—and, in the light of the challenge posed, also suggesting doubt about whether the community will take up this task that has been set before them. As will occur twice more in the work, the tritone is resolved onto the alien key of F major—which might suggest hope, but, in its jarring and alien effect, might also suggest rupture and uncertainty.

****

2. *Dies Irae*

Chorus

Dies irae, Dies illa,	This day, this day of wrath
solvet saeclum in favilla:	shall consume the world in ashes,
teste David cum Sibylla.	as foretold by David and the Sibyl.
Quantus tremor est futurus,	What trembling there shall be
quanto Judex est venturus,	when the judge shall come
cuncta stricte discussurus!	to weigh everything strictly
Tuba mirum spargens sonum	The trumpet, scattering its awful sound
per sepulchra regionum	across the graves of all lands
coget omnes ante thronum.	summons all[30] before the throne.
Mors stupebit et natura,	Death and nature shall be stunned
cum resurget creatura,	when mankind arises[31]
judicanti responsura.	to render account before the judge.

This doubt is shortly reinforced by the way in which the choral forces plow straight onward, with no hint of critique or reflection, into the next section of the traditional Requiem Mass, the medieval poem *Dies Irae*. Traditional expressions of mourning are insufficient, but not wrong-headed. Things are otherwise with this all-too-familiar text, whose abhorrent sentiments—to anyone at all inclined to pacifism, especially emotional pacifism—are uttered without critique by the chorus. Moreover, the problems that anyone with the sensibilities of Britten and Pears must find with this text have even eluded critics, accustomed as they are to the *Dies Irae* as a familiar part of many Requiem masses, and always a source of thrilling musical effects. While critics say that this music is derivative of Verdi, and link it with the prior movement as an expression of tradition that needs to be challenged, they do not distinguish it

---

[30] As usual, I follow the English version given in the first recording, but it is inaccurate here: *coget*, like the other verbs in the sequence, is a future tense.

[31] Once again: future tense in Latin. I also take issue with "mankind" for *creatura*, which means all creation—though in what follows it appears to be only humans who are asked to render an accounting.

sufficiently from the first movement, whose words of mourning are not rejected, even if they prove insufficient—or, indeed, from subsequent texts whose Christian sentiments Britten clearly endorses wholeheartedly, the Agnus Dei above all.

Britten does not reject all elements of traditional religion, nor does he see all religion as inadequate to guide people in thinking about war. His admiration for the life and ideas of Jesus is unequivocal, and it guided his profound critique of war in the Donne Sonnets. But he certainly does reject those elements of traditional religion that validate war by appeal to divine authority and ask us to model ourselves on a God who makes aggressive war. (Let us not use the facile contrast between the religions of the Old Testament and the New. There are peace and mercy in the Old Testament, and there is plenty of retributive anger in the New, albeit not in the life and sayings of Jesus. The *Dies Irae* is a medieval Christian hymn with no basis in biblical text.)

The *Dies Irae* depicts God as a harsh and angry judge of human wrongdoing—including lack of proper submission to traditional religious authority. It valorizes a priestly culture in which all human errors are recorded and can only find atonement by groveling submission to ecclesiastical authority in rituals of confession and absolution. It was used to terrorize people into obedience. By calling the Last Judgment a Day of Anger, the poem depicts punishment as harsh retribution for human disobedience—not as deterrence, or reform. This retributive, even violent, spirit toward opponents is precisely what the culture of peace is opposed to, and finds at the root of war. For related reasons the *Dies Irae* was dropped during the Vatican II reforms of 1969–1970, which favored texts expressive of hope, love, and faith, rather than those expressing anger, fear, and despair (which Archbishop Annabale Bugnini, chief architect of many of the reforms, called a "negative spirituality"). So it was already on its way out even in the Roman Catholic liturgy. It plays no role at all in forms of funeral service recommended for Anglican worship, whether in 1962 or today. Although there is more flexibility in the Anglican funeral service than in the Roman Catholic Mass, the sentiments expressed and the texts chosen—for example in the recent funeral service for Elizabeth II—are ideas of mercy, love, consolation, and peace—and thanks for the life and service of the departed. It would have been profoundly shocking to have included the *Dies Irae* there or in any other modern Anglican funeral, imperfect though all human beings surely are. (And music lovers would know that its sentiments had been rejected long before, in Mozart's Freemasonic religion of love, as he makes clear by depicting the Queen of the Night in *Die Zauberflöte*, the spirit of revenge, as a representative of the idolatrous Roman Catholic Church.)

In 1996, the Church of England officially renounced the idea of eternal punishment as a morally defective image of God: "Christians have professed appalling theologies which made God into a sadistic monster and left searing psychological scars on many." Stating that acceptance of such ideas had long faded, the report continues: "There are many reasons for this change, but amongst them have been the moral protest from both within and without the Christian faith against a religion of fear, and a growing sense that the picture of a God who consigned millions to eternal torment was far removed from the revelation of God's love in Christ."[32] There is no doubt that this change was well under way in the 1960s and that the Coventry clergy professed no such "appalling" theology.

In short, Britten—and the Coventry prelates—are sure to have seen the *Dies Irae* as expressive of false and harmful religious sentiments. The task Britten undertook was to write a setting of the traditional Latin Requiem Mass, which contained it. But he (and his Coventry hosts) would want to urge its rejection as a view of the world, as indeed he does, while endorsing the Christian sentiments of other sections, which are more congenial, especially the Agnus

---

[32] Associated Press (1996), https://web.archive.org/web/20210320053853/https://apnews.com/article/611c8aa8904dde105806f6c05485f995.

Dei, and while urging that more neutral sections, for example the *Requiem Aeternum* are insufficient and must be surpassed by deliberation about future peace. The *Dies Irae* is not even traditional religion, as of 1962: it is old false religion, something to be struggled against and left behind. The fact that critics—even those who feel vague discontent with this part of the *War Requiem*—have not understood this fundamental theological point is itself discouraging, showing how difficult it is to eradicate a love of retributive anger from Christian doctrines and sentiments. It seems, too, that many musicologists are not very familiar with developments in Anglican theology, or curious about what has happened in Christian thought since the Middle Ages!

Thus the text of the *Dies Irae* figures theatrically in the work as an opposing character, like a persecutory character in a Britten opera—say, the crowd in *Peter Grimes*. That does not mean that brilliant music cannot be used to express this character and point of view. Britten is a theatrical composer, skilled at representing a variety of points of view, not just those with which he agrees. But since some features of the Mass are peace-loving and others (the *Requiem Aeternum*) neutral, Britten must guide the listener through this thicket.

One further complication must be introduced: the *Dies Irae* is not entirely the voice of the opposition. It has sections expressing Christ's gentleness and mercy and His sacrifice for humans: in particular the Recordare, Jesu pie section. Britten is of course perfectly aware of these internal differences within traditional religion, and he agrees, as he long ago insisted at the tribunal, with Christ's example and teaching. So he must deal with this difficult text in a subtle way.

Britten tackles the *Dies Irae* problem in three ways. First, he makes most of his *Dies Irae* express, musically, the ideas of war, as those sound-ideas have already been established in the first movement—suggesting in no uncertain terms that this part of traditional religion is mistaken, productive of harm, and should be rejected. Second, he develops his critique of emotional war-mongering through the Owen poems in this movement and in the subsequent Offertorium and Sanctus, in a variety of different and insightful ways. Third, he develops a very different, harmonious. and constructive, relationship between the Owen critique of war and Jesus's message of mercy, love, and peace, both in the Recordare and Lacrimosa in this movement and, later, in the culminating movement of his musical "argument," the Agnus Dei. In this way he creates a basis for reconstruction of traditional Christianity and reconciliation between tradition and his passionate critique.

The music of Britten's *Dies Irae* has disturbed many commentators because of its apparently derivative and un-Brittenlike qualities. Resemblances to Verdi's *Requiem* are dense here: structural (the recapitulation of the opening material before moving on to the Offertorium); rhythmic (similar patterns in Quantus tremor—Boyd finds a resemblance to choral asides in opera), vocal (the casting of female and male voices, both choral and solo (female soloist in Liber scriptus, all female choral voices in Recordare, all male choral voices in Confutatis maledictis), even melodic (Liber scriptus especially); more generally a sense that both are reaching for very similar theatrical effects, using similar orchestral resources (not surprisingly, the use of brass in Tuba mirum, but elsewhere too).

Boyd suggests that a likely reason for the continual references to Verdi is to create a familiar point of departure for the audience, a background against which Britten's uniquely Brittenesque deployment of resources in the Owen poems can stand out all the more clearly. This is fine as far as it goes, but we must now observe that this familiar background is all too familiar: it is war music, as Britten has set up this idea in "What passing bells." The whistling and banging, the use of martial fanfares and other militaristic sounds from the brass, and more generally the overall sense of tumult, disorder, and danger—all this is now developed at far greater length than it was in the previous movement—but it is essentially the same music. This should cause unease in sensitive members of the audience even before Britten's explicit critique gets going—as hearers notice that ideas of the Last Judgment in their own religion are very like the warlike anger that devastated the lives of soldiers in the previous movement. How can this be? Aren't we supposed to be on the side of the angry God who calls all mortals to account? Terrified of this God, but terrified because we see God's cause and God's conduct as just? But how can we be on the side of this God, or seek to model ourselves on this God, who has given us a model of retributive anger that has apparently unleashed the horrors of war in Europe? In *Our Hunting Fathers*, the origin of religious ideas was seen as inside human beings, in our terror of our own bodies, our hatred of outsiders, our frenzied pursuit of self-escape. Here the diagnosis is not yet fully clear, but the devastation wrought by retributive anger is clear already.

Most of the audience will not have reached this point explicitly. Most will be enjoying the drama. And yet a vague unease sets in— what, really, should we be thinking of the pleasure this music takes in emotional warfare? And the discontent also may take, as it so often has taken, the form—Is this really Benjamin Britten? Why does it sound so unlike his sincere utterances of his viewpoint, and indeed it is alien to his personal sensibility?

The familiar text with its Verdi-influenced setting will eventually serve as a touchstone of another sort for the audience, who are challenged to ask themselves: which parts of this shall we accept, and which parts reject? Later, too, Britten will further complicate his reckoning with traditional Christianity by showing that some of the elements he indicts are buried deep within human beings and hard to eradicate. (He will do this by allowing the martial music of the main orchestra to invade and corrupt the world of the soloists.)

Baritone

Bugles sang, saddening the evening air;
and bugles answered, sorrowful to hear.
Voices of boys were by the river-side.
Sleep mothered them; and left the twilight sad.
The shadow of the morrow weighed on men.
Voices of old despondency resigned,
bowed by the shadow of the morrow, slept.[33]

As the hushed phrases of *Mors stupebit. . . . reponsura*—expressing human terror before divine anger—fade away in the main chorus and orchestra, the Chamber orchestra and the baritone soloist take over in the first of the Owen poems used in this movement. In place of the frenzied activity of the *Dies Irae*, with its punitive anger and abject terror, we now have lonely soldiers, mere boys, sleeping by a river. Bowed down with war's heaviness, they sadly await the battle on the next day, but are gently lulled by sleep, as nature proves a kinder mother than the vengeful God. (This idea of gentle mothering looks ahead to "Futility" in the Lacrimosa section.)

The musical setting incorporates themes from the *Dies Irae*, as the woodwinds replace the thrilling martial trumpets, so that the sounds of war are "subdued and etiolated," as Cooke nicely puts it.[34] Instead of the drama of the Apocalypse, these are ordinary end-of-day sounds, and as the horns heavily reply, the world of the young men is impregnated by a weighty sorrow. Although bugles are part of the music of war, they also have a more intimate human meaning

[33] Owen, untitled draft, in *Collected Poems*, p. 128.
[34] Cooke (1996, p. 63).

(for example, in their use in "Taps"), reminding us of the human cost of war. After "sleep mothered them," comes, as Philip Kitcher observes, "a long phrase, tracing an arc of pain, as the voice ascends, in f minor steps, from a low B flat to a high F sharp, from which it descends in chromatic steps to E flat. At this point, first the harp, then the horns, quietly continue the arpeggios, recapitulating the elegiac music of the opening. The baritone then descends a tritone, to sing a single word, 'slept,' on a low A."[35]

The mood throughout is elegiac, except for the fact that the sorrow that burdens the young men is not about them as particular people, as in a traditional elegy—even though they are the ones who are about to die. Instead, these are "voices of old despondency"— the elegy is for the whole history and tradition of war-making, endemic to all human cultures, and a burden on all humanity's youth. We hear the vulnerability of youth in the delicate triplets in the winds, accompanied by strings and harp. In the horns we hear the shadow of the morrow, but, really, of all of human history.

Soprano

Liber scriptus proferetur,	The written book shall be brought
in quo totum continetur,	in which all is contained
unde mundus judicetur.	whereby the world shall be judged.
Judex ergo cum sedebit	When the judge takes his seat
quidquid latet, apparebit:	all that is hidden shall appear:
nil inultum remanebit.	nothing will remain unavenged.

Chorus

Quid sum miser tunc dicturus?	What shall I, a wretch, say then?
Quem patronum rogaturus,	To which protector shall I appeal
cum vix justus sit securus?	when even the just man is barely safe?

Soprano and Chorus

Rex tremendae majestatis,	King of awful majesty,
qui salvandos salvas gratis,	who freely savest those worthy of salvation,
salva me, fons pietatis.	save me, fount of pity.

---

[35] Kitcher (forthcoming).

As in Verdi, the Liber scriptus is given to the soprano soloist (in Verdi it is a mezzo-soprano), who blazes out like a trumpet, sounding the words of divine judgment: nothing shall remain unavenged. The chorus joins, acknowledging the awesome power and might of the vengeful god, and begging desperately to be saved, as the music fades to a hushed pianissimo.

Tenor and Baritone

Out there, we've walked quite friendly
   up to Death:
sat down and eaten with him, cool and bland, —
pardoned his spilling mess-tins in our hand.
We've sniffed the green thick odour of his
   breath, —
our eyes wept, but our courage didn't writhe.
He's spat at us with bullets and he's coughed
shrapnel. We chorused when he sang aloft;
we whistled while he shaved us with his
   scythe.
Oh, Death was never enemy of ours!
We laughed with him, we leagued with him,
   old chum.
No soldier's paid to kick against his powers.
We laughed, knowing that better men would
   come,
and greater wars; when each proud fighter brags
he wars on Death — for Life; not men —
   for flags.[36]

As the chorus and the main orchestra fall silent, the chamber orchestra enters in a rapid syncopated rhythm of staccato triplets, marked "Fast and gay." This Owen setting is a Britten tour de force, lasting under two minutes and expressing the giddy bravado that is the other side of the night's heavy sadness. Young men brought up on the culture of war, taught that it is glorious, often go out

[36] Owen, "The Next War," quoted in full.

to battle with just such bravado—but the joy is highly unstable, mingled, as it is, with terror. (Think of Nikolai Rostov's entrance into battle in *War and Peace*.) Here the soloists are not weighted down, but are positively manic in their movement toward death, singing in unison a "splendidly blasé melody"[37] with much staccato and dotted rhythms, and, in the orchestra, timpani as in a parody of martial music. The horn's bugle call from "Anthem for Dead Youth" is heard along with "shrieking chromatics on high wind and violins representing the soldiers' manic whistling,"[38] and also the whistling and whizzing of bullets. The repeated and accented "shrapnel" suggests that it is flying around them. The melismatic "laughed" is a ghastly false laugh, undercutting the poem's transition to optimism. The final lines, which in the poem itself seem to be an optimistic affirmation of the overcoming of war, are hushed and uncertain here, mere shreds of hope, and fade into nothingness.

Chorus

Recordare Jesu pie,	Remember, gentle Jesus,
quod sum cause tuae viae:	that I am the reason for Thy time on earth,
ne me perdas illa die.	do not cast me out on that day.
Quaerens me, sedisti lassus:	Seeking me, Thou didst sink down wearily,
redemisti crucem passus:	Thou hast saved me by enduring the cross,
tantus labor non sit cassus.	such travail must not be in vain.
Ingemisco, tamquam reus:	I groan, like the sinner that I am,
culpa rubet vultus meus:	guilt reddens my face,
supplicanti parce Deus.	Oh God, spare the supplicant.
Qui Mariam absolvisti,	Thou, who pardoned Mary
et latronem exaudisti,	and heeded the thief,
mihi quoque spem dedisti.	hast given me hope as well.
Inter oves locum praesta,	Give me a place among the sheep
et ab haedis me sequestra,	and separate me from the goats,
statuens in parte dextra.	let me stand at Thy right hand.
Confutatis maledictis,	When the damned are cast away
flammis acribus addictis,	and consigned to the searing flames,

---

[37] Cooke (1996, p. 65).
[38] Ibid.

voca me cum benedictis.	call me to be with the blessed.
Oro supplex et acclinis	Bowed down in supplication I beg Thee,
cor contritum quasi cinis	my heart as though ground to ashes:
gere curam mei finis.	help me in my last hour.

In this section of the *Dies Irae*, the tone changes. Instead of depicting a vengeful God the Father, the poem shifts to a focus on the gentle and merciful nature of Jesus. Here, as in Verdi, the chorus splits: only female voices, softly surging upward, sing the tender merciful music of "Recordare . . . in parte dextra." These voices are, in effect, the gentle sheep, Jesus their shepherd. Significantly, this section is in B flat major, one of the key signatures Britten associates with peace. However, the respite is brief: the perspective of retribution returns, in the key of E minor/ G major, with a rapid staccato onslaught accompanied by bugle-like horns, as the male voices take up the perspective of God's vengeance in "Confutatis . . . finis." This section, then, reminds the audience that the *Dies Irae* text, like the religious tradition from which it emerges, is not simple. It contains the materials of war, but it also contains the basis for peace. At this point, however, the perspective of war wins out.

Baritone

Be slowly lifted up, thou long black arm,
great gun towering toward Heaven, about
　　to curse;
reach at that arrogance which needs thy harm,
and beat it down before its sins grow worse;
but when thy spell be cast complete and whole,
may God curse thee, and cut thee from our soul![39]

---

[39] Owen, "Sonnet: On Seeing a Piece of Our Heavy Artillery Brought into Action," a poem of fourteen lines, of which Britten has selected six.

In what Cooke aptly describes as a "thrilling surge," the music "spills directly into" the baritone solo.[40] This is a crucial juncture in the work, and it must be interpreted with the greatest care. On the surface, the Owen poem, "On Seeing a Piece of Our Heavy Artillery Brought into Action" (reduced by Britten to six lines)—while condemning the use of heavy artillery with ironic disparagement (the gun is lifted to heaven to curse, not to pray or bless)—nonetheless grants that force is sometimes a necessary response to great harms, one that must eventually be transcended by getting rid of these weapons and the parts of our souls that wish to use them. It is here that one might find Britten acknowledging that World War II was a just and necessary war, and yet we must seek to go beyond it. In comments of great subtlety, Philip Kitcher does so construe both poem and song.[41]

This would be a great surprise, given all the evidence of Britten's unswerving lifelong commitment to unqualified pacifism in both emotions and actions (Chapter 5). There is no shift of view in his statements and actions. From the tribunal straight on to *Owen Wingrave* and the energetic work of both Britten and Pears for unilateral nuclear disarmament, the position is the same—and repeatedly reasserted each time the two applied for visas to enter the United States (see Chapter 5). But even should one grant that Britten might have shifted his view about warlike acts right after visiting Belsen and then shifted back later, it seems to me impossible to maintain that he ever changed his view about what I have called "emotional pacifism,"—and the use of force is endorsed emotionally in the poem, rather than with detached reluctance. But there is worse trouble ahead for the Kitcher reading: for the very decision to do away with the weapons of war is announced with terrible retributive anger, from the perspective of the God of vengeance: "May God curse thee, and cut thee from our soul." War

---

[40] Cooke (1996, p. 65).
[41] Kitcher (forthcoming).

is cast out by the spirit of war, not by a conversion to the spirit of gentleness and peace. I am pretty sure the poem itself (with the aggressive alliteration on "curse" and "cut") is meant to show us that humans cannot even contemplate ending violence without deploying a spirit of violence within themselves. Thus, violence is not ended, and the very prayer to end it betrays its own impossibility, given people as they currently are. Owen, however, once speaks approvingly of retributive vengeance in a letter (Chapter 5), so it is difficult to draw a definite conclusion about his poetic intentions.

But whether or not this irony is intended by Owen, it is certainly intended by Britten. For something unprecedented takes place in the music: the martial trumpets of the main orchestra invade— or even, one might say, conduct an assault on, the world of the chamber orchestra, the first instance of such mingling, and the most disturbing, since the fanfares appear to contradict the spirit of the solo. The martial trumpets clearly suggest that the point of view of the baritone solo, which purports to be against war, is infected by the spirit of the *Dies Irae*. Similarly, the timpani are drawn directly from their use in Confutatis maledictis—so beating down the arrogance is seen as an act of the vengeful God. Moreover, four of the poem's six lines end with tritones, suggesting a deep pessimism about the project of ending war, given human beings as they are. Cooke even suggests that the tritones, recalling their earlier use in speaking of "*requiem aeternum*," mock the very idea of peace and rest.[42] The final incursion of the trumpets ushers in the recapitulation of the *Dies Irae*, as Cooke says "a fittingly violent response to the baritone's concluding wish."[43]

My own view, developed in Chapter 5, is that it is possible to use force in defense of self or others without deploying the spirit of warlike retributive aggression—but it is surely very difficult.

[42] Cooke (1996, p. 65).
[43] Ibid., p. 66.

World War II saw excesses, such as the bombing of Dresden, that did not flow from a desire to end hostilities and to establish a regime of justice. Once people begin to use violence, and have to engage in acts of killing, these acts are all too likely to stir up the roots of violence within them. So if Owen and Britten are not fully fair in their critique of "just war," they do point to a terrible problem in the depths of the human personality: how can such a war be conducted without drawing on, and in the process strengthening, the roots of aggression and violence inside us? As I mentioned in Chapter 5, Nelson Mandela records that he needed most of his twenty-seven years of imprisonment to extirpate his own desire for retributive violence, and he always needed to rein in the desire for retribution in his followers. How can we expect this sort of patient inner effort from each and every citizen of a modern nation?

Chorus

Dies irae, dies illa,
solvet saeclum in favilla:
teste David cum Sibylla.
Quantus tremor est futurus,
quando Judex est venturus,
cuncta stricte discussurus!

This day, this day of wrath
shall consume the world in ashes,
as foretold by David and the Sibyl.
What trembling there shall be
when the judge shall come
to weigh everything strictly.

Soprano and Chorus

Lacrimosa dies illa,
qua resurget ex favilla,
judicandus homo reus:
huic ergo parce Deus.

Oh, this day full of tears
when from the ashes arises
guilty man, to be judged:
o Lord, have mercy upon him.

Tenor

Move him into the sun –
gently its touch awoke him once,
at home, whispering of fields unsown.
Always it woke him, even in France,
until this morning and this snow.
If anything might rouse him now
the kind old sun will know.

Soprano and Chorus

Lacrimosa dies illa . . .

Oh, this day full of tears . . .

Tenor
Think how it wakes the seeds —
woke, once, the clays of a cold star.
Are limbs, so dear-achieved, are sides,
full-nerved — still warm — too hard to stir?
Was it for this the clay grew tall?

Soprano and Chorus
... qua resurget ex favilla ...   ... when from the ashes arises ...

Tenor
Was it for this the clay grew tall?

Soprano and Chorus
... judicandus homo reus.   ... guilty man, to be judged.

Tenor
— Oh what made fatuous sunbeams toil
To break earth's sleep at all?

Chorus
Pie Jesu Domine,   Gentle Lord Jesus,
dona eis requiem.   grant them rest.
Amen.   Amen.

This section of the *Dies Irae* marks a new departure in the relationship between soloists and main orchestra and chorus. In *Requiem Aeternum* the chorus provided a distant background of mourning, not objectionable as such, but needing challenge and the education about war's reality that is supplied by the soloist and the chamber orchestra. In much of the *Dies Irae* the chorus and main orchestra play the role of an operatic antagonist to the soloists' depiction of war's awful reality. Now we begin to see a new relationship of real reciprocity in mourning and in a turning to the body of Jesus—incomplete but promising.

The Soprano's broken descending phrases sound like sobs (a mourning mother, says Kitcher)—a less abstract and distant kind of mourning than in *Requiem Aeternum*. Once this pattern has been established, the tenor enters, singing the words of Owen's "Futility," a poem about one particular dead soldier. Against a very spare background—soft tremolo on strings and woodwinds—the tenor gently evokes the feeling of a body warmed by ordinary daylight. His phrases delicately touch the fallen soldier, making contact with hope for our bodily humanity—even if that hope is snatched away at the end, when the reality of death dawns on the speaker.[44] I would add that the sense of warmth and hope is more in the music, which caresses the fallen soldier, than in the poem itself, which can seem detached and bitterly ironic. At this point, the Chorus reenters, responding to the idea of the soldier's body, and the warmth of their mourning complements the compassion of the solo.

As the poem continues, the tenor's phrases become more agitated, asking why such things happen and striking a note of despondent protest. Here Kitcher locates a "tension" between the tenor soloist and the chorus/soprano soloist, since they do not appear to hear his protest, but continue to mourn. Of course, their text has to be the traditional text of the Mass. Nonetheless, the responsive intensity of their mourning does seem to answer the soloist's claim of irreplaceable loss. There is surely no incompatibility between mourning and asserting that such a loss is wrong and unacceptable. (And although some of their words still allude to human guilt and the last judgment, there is only gentle sorrow in their music.) Finally, after the tenor ends his solo, they deliver what is in effect their answer to his protest: the presence and gentleness of Jesus. *Pie Jesu domine, dona eis requiem* (with the mournful tolling of tubular bells, again striking the C-F # tritone, suggesting that peace may be unstable and inconclusive). Only in the Agnus Dei will the full significance of Christ's body be shown, offering a retort to the makers of war. Here already, however, it appears that the chorus and soprano are ready to learn from the tenor soloist and to join him in a mourning that acknowledges war's terrible toll and the irreplaceable loss of young bodies. Like Wiebe, then, I see signs of hope and possible renewal in this section, which ends the *Dies Irae*. The prayer for rest

---

[44] See Wiebe (2012, pp. 213–16), who calls this movement "a central site of potential renewal in the *War Requiem*."

sung by the chorus resolves onto the F major chord, thus ending the *Dies Irae* on a tentatively hopeful note.[45]

*****

3. Offertorium

Boys' Choir

Domine Jesu Christe, Rex gloriae,	Lord Jesus Christ, King of glory,
libera animas omnium fidelium	deliver the souls of the faithful
defunctorum de poenis inferni,	departed from the pains of hell,
et de profundo lacu:	sand the bottomless pit:
libera eas de ore leonis,	deliver them from the jaws of the lion,
ne absorbeat eas tartarus,	lest hell engulf them,
ne cadant in obscurum.	lest they be plunged into darkness.

Chorus

Sed signifer sanctus Michael	But let the holy standard-bearer Michael
repraesentet eas in lucem sanctam:	lead them into the holy light,
quam olim Abrahae promisisti,	as Thou didst promise Abraham
et semini ejus.	and his seed.

Tenor and Baritone

So Abram rose, and clave the wood, and went,
and took the fire with him, and a knife.
and as they sojourned both of them together,
Isaac the first-born spake and said, My Father,
behold the preparations, fire and iron,
but where the lamb for this burnt-offering?
Then Abram bound the youth with belts
  and straps,
and builded parapets and trenches there,
and stretched forth the knife to slay his son.
When lo! an angel called him out of heaven,
saying, Lay not thy hand upon the lad,
neither do anything to him. Behold,
a ram, caught in a thicket by its horns;
offer the Ram of Pride instead of him.
But the old man would not so,
but slew his son, —
and half the seed of Europe, one by one.

---

[45] See Shrock (2017, p. 422); also Elliott (2006, p. 143).

Boys' Choir

Hostias et preces tibi Domine	Lord, in praise we offer to Thee
laudis offerimus; tu suscipe pro	sacrifices and prayers, do Thou receive them
animabus illis, quarum hodie	for the souls of those whom we remember
memoriam facimus: fac eas, Domine,	this day: Lord, make them pass
de morte transire ad vitam.	from death to life.
Quam olim Abrahae promisisti	As Thou didst promise Abraham
et semini ejus.	and his seed.

Chorus

... Quam olim Abrahae promisisti	... As Thou didst promise Abraham
et semini ejus.	and his seed.

The Offertorium turns from the depiction of God's punishment to praise of God's glory. It emphasizes the covenant God made with Abraham: God's promises of redemption, offspring, and deliverance into the "holy light." Thus far, traditional ritual has raised an acute issue about the moral worth of the traditional image of God. The punishing God is deeply problematic and closely linked to ideas about war that Britten repudiates, but the image of a merciful and loving Jesus remains a good guide for thought and action. The Offertorium raises a new set of questions about religion: what do its promises come to? Does God intervene in human affairs, and can we rely on a divine covenant to help us out of the moral mess we have created in our world? The question of whether the *War Requiem* is an optimistic or a pessimistic work is really several distinct questions, but one surely is this one: can we hope that extra-human aid will assist us in our struggle to create a world of peace?

To understand Britten's work in this movement, we must first confront the story that lies at its textual core: the story of God's decision to test Abraham by demanding that he sacrifice his son.

The biblical story of Abraham's aborted sacrifice of Isaac, known as the Akedah, has been a point of contention throughout the history of Judaism and Christianity. The story is closely linked to God's covenant with Abraham in Genesis 17, which promises copious offspring to Abraham, conditional on his loyalty to God. This promise is renewed in Genesis 22 after Abraham displays obedience by his willingness to sacrifice his beloved son (and after an angel puts a stop to the sacrifice). On its face, the story praises absolute obedience to a divine command, no matter how horrible. Abraham was doing the right thing by preparing in all seriousness to kill his son, and God, pleased with his obedience, rewards him by cutting the sacrifice short. Some people have indeed understood their religion (whether Judaism or Christianity) as based on unquestioning obedience, and have understood the story according to its most obvious meaning. The philosopher Soren Kierkegaard (1813–1855) even argued that the tale shows Abraham as a "knight of faith," willing to suspend ethical laws for the sake of faith, which Kierkegaard regarded as superior to ethics.

However, over the ages it has been difficult for believers in a loving and just God to accept the idea that God would be pleased by Abraham's evident willingness to kill his own son, prior to the divine intervention that stops the sacrifice. Numerous strategies have been tried to make acceptable moral sense of the story. One common view, and the dominant view among the ancient Jewish rabbis, is that all along God had no intention of allowing the sacrifice to take place *and* that Abraham was fully aware of that, and therefore never formed a morally defective intention. Instead, both Abraham and God intended to display the heinousness of child sacrifice.

Another common interpretation is that God actually wants to see whether Abraham will do somethingj morally horrible, just because he is told to do it, or whether he has developed mature moral faculties. On this account Abraham fails the test. A variant of this strategy, more favorable to Abraham, was that of the great Jewish philosopher Maimonides (1138–1204), who said that Abraham does not sacrifice Isaac because he ultimately realizes that to do so would be idolatrous worship, not genuine worship.[46]

---

[46] I owe this to my colleague Josef Stern, who has developed an interpretation of Maimonides in his Gruss lectures, ultimately to be published as a book.

For religions like that of the Freemasons, however, or Reform Judaism, both of which deny the literal truth of the Bible, a more direct route is available: God was simply wrong, cruel; the story portrays a God created by benighted human superstition, and this God is not worthy of worship. I have often heard this approach in my synagogue and have myself given a talk with that idea, which was not received as at all shocking, since Reform reads the Bible historically, as including a lot of human error. People should not be duped by such tales. The core of true religion is the moral law.

Mozart's *Idomeneo* (1781) takes this anti-superstition line. The Greek world of the opera is a thinly veiled allegory for the superstitions of most received religions of Mozart's time (especially Roman Catholicism), which his Freemasonic group[47] sought to replace by a religion based on love, fraternity, and reason. Idomeneo asks Neptune to deliver him from the storm and promises in return to sacrifice the first person he sees on landing on the shore. As it happens, the first person is his own son, Idamante. As he later prepares for the sacrifice, Idomeneo says that his human nature rebels against the deed; the chorus assails Neptune's harsh rigidity. Nonetheless, Idomeneo gets almost to the point of slaying his son. Then a Voice (whose?) announces that Love has conquered. From now on the kingdom will be governed (not by the old gods but) by Ilia and Idamante, a loving couple—who have already been shown to favor freedom, flexibility, reciprocity, and brotherhood. (Idamante has liberated all the Trojan prisoners and made them equals of the Greeks.) Mozart's audience could not help hearing a subtle critique of the biblical narrative, similar to *The Magic Flute*'s more overt critique of conventional religion in favor of Freemasonic reason and fraternity.

So when Britten approaches the traditional biblical story, he does so in a context of much discussion and criticism of the story's surface

---

[47] Mozart formally joined the Freemasons only in 1784, but the views that brought him to take this step are already on view in this earlier opera.

reading. And even though Anglicans have never been Freemasons, they are free to criticize biblical texts to a somewhat greater extent than either Roman Catholics or most other Protestants. So in the context of Coventry—not to mention the Quaker circles frequented by Britten and Pears—it would have been entirely appropriate and unsurprising for Britten to join this critical tradition. He does so, however (along with Owen) in an entirely original way, consistent with Mozart's Freemasonic humanism, but with far less optimism about the power of love to rein in human aggression.

The theme of threatened innocence often attracted Britten, and he had already composed one version of the Akedah in Canticle II (opus 51, 1952), first performed at a fundraiser for the English Opera Group—right after the premiere of *Billy Budd*, whose themes are closely related. Part of the series of five Canticles, and following the much-admired Canticle I (see Chapter 6), it is written for a tenor (Pears at the premiere), a contralto, or countertenor (Kathleen Ferrier at the premiere), and piano (Britten at the premiere). The text is from an anonymous Chester Mystery Play. Like a mini-opera, it dramatizes the story at length. Philosophically, it could be read as compatible with the traditional praise-of-obedience reading, but the accent is placed so strongly on the horrible danger to innocent life, and on the beauty of the loving commandment to spare the child, that some type of critical reading is suggested, at least in the music—whether of the sort that holds that God never meant any wrong to occur or of the sort that looks skeptically on the idea of immoral obedience.

The tenor portrays Abraham, the contralto or countertenor Isaac, and the parts of the original text that are third-person narration are dropped, so it is a fully dramatic work. God's voice, both at the beginning and in the critical intervention (here it is God, not an Angel of God, as in the biblical text, who orders Abraham not to sacrifice his son), is portrayed by both singers, singing in close harmony, occasionally in unison, and in a muffled way as if from a great distance, with very little vibrato. The emotions of both father and son are richly depicted: Isaac's shock and fear, Abraham's agony. And because the text is anachronistic, Abraham asks Jesus to pity him, and the Trinity to bless Isaac. The piano accompaniment, at first sparse, builds to a virtuosic climax. The voice of God is so far from expressing any aggressive intent, so determinedly peaceful and composed, that the musical interpretation inclines to a reading according to which God never wanted violence. God's voice seems admirable, not corrupt, but also sounds very dreamlike and far away.

Now to the setting of the Akedah within the Offertorium. The movement begins with distant praise of God from the boys' choir, accompanied by the organ, like a faraway dream. The chorus and full orchestra then join at "Sed signifer sanctus Michael," and the music abruptly changes character to a cheerful G major, becoming up-tempo and immediate, with syncopation and accentuation, building to a dramatic fugue at "quam olim Abrahae." Both the knife-sharp rhythms and the increasing use of brass suggest the war music of the *Dies Irae*—thus casting doubt on the benign vision of the text and suggesting a link between Abraham and war-making.[48] The jaunty fugue suggests pleasure in the thought of battle. The fugue's subject is borrowed from the music that in Canticle II accompanies preparation for sacrifice.

The chamber orchestra now enters, continuing in G major, and picking up the rhythm and style of the fugue. As in "Bugles Sang," the woodwinds take over the role of depicting cheerful military music. And now the baritone begins the Owen text, singing both Abraham's utterances and narration about what he does, while the tenor sings Isaac's speeches and his part of the narration. Abraham's "and a knife" accents that word strongly and ominously. At Isaac's ""Father, behold the preparations," the tempo slows and the music

---

[48] For related observations, see Couderc (2013, p. 16); Cameron Pyke, "Shostakovich's Fourteenth Symphony: A Response to *War Requiem*," in *Benjamin Britten: New Perspectives on His Life and Works*, edited by Lucy Walker (Woodbridge, UK: The Boydell Press and the Britten-Pears Foundation, 2009, p. 343).

softens. In music borrowed from Canticle II, and described correctly by Cooke as "lush, almost romantic,"[49] accompanied only by a soft tremolo on strings and harp, Isaac inquires about the sacrifice. Then the jaunty music returns, as Abraham makes his preparations for the sacrifice, accompanied by a menacing gong and a marcato syncopated bassoon solo. As he builds his parapets and trenches, we hear fragments of the fanfares from the *Dies Irae* and the wailing of shells from "Anthem," on woodwinds and horns. The word "knife" again receives strong emphasis.

There is now a remarkable shift. As in Canticle II, the two singers, joining in close harmony, sing the words of the Angel (God in the Canticle), very serenely and gently, and as if from a great distance, in the new key of C major, symbolizing purity. As Cooke notes, the "chords outlined by strings and harp are made curiously luminous by their Stravinskian omission of the fifth, and the vocal recitation is deliberately archaic."[50] We have entered the terrain of Britten's "peace family" (Chapter 5). The phrase "Offer the Ram of Pride instead of him"—another melody borrowed from the canticle—contains a curious and remarkable effect. The C major at this point is Lydian-inflected, and hence it contains both C and F sharp, the tones of the ominous tritone, where the words "the Ram of Pride" occur. The tritone denotes the sin of Pride, and the phrase is thus, as Cooke says, the *diabolus in musica* that was traditionally banned from medieval music.[51] Even in this pure world, human Pride sneaks in.

Pride, in the Christian tradition—as Britten would surely have known—is not confident self-assertion (as in a Gay Pride march), it is the sin of seeing only yourself and not acknowledging the reality of other people. In Dante's *Purgatorio*, the proud are bent over like hoops, so that they can see only parts of their own bodies.[52]

---

[49] Cooke (1996, p. 68).
[50] Ibid.
[51] Ibid.
[52] See Nussbaum *Citadels of Pride: Sexual Assault, Accountability, and Reconciliation* (New York: W. W. Norton, 2021).

The suggestion of the music is that even when the voices of peace are sounding, human beings cannot hear them, because they are mastered by their own narcissism and their overweening drive to dominate others.

As the Angel concludes, the cheerfully aggressive fugal theme returns—as if the Angel's utterance falls on deaf ears—and in the new key of E major, whose sharpness contrasts with the C major's purity. However, at "but slew his son" the key briefly shifts back to the Angel's C major triad, clashing sharply with its tonal context,[53] and showing that Abraham's response is not simple ignorance but deliberate defiance of the Angel. The two voices repeat "and half the seed of Europe" over and over again, suggesting that human war-making will likely have no end. Meanwhile, the boys' choir enters from an impotent distance, and in their accustomed archaic idiom, singing praises to God. The chorus and full orchestra enter for a hushed, compressed, and seemingly defeated recapitulation of the covenantal fugue.

In Owen's version of the Akedah, effectively dramatized by Britten, blame is directed not to a traditional and morally obtuse God—God in the story is a distant figure with impotent good intentions—but rather to willful and hate-filled human beings. Abraham has no excuse. He might have saved his son, and indeed is ordered by the Angel to do so. He acts without clear motive, apparently out of a desire for violence itself and a disdain for the message of peace. Thus he displays the perverse and cruel aggressiveness of which humanity has been all too capable, again and again. In the Coventry context, his murder of Isaac reminds listeners of the mad hate-filled destructiveness of the Axis powers, a horror through which they have recently lived. Even the dearest and most beloved can be sacrificed to satisfy the blood-lust of the warmaker; thus aggressive warmakers destroy their own youths and families, as well as their enemies, in pursuit of their horrible project. These

---

[53] See Cooke (1996, p. 69).

aggressive forces were not halted by divine intervention. Just as the Angel could not stop Abraham, so centuries of Christian teaching have not halted the warmakers. Like Mozart, Britten depicts the voices of love warning against slaughter; unlike Mozart, he shows Abraham's aggression as internally generated, not commanded by easily refuted superstition—and then displays the impotence of the voices of peace, whether understood as human or divine. If the audience is morally alert, they will begin to realize that this danger is very likely inside us all. It is not the peculiar property of other groups or nations that might be depicted as enemies and branded as evil.

Then how, if at all, can the Abrahams of the world be stopped? Kitcher argues that by raising this question so vividly, Britten is conceding the necessity of military force in World War II and conflicts like it. When we are dealing with an Abraham, after all, persuasion will not work: even the Angel had no effect on his obdurate evil-doing. But it is one thing for Kitcher to reason this way himself—and up to a certain extent I agree with him—quite another to show that military force is Britten's own solution to the Abraham problem. Such a solution in this context would be superficial, suggesting that British people are immune from Abraham's sin. It would make the work all about the badness of Germans, and this is surely far from the work's intent. The poem and the music suggest, instead, that the inclination to lash out in retributive violence is inside us all. Without constant self-cultivation and self-monitoring we cannot hope to escape it. In that sense my critique of the pacifism of acts seems to me irrelevant to this part of the work: it is about the need for a profound reorientation toward emotional pacifism, which even nonpacifists in the World War II case must urgently undertake.

The *War Requiem* is about emotions, not acts, and about the future, not the past. Here Britten offers a very stern warning for the future: bring up people who will not be like Abraham, who will be guided by love and not by the lust for power and blood. And: do not

think that our societies will be rescued by external angelic intervention. If we are ever to prevail over what is worst in our history, we
have to create change ourselves, and this means, first and foremost,
within ourselves.

*****

4. Sanctus

Soprano and Chorus

Sanctus, sanctus, sanctus	Holy, holy, holy
Dominus Deus Sabaoth,	Lord God of hosts.
Pleni sunt ceoli et terra gloria tua.	Heaven and earth are full of Thy glory.

Hosanna in excelsis.	Hosanna in the highest.
Sanctus	Holy
Benedictus qui venit in nomine Domini.	Blessed is He that cometh in the name of the Lord.
Hosanna in excelsis.	Hosanna in the highest.
Sanctus.	Holy.

Baritone

After the blast of lightning from the East,[54]
the flourish of loud clouds, the Chariot Throne;
after the drums of Time have rolled and ceased,
and by the bronze west long retreat is blown,
shall life renew these bodies? Of a truth
all death will He annul, all tears assuage?—
fill the void veins of Life again with youth,
and wash, with an immortal water, Age?
When I do ask white Age he saith not so:
"My head hangs weighed[55] with snow."
And while I hearken to the Earth, she saith:
"My fiery heart shrinks aching. It is death.
Mine ancient scars shall not be glorified,
nor my titanic tears, the sea, be dried."

[54] Owen, "The End," complete; spacing as in the original.
[55] Owen's original has "weighted," but both the vocal and complete scores, and the libretto of the recording, have "weighed," and the vocal line requires a monosyllable, though it would have been very easy to substitute two eighth notes for the quarter note." "Weighted" seems metrically required and is more suitable in meaning. It appears that Britten has made an error.

The Sanctus strikes, from the beginning, a tone of distance and estrangement. Its glittering tremolos use a combination of percussion instruments—vibraphone, glockenspiel, bells, antique cymbals toned to the tritone C and F sharp—that shows the influence of Indonesian gamelan music on Britten, who was much impressed by the gamelan during a visit he and Pears took to Bali. The effect is dazzling, slightly hypnotic, but also foreign, distant, and in the repetitious use of the tritone, vaguely ominous. The suggestion is that God has receded to a very remote distance, no longer caring for erring mortals—as the Offertorium, by demonstrating God's failure to intervene successfully in the sacrifice of Isaac, had already shown. The music is suggestive of a ritual, but one without a clear purpose or object.[56] The Offertorium had shown an urgent need for acute critical thought to halt human wickedness, but the participants in this ritual refuse to think.

In terms of the actual celebration of the Mass, the use of bells possibly evokes the Roman Catholic use of the Sanctus bell during this part of the ritual—thus suggesting to a primarily Anglican audience an alien tradition, perhaps even one that is authoritarian rather than deliberative.[57]

The chorus now enters in a lengthy passage of unsynchronized chanting, followed by the blaring of trumpets and the shout of "Hosanna," all this suggesting a habitual observance with no independent thought. Even the Soprano's lovely Benedictus fails to humanize this alien world.

The Baritone now enters, with a setting of Owen's extremely grim poem "The End." The text offers no hope for humankind, or even for the earth. Instead of resurrection of souls and bodies, the final moment offers only death. The musical setting too is alienating,

---

[56] Cooke (1996, p. 70) calls it "hypnotic."

[57] I am grateful to Andrew Biondo and Alison LaCroix for discussion of the Roman Catholic Sanctus bell and its meaning. Obviously, though, for a Catholic listener this would not be a moment of distance or estrangement, since the bell marks the moment when the transubstantiation occurs. Whether Britten intended a somewhat critical reference to Roman Catholic ritual is unclear to me.

because it has no tonal center and passes through all twelve tones, as well as having what Cooke rightly calls "a disturbingly thin texture recalling Webern."[58] There seems to be nothing to live for in this world. Ritual is empty, human life without hope. Even the earth itself is ready to die. This is the bleakest moment in the *War Requiem*, since even human wickedness might be corrected or atoned for. Here there is not even wickedness: here is the emptiness of despair.

Britten, then, approaches Schopenhauer's pessimism: all human efforts seem futile, and life on this earth with it. The music expresses a cold detachment that was not actually the type of music Schopenhauer liked (recall that he loved the operas of Rossini), but the music that is called for by his stance toward life.

*****

5. Agnus Dei

TENOR
One ever hangs where shelled roads part.
In this war He too lost a limb,
But His disciples hide apart;
and now the Soldiers bear with Him.

CHORUS

Agnus Dei,	Lamb of God,
qui tollis peccata mundi,	that takest away the sins of the world,
dona eis requiem.	grant them rest.

TENOR SOLO
Near Golgotha strolls many a priest,
And in their faces there is pride
That they were flesh-marked by the Beast
By whom the gentle Christ's denied.

CHORUS

Agnus Dei,	Lamb of God,
qui tollis peccata mundi,	that takest away the sins of the world,
dona eis requiem.	grant them rest.

---

[58] Cooke (1996, p. 71).

TENOR
The scribes on all the people shove
and bawl allegiance to the state,

CHORUS	CHORUS
Agnus Dei,	Lamb of God,
qui tollis peccata mundi...	that takest away the sins of the world ...

TENOR
but they who love the greater love
lay down their life; they do not hate.[59]

CHORUS	CHORUS
...dona eis requiem sempiternam.	... grant them eternal rest.

TENOR	TENOR
Dona nobis pacem.	Grant us peace.

With Owen's "The End" we reached the bleakest moment of the work's reflection, albeit after finding moments of hope along the way, connected to the worth of real soldiers and with the example of Christ. These shreds of hope, these reasons for living in the face of death, are made much more substantial in the culminating moment of the Mass, where Christ's body is revealed.

As we arrive at the Agnus Dei, where, traditionally, Christ's mercy is made manifest, the structure usual in the work inverts itself: the Owen poem, "At a Calvary Near the Ancre," sung by the tenor, takes the lead, and the boys' choir sings the Latin words only after each stanza of the Owen poem.[60] A second structural difference is, I believe, even more important: typically, though not always, the soloists are detached from the choirs, as if challenging them. Here they address one another, so to speak, in alternating stanzas, with something like mutual awareness and reciprocity, although the boys are still very distant.

In music of stark simplicity and haunting beauty, in the key of D major, so often associated with love and peace, with a nakedness referring to—and honoring—the naked vocal lines of the Verdi

---

[59] Owen's poem "At a Calvary Near the Ancre," quoted in full. This poem is not in the British Museum manuscript; the text is taken from a draft in Owen's mother's handwriting. The text used by Britten is that of the *Collected Poems*, apart from substituting "bawl," a clearly superior reading, and present in the Blunden edition of 1931, for "brawl." See Owen (1963).

[60] See also Mitchell (1999, p. 208). But he refers to the boys' choir as a background, which I think is not correct, given the reciprocity between the choir and the soloist.

Agnus Dei, the tenor solo tells us not of mercy from the other world, but, instead, of the death of a human Christ (emblem of the young men of Europe), crucified by the war machine.[61] The voice of Peter Pears, with its sui generis combination of humanity and purity of diction and intonation, expresses the persona of the human Christ, almost naked against a very sparse orchestration and the distant Latin chant of the boys' choir. As Cooke observes, the use of F sharp suspensions onto C major chords, at the words "hangs," "disciples," and, later, "love," creates a powerful and poignant impression of a human purity tormented by malice and sin.[62] This young human Christ is laying down his life for the sins of the world. In place of any mercy for these guilty sinners, however, we find a savage indictment of the social institutions that put Christ to death, including organized religion itself, as coopted by makers of war. (Not, then, the Coventry clergy, or any others—the audience—who will heed the music's call for a future of peace.) Donald Mitchell perceptively notes the accents marked on "flesh-marked" and the use of the side drum, the only percussion in the entire movement, to underline the "ensuing indictment," namely: "The scribes on all the people shove / And bawl allegiance to the state." "The side drum," Mitchell continues, "undoubtedly, serves as a reminder of the weapons to which an oppressive state will have recourse."[63]

Here I must insert a small and by now predictable voice of protest. Owen's words "and bawl allegiance to the state" are utterly contemptuous of any and all states to whom soldiers may have allegiance. Even if this may be a plausible view of the opposed states in World War I, it is not a correct, or even honorable, view of World War II. The Allied nations were right to oppose the Axis and to ask their young people to do so. Most followed that allegiance not as

---

[61] See the excellent musical analysis of this movement in Cooke (1996, pp. 71–73).

[62] Cooke says "flawed purity," but the emphasis is on Christ's full humanity, not on any fault.

[63] Mitchell (1999, pp. 208–9).

dupes but as honorable agents of the state's good goals. The state is not a distant "other," but part of the self of each common soldier. (Consider President Zelenskyy, appearing before the U.S. Congress in the attire of a common soldier.) And yet, this flaw does not alter the terrible fact that the poem displays: precious human lives have been laid waste owing to the demands of insatiable human aggression. War itself, and the original aggressors, have crucified the body of Europe's young men.

Apparently, then, there is no redemption to be found in otherworldly religion or in national pride. (Even if, as I urge, national causes are sometimes justified, they do not redeem the terrible waste of life that war has inflicted. Moreover, we should acknowledge that the tendencies that lead to war inhabit all of us.) The music expresses, with a stark sadness, the emptiness of a world into which people hoped God would intervene. Mitchell correctly emphasizes the movement's "unequivocal insistence on the baneful tritone (C-F#), the Requiem's unappeasable and all-pervasive leading motif."[64] Instead of being redeemed, human violence runs riot, as it already has in the Offertorium. The linearity of the ascending and descending sequences jolts listeners, preventing us from getting our bearings: F# descends to B in a B minor pentachord, followed by an ascending C major pentachord. The sequences seem to clash with one another at every turn.[65]

At the end of the movement, the text of the Latin Mass in the tenor line is changed: instead of a final *dona eis requiem sempiternam*, "give them eternal rest," which the chorus still sings, the tenor sings *dona nobis pacem*, "give us peace." The original score shows that this change was inserted in Pears's handwriting, a bold expression of his pacifism, but also a return to the world of the everyday and of the audience, since these are the words of the daily Mass, by contrast with the Requiem Mass. We are left with the beauty of Christ

---

[64] See Mitchell (1999, p. 208).
[65] I owe this observation to Anne Robertson.

and of his sacrifice—and with the possibility, if we will seize it, of a purely human peace. The idea that a kind of redemption could be achieved through the suffering of Christ inhabits numerous works of Britten, perhaps especially the epilogue of *Billy Budd* (1951). This is among its most wonderful expressions.

But what is the source of hope, even joy, in this wonderful movement? We must now state the obvious: the music is extraordinarily beautiful. It presents a Christ who is beautiful, lovable, and very human. The beauty is in the sheer nakedness of the vocal line, as sung by Peter Pears's voice, with its intelligence and clarity in articulating the text, and the very human immediacy that was always his hallmark.[66] As we saw in Chapter 4, Britten was inspired by the voice and physical presence of Pears throughout their thirty-nine year partnership. He wrote more or less everything he wrote in order to express a deep, loving and joyful, response to that body and voice, and one can hardly interpret this text without asking what it says about human love and how the music reveals, in voice, the beloved body.

Britten and Auden long ago suggested that the makers of law and the makers of war avoid acknowledging their own bodies and bodily desires. They are so eager to rid their dwellings of dirt and disorder that they project the messy phenomena of human embodiment, including bodily desire, onto outsiders (whether Jewish or homosexual) who then come to represent the ungovernable body, seen as a kind of dirt that must be removed. This refusal to come to terms with embodiment is compounded by the tradition of "manning up," pretending that one is above pain. The Agnus Dei, with its naked beauty, gazes lovingly at a beautiful beloved body, beautiful but in great pain. It is quite literally the *Hoc*

---

[66] A very good description of the effect of his voice is presented by pianist Murray Perahia, who often accompanied him: "It didn't have this great singer's kind of polish to it, so you felt the person immediately from it. . . . You felt that everything was very sincere: the emotions came to you straight—a little understated perhaps, and I loved that. I loved that they weren't in Technicolor." See Carpenter (1992, p. 183).

est corpus meum of the Mass: but in place of the lofty abstractions of tradition we have a vibrant particular human being, fully and unmistakably human, lovable and loving. Britten has written such musical love letters before—above all in the Michelangelo Sonnets and in Canticle I. But now he boldly asserts (as he did in the Donne Sonnets) that the experience of human love and human beauty is key to understanding the meaning of Christ's sacrifice and the possibility of any redemption that might come from that. Similarly, in the daily Mass, at the conclusion of this hymn, the priest holds up the host for everyone to see, saying "Ecce Agnus Dei."[67] This emphasis on incarnation is what Britten has in mind: the celebrants (the audience) must actually behold the body and see it as beautiful.

In her study of Britten's postwar works, many of which are in some manner Christian, musicologist Heather Wiebe describes an "incarnational aesthetic" that repeatedly produced works on sacred themes but with a marked human earthiness. Hence, as I've noted, his preference for an earthy "impure" boys' choir sound, rather than one artificially prettified.[68] Wiebe (see above) persuasively reads this as a rejection of a prettified Victorian Christianity in favor of a Christianity of this world. Here in the Requiem, by casting Pears in the role of Christ, or, we might say, by depicting Christ through the loved voice of Pears, Britten depicts the Incarnation, representing the body of Christ as both uniquely beautiful and lovable, and also as immensely vulnerable and fully human. And through the particular, the music swells out to embrace the universally human, the body that war crucifies, the body that must in some manner be permitted to rise again. The Owen text is tragic, but the expression of human love in the musical setting signals hope because that love is plainly not dead, and therefore love is not dead.

---

[67] I owe this observation to Andrew Biondo.
[68] Wiebe (2012, ch. 2).

I have used the words "beauty" and "love." What do these words mean here? "Beauty" is no mere aesthetic attribute; it signifies the inner and the outer, body and soul, together. (If we used ancient Greek, it would be the *kalon*.) The surface of a person summons us to wonder and delight, and then, rapt before it, we become able to see depths of goodness and potentiality that lie beneath. This play of outer and inner is familiar from the Michelangelo sonnet "Spirto ben nato" and also from the Donne sonnet "What if this present" (for both see Chapter 4), which makes the bold claim that, just as the beauty of earthly lovers is seen as a sign of inner beauty, so too Christ's earthly beauty is a sign of his capacity for mercy. The beauty in Pears's singing of Britten's vocal line, and in the line itself, is musical beauty, the work claims, of a sort that inspires wonder and at the same time gestures to a hidden inner human goodness that redeems.

And love? Once again, it is love embodied—for what is music if not bodily?—and love that includes rather than excludes the erotic element in love, love that sees the erotic as fully merged with inner and spiritual love. As in the Donne sonnet, Christ's body is seen as a fully human body, including, not excluding, the erotic—a traditional motif in Christian visual art.[69] Christ's

---

[69] The idea that Christ, to be seen as incarnate, must be seen as fully sexual, both desired and desiring, is no weird innovation of a gay subculture. It is a traditional aspect of the depiction of Christ in art. In *The Sexuality of Christ in Renaissance Art and in Modern Oblivion* (1983), the great art historian Leo Steinberg (1920–2011) has shown that artists of the Renaissance prominently draw attention to the genitals of the infant Christ and to His genital area after death. The rationale, he argued, was to make clear what Incarnation implies and to emphasis Christ's kinship with imperfect humanity. It is perhaps no accident that this rediscovery of the obvious was made by a Russian Jew and Holocaust refugee. Traditional proper Christianity had refused to see these elements out of the same bodily shame and obtuseness that the Britten work, as I claim, undermines. Oddly, Steinberg's insight (or rather sight, since seeing what is plain on the surface is not insight except against a background of willful blindness) is anticipated in Jeremy Bentham's (1823/2013) remarkable book *Not Paul But Jesus*, a small part of which was originally published under a pseudonym in 1823, but which was published in its entirety only in 2013, as an ebook from the Bentham Project at University College, London. Bentham argues, first, that authentic Christianity is not hostile to the body and sexuality; he then goes much further, arguing with close attention to several biblical texts, that Christ both accepted and even practiced same-sex conduct. One doesn't have to believe

love—and the love to which Christ summons us—is a love encompassing the body and its sexuality, seeing these as not shameful or to be concealed—not in the least at odds with the soul and its goodness.

Thus the answer to the perennial question, "Is the *War Requiem* "about" Britten's homosexuality?" is a refusal of the question. The question assumes that there is something problematic about sexual love in general, and about same-sex love in particular. Britten's vision bypasses this (and had already exposed the problems in such ways of seeing the world as early as "Our Hunting Fathers"). It is "about" a way of being human, one that sees the body in the soul and the soul in the body, and both as isomorphic with Christ's body, and Christ's love. It is a way of seeing others in society that makes possible a very basic way of being happy together—"out on the lawn," or at the Mayday festival, as spring emerges out of frozen winter. The Loxford of *Albert Herring* scrutinized each person for purity—meaning avoidance of bodily desire. It was therefore an unhappy place, especially for women. Britten is repudiating that false sort of Victorian Christianity and is urging us to accept a richer embodied vision of a flourishing life.[70]

Since I have concurred with aspects of Donald Mitchell's interpretation of this movement, I must now record a note of dissent. At the end of his analysis, Mitchell speaks of "the (righteous) anger that erupts in the Agnus Dei."[71] I believe that this ascription of a spirit of anger to the movement's viewpoint to be profoundly

the claim about practice (Steinberg emphasized the motif of chastity as self-control), in order to believe the rest.

The theme of self-control played a large part in Britten's sexual life, according to both Carpenter (1992) and John Bridcut, in his excellent study, *Britten's Children* (London: Faber & Faber, 2006). Bridcut argues that Britten felt desire for a series of teenage boys, but always restrained this desire and never acted on it. He interviews all the candidates, who uniformly say that they felt totally safe with him and were not abused.

[70] For a valuable interpretation of the entire movement, which also sees this movement as the crux of the work, see Evans (1979, p. 462).

[71] Mitchell (1999, p. 209).

wrong, both philosophically (in terms of Britten's beliefs and commitments, which he typically follows through with unerring musical judgment), and musically. The pacifist tradition of which Britten was a leading exponent totally eschewed the spirit of anger, even though some of its members were willing to countenance the resort to physical violence in self-defense. Furthermore, the utter rejection of anger is a repeated theme in Britten's wrestling with this theme, as Chapter 5 has shown (and Mitchell here draws attention to some of the same passages I discuss there); From the early *The World of the Spirit* (1938) to the later *Voices of Today* (1965) and *Owen Wingrave* (1970), there is repeated emphasis on the gentleness of the spirit of peace, on the need to replace the angry spirit with a spirit of love. We should recall that *Voices for Today* includes as leading texts the gospel text "Love your enemies; do good to those that hate you" and a text from Ashoka, "The Beloved of the Gods wishes that all people should be unharmed, self-controlled, calm in mind, and gentle."[72] And at a climactic moment in *Owen Wingrave*, Owen describes the haunted room at Paramore, crying out: " 'The anger of the world is locked up there, the horrible power that makes men fight.' " Britten does not distinguish between righteous and nonrighteous anger; he says, get rid of that doomed retributive emotion and act in a spirit of gentleness and love. (Here as elsewhere: Britten's non-anger does not entail the sort of pacifism that I have criticized. "Emotional pacifism" is compatible with a military response to aggression in defense of self and others, difficult though it always is for flawed humans to retain emotional balance in the process of just defense.)

Nor does the music of the Agnus Dei speak otherwise. The anger in the movement is entirely in the persona of the warmongers. Christ's music is serene, gentle, and loving. One would hardly expect otherwise, in a setting of "But they who love the greater love lay down their lives, they do not hate." And the

---

[72] Ibid., p. 191.

setting of that line is indeed loving and serene. Mitchell's comment shows us how difficult it is, in modern societies hooked on anger, to comprehend that there can be resistance to war and injustice, and indeed an emphatic protest against war and injustice, conducted in a spirit not of anger but of love and peace. It is not too surprising, given traditional associations of masculinity with anger, that the music is misheard, even by this very distinguished interpreter.

Just as significant an error in Mitchell's reading is his failure to describe the validation of human love in the beauty and freedom of the musical line. He therefore offers a reading of the movement that is unrelievedly pessimistic, whereas I argue that we can't help hearing hope—even hope for peace—in the beauty and lovability of the human being, human love, and the human Christ.

*****

6. Libera Me

Chorus

Libera me, Domine, de morte aeterna,	Deliver me, O Lord, from eternal death
in die illa tremenda:	in that awful day
quando coeli movendi sunt et terra: /	when the heavens and earth shall be shaken
dum veneris judicare saeculum per ignem.	when Thou shalt come to judge the world by fire.

Soprano and Chorus

Tremens factus sum ego, et timeo dum discussio venerit, atque ventura ira.	I am seized with fear and trembling, until the trial shall be at hand, and the wrath to come.
Libera me, Domine, de morte aeterna.[73]	Deliver me, O Lord, from eternal death.
Quando coeli movendi sunt et terra.	When the heavens and earth shall be shaken.
Dies illa, dies irae, calamitatis	That day, that day of wrath, of calamity
et miseriae, dies magna et amara valde.	and misery, a great day and exceeding bitter.
Libera me, Domine.	Deliver me, O Lord.

[73] In both Latin and English, the punctuation in these stanzas is odd, but I follow the original recording's libretto.

Tenor

It seemed that out of battle I escaped
down some profound dull tunnel,
      long since scooped
through granites which titanic wars had groined.
Yet also there encumbered sleepers groaned,
too fast in thought or death to be bestirred.
Then, as I probed them, one sprang up,
      and stared
with piteous recognition in fixed eyes,
lifting distressful hands as if to bless.
And no guns thumped, or down the flues
      made moan.
"Strange friend," I said, "here is no cause
      to mourn."

Baritone

"None," said the other, "save the undone years,
the hopelessness. Whatever hope is yours,
was my life also; I went hunting wild
after the wildest beauty in the world,
for by my glee might many men have laughed,
and of my weeping something had been left,
which must die now. I mean the truth untold,
the pity of war, the pity war distilled.
Now men will go content with what we spoiled.
Or, discontent, boil bloody, and be spilled.
They will be swift with swiftness of
      the tigress,
none will break ranks, though nations trek from
      progress.
Miss we the march of this retreating world
into vain citadels that are not walled.
Then, when much blood had clogged their
      chariot-wheels,
I would go up and wash them from
      sweet wells,
even from wells we sunk too deep for war,
even from the sweetest wells that ever were.
I am the enemy you killed, my friend.
I knew you in this dark; for so you frowned
yesterday through me as you jabbed and killed.
I parried; but my hands were loath and cold.
Let us sleep now . . ."

Boys, then Chorus, then Soprano

In paradisum deducant te Angeli:
in tuo adventu suscipiant te Martyres,
et perducant te in civitatem sanctam
      Jerusalem.

Into Paradise may the Angels lead thee:
at thy coming may the Martyrs receive thee,
and bring thee into the holy city Jerusalem.

Chorus Angelorum te suscipiat,	May the Choir of Angels receive thee
et cum Lazaro quondam paupere	and with Lazarus, once poor,
aeternam habeas requiem.	may thou have eternal rest.

Boys

Requiem aeternam dona eis, Domine:	Lord, grant them eternal rest,
et lux perpetua luceat eis.	and let the perpetual light shine upon them.

Chorus

In Paradisum deducant, *etc.*	Into Paradise, *etc.*

Soprano

Chorus Angelorum te suscipiat, *etc.*	May the Choir of Angels, *etc.*

Tenor and Baritone

Let us sleep now.

Chorus

Requiescant in pace. Amen.	Let them rest in peace. Amen.

For the most part, the *War Requiem* is a bleak work. It has taken listeners down into the depths of ugly retributivism, so tempting for flawed human beings and their political and religious institutions. It has depicted the terrible costs of war on young bodies. And with "The End" it has taken the listener further, into a Schopenhauerian detachment that finds no hope for human life and no positive value in it. I have argued, however, that along the way it offers glimpses of joy, love, and hope. "Anthem for Doomed Youth" suggests that reflection by those who mourn may begin to see war's costs correctly: the "tenderness of silent minds" may begin to deliberate about creating a world without war. "Futility" has depicted the bodies of soldiers as precious, mourned and caressed by the sun. And in the Agnus Dei the worth of human love, and of Christ as an embodied symbol of that love, is radiantly affirmed.

But what about the future of Europe? What about the Coventry project of reconciliation with and between nations? The possibility that incarnate love might lead to a European reconstruction is confronted at the end of the work in the setting of Owen's "Strange

Meeting," included as part of the Libera Me—the movement of the Mass in which the agonized soprano voice begs God for a chance of freedom from the tyranny of death.

The movement begins with a Mahlerian funeral march—so often used by Britten to accompany thoughts of war. At first hushed, it builds gradually, adding percussion and brass.[74] The soprano enters at "Tremens factus," with an urgent plea, and the combined forces build to a furious recapitulation of the *Dies Irae*, with fanfares and drums, which gradually fades to a hushed pianissimo, then to a silence. In a sense we are back where we were—in the middle of war's horrors with their accompanying terrors. And yet, after "The End," strong and vibrant human emotion is almost a relief, a sign that humans are alive and possibly capable of thought and change.

Out of the silence, the two soloists begin the final Owen poem of the work, "Strange Meeting."

The poem depicts the reconciliation of two soldiers who meet after both are dead, one British and one German. The setting is some mythic realm beyond death—but Britten pointedly omits lines of the Owen poem, giving the meeting place as Hell. Religious cosmology is replaced by a world of human imagination and emotion.[75] And the deliberate casting of Pears and Fischer-Dieskau, whose heavily accented English is an important part of the aesthetic effect, makes the poem resonate against postwar projects of Anglo-German reconciliation and reconstruction.

Britten heavily edited this poem, in some cases shortening merely, in others shaping the meaning. As mentioned, he omits lines in which the first speaker says that the meeting takes place in Hell. Very significantly, he omits the misogynistic lines, after "wildest beauty in the world" that say, "Which lies not calm in eyes, or braided hair, / But mocks the steady running of the hour, / And if it grieves, grieves richlier than here"—imputing placidity and

---

[74] On further allusions to Verdi here, see Cooke (1996, pp. 73–74).

[75] Theologically, the Coventry clergy and most of the audience would surely reject the suggestion that these men, victims of war, are in Hell.

deficient emotionality to women back at home. Again, and also significantly, he omits the lines "Courage was mine, and I had mystery, / Wisdom was mine, and I had mastery," redolent of the elitism that Owen at times expresses but Britten does not. The line "Even from wells we sunk too deep for war, / Even from the sweetest wells that ever were" is Britten's rewriting of "Even with truths that lie too deep for taint," and Britten then omits three more lines about the "I" and his projects—which, again, suggests elite knowledge rather than a communal project of reconstruction, as in Britten's version.

The poem is sung almost *a cappella* at first, with only brief interventions: chords from strings and harp, brief solos from oboe, bassoon, clarinet, flute, and horn. And although the German soldier is "lifting distressful hands as if to bless," when he speaks, he does not endorse conventional religious ideas. Instead, he talks of hopelessness (to a single oboe's accompaniment), of unrealized hope (against a harp). When he speaks of nations returning to war, the sounds of war are heard. But then, when he begins to speak of his desire to offer a purely human consolation ("I would go up and wash them from sweet wells"),[76] the violins enter, and eventually the rest of the strings, a warmer sound, swelling out. The climactic declaration, "I am the enemy you killed, my friend. . . . Let us sleep now" is delivered *a cappella*—but then the choir takes up the last line, "Let us sleep now," and the choral voices curve around the soloists as the refrain swells outward.

The poem is in a way highly pessimistic: the "truth" will remain "untold," the "pity of war" will be unrecognized, and nations, heedless of the warning, will "trek from progress." Blood will clog their chariot wheels, and all the baritone can do is, counterfactually, to tend the sick and the dying. And yet: Owen intended his entire poetic oeuvre as a warning about the "pity of war." Britten has endorsed a similar account of what he is trying to accomplish in

---

[76] Cooke (1996, p. 76) notes that the baritone solo uses perfect fourths, signifying, he argues, resignation to his fate, by contrast with the many augmented fourths that precede in earlier movements

this work. And here is the work, performed and "told," on a high public occasion on which the future of Europe is being debated. The speaker, then, was perhaps wrongly pessimistic: his warning is in fact being spoken, the pity of war displayed. What remains to be seen, of course, is whether the warning will be heeded.

Furthermore, both poem and setting emphasize the human worth of both the English and the German soldier. The German, in particular, is given thoughts of beauty and worth, and emotions of universal love and compassion. Neither wants revenge. Indeed, the German notes that, though he "parried" defending himself, his hands were "loath and cold." So both poem and its nakedly beautiful setting ask listeners to recognize the human worth that has already been the core of the Agnus Dei, and to see it as inherent in all humans, "friend" and "enemy" alike. These sentiments are very much in keeping with the Marshall Plan and other projects of postwar reconstruction and reconciliation—which, by 1962, late in Konrad Adenauer's successful term as chancellor, were well under way. Reconciliation and reconstruction are possible. In fact, by then, they had already happened, and by now we can appreciate the stability of the foundations that had been laid, with Germany taking the lead in Europe as one of its most stable and successful democracies, and as a committed defender of democracy elsewhere.

The poem and work do not predict a utopia, however. The idea that when people do not receive the Owen/Britten warning and take it to heart, they will "trek from progress" and return to aggression is also part of the poem. And this idea, too, had already been realized in 1962, with the Soviet Union's totalitarian regime and its persecution of artists and writers—even Vishnevskaya, unable to sing at the work's premiere. Today that same aggressive totalitarian spirit continues under another name, and it is creating human tragedy in Ukraine, as well as risk for all the nations of Europe. So the very performance conditions of the work show that human beings can work together to make things better, that democracies can be stable friends across a history of difference—but also that human aggression, Hydra-headed, springs up in another place and makes war, despite the work's warnings. What does the work say about this?

What I would say is: make peace, cement alliances, but be vigilant, and be prepared to use force in defense of democracy. This of course is not what Britten is ever prepared to say. He can say the first part, and he can then say: but if trouble comes, as it surely will, given human frailty, remember that human beings and human life are worthwhile, despite their imperfection. And vigilantly cultivate your inner world: subdue aggression and foster the spirit of peace. And perhaps that is a fine enough message for an apolitical artist to give the world. The rest is up to the audience.

*****

The boys' choir takes up the otherworldly religious text, speaking of angels leading the dead person into Paradise, but those voices are distant, and it is the two particular humans who have immediacy. They do not even acknowledge conventional religious ideas; they simply speak to one another. In a world where conventional ideas of divine grace have failed to intervene—indeed, even at times been corrupted and expropriated by nationalistic politics—human compassion and the ability of humans to overcome hatred must take the lead, becoming the full embodiment of the murdered Christ (after all, Pears, who was the murdered Christ, is now the British soldier). Cooke remarks: "This unique conjoining of all the performing groups (spanning some forty-seven staves of full score, mostly subdued in dynamics) singing the same music, serves as a fitting representation of the reconciliation with which the Owen setting ends."[77] As Wiebe emphasizes, the work performs both rupture and continuity,[78] since the humanity of Christ is, of course, part of traditional religion, though slighted by some religious elites. The advice to humans is not to wait for external intervention from the

---

[77] Cooke (1996, p. 76).
[78] See Wiebe (2012, ch. 6).

heavens: instead, we must arrange to have mercy on, and to love, one another.

In a purely human world, however, there are no neat endings, and Britten disrupts the final reconciliation by the reintroduction of the tritone C-F sharp on the tubular bells, which twice discordantly check the voices in their attempt to repeat, "Let us sleep now" / In paradisum. As if dejected, the chorus takes up the tritone for the final Requiescant in pace, as a resolution into the alien key of F major (as at the end of both the Requiem Aeternam and the *Dies Irae*) ends the work on a profoundly unsettling and ambiguous note: does the resolution express a possibility of hope, or a further stage of dejection?[79]

Britten was always opposed to prettiness and sentimentality. Once, objecting to a description of his boys' choir as "angelic," he remarked that this "may bring some unhappy echoes of the end of Walt Disney's soupier films!"[80] It is then fitting that he offers no pat ending. European reconstruction, British decency, and international peace are for the audience to construct. Each audience. Whether we will take up that challenge is unclear.

A work like this offers no easy formula for law and policy. Instead it offers something more valuable, an emotional and intellectual confrontation with difficulty and contradiction, with tragedy and hope and enormous uncertainty, with all the material of sound public deliberation. Britten's whole career makes the case that a confrontation with difficult and daring works of art is something Britain's narrow and puritanical public culture needs; and his work to create the Aldeburgh Festival showed his determination to build an artistic infrastructure for his region and nation.

As the work ends, we are left, then, with political reconciliation in grave doubt—but with human love, and, with and in it, music, alive and magnetically beautiful. That was 1962. Today, as I write this in 2023—and in your time, whenever you read this—the same conclusion seems just right.

---

[79] See Cooke (1996, pp. 76–77). Compare Rupprecht (2001, pp. 218–19).
[80] Wiebe (2012, p. 61).

Conclusion: The Way Forward

Britten's wonderful work may seem, today, to have been written in vain. Such a work cannot have influence on public thought if it is not performed and heard. But over the years since the work was first performed, the centrality of classical music in both American and European public culture seems to be declining. Symphony orchestras around the world continue to attain a very high level of musical performance, but they do so, in the United States, largely through the support of private donors, and in Europe through governmental support, which is always a risky business. For earlier generations, a work such as Beethoven's Ninth Symphony could play a central role in public culture, both expressing and shaping aspirations for the future of humanity. When first performed in Great Britain, Benjamin Britten's work seemed poised to take on a similar centrality. Today the musical choices of younger listeners are tremendously varied, and classical music has to compete to maintain even a share of people's attention. Britten, furthermore, is less well known than he should be in the United States, or at least less central and even (to a lesser extent) in Europe: he is seen primarily as a key English composer. This undeserved relative neglect produces yet further neglect, as opera companies shrink from producing his works lest audiences stay away. My own home opera company, Lyric Opera of Chicago, has not staged a Britten opera since a wonderful mounting of *Billy Budd* in 2001—although the more experimental and smaller-scale Chicago Opera Theater staged a superb *Albert Herring* (rather poorly attended) in 2023.

It is not yet time to panic, however. First of all, it is important to realize that classical music was actually a relatively narrow and

The Tenderness of Silent Minds. Martha C. Nussbaum, Oxford University Press.
© Oxford University Press 2024. DOI: 10.1093/oso/9780197568538.003.0007

elite experience for centuries, limited to those affluent and socially well placed enough to attend live concerts, or musically educated enough to read scores or play them on the piano—until the advent of recording put these works within the reach of a mass audience. Prissy culture critics decried this democratization of the classics—think, for example, of Walter Benjamin's *The Work of Art in the Age of Mechanical Reproduction* (1935)—but the new technology has been immensely salutary, both broadening access and deepening it, through the possibilities it affords of both repeated listening and listening to different interpretations. And now someone who wants to experience a work of Britten does not even need to own a vinyl record or CD: online streaming puts all these works in people's rooms at the click of a cursor. This includes the original recording of the *War Requiem*, all of which is available for free on YouTube. When the *War Requiem* is performed, it occasions great excitement, as it did when the Boston Symphony Orchestra performed it to sell-out crowds in 2022. But people who do not have access to a live performance still have easy access to the work. Furthermore, Britten's deliberate outreach to the amateur musician, a lifelong commitment of his, led him to compose the *War Requiem* as a work that can be performed by amateur choruses, as indeed it was at its premiere, and by high-quality amateur orchestras, so long as professional soloists take the three solo roles. The easy access such amateur musicians have to recorded versions of the work improves their performance, and the chance to listen before attending improves the performance of the audience. People anywhere in the world can take the emotional path this work maps out, even if they are unlikely ever to attend a live performance. (I myself have never been present at a live performance of the *War Requiem*, although I have attended live performances of *Peter Grimes, Billy Budd, Albert Herring, Turn of the Screw,* and *The Rape of Lucretia,* not to mention related works such as Verdi's *Requiem* and nine of the ten Mahler symphonies, plus *Das Lied von der Erde.*)

I hope this book will cause more people to experience the *War Requiem* one way or another, because I think it is one of music's deepest and most complex confrontations with the causes of war and the prospects of peace. But, like reading Wilfred Owen's poetry, it must always remain a personal choice, and it is unlikely ever to attain the ubiquity of Beethoven's Ninth. This has advantages as well as disadvantages: the work is unlikely to become sentimentalized or debased, robbed of its emotional power by too frequent or too casual repetition. It is also not likely to be appropriated by tyrants, as Beethoven has been. I can also live happily with the fact that this work is not likely to be a source for TV commercial jingles, or played in disconnected bits at public events of various sorts, the way many parts of Beethoven's symphonies are. It needs to be heard as a whole and listened to seriously.

Britten's work constructs just one path to its goal—serious public deliberation about how to achieve future peace and reconciliation among nations, a goal requiring both personal and social change. (Really, as I shall insist, it constructs more than one path, as listeners enter the work at different points and hear different things in it.) But there are many ways of pursuing Britten's goal, nor are they mutually exclusive. People can seek out many different musical works in different traditions, including jazz and popular music; they can engage with drama, poetry, novels, works of visual art, architecture, and dance. They can look for guidance to the many religious traditions that do seriously pursue peace and its inner emotional prerequisites. They can ponder philosophical works bearing on these ideas. They can join groups and movements of peaceful resistance to injustice, wherever they find them in their society. They can do all of these things and more. And they can then come together to discuss their experiences and what these experiences suggest for political and social questions facing them. Our efforts to pursue Britten's goal hardly stand or fall with his distinguished work, although I believe it to be one of our most profound works of art on the topic, the *War and Peace* of music, so to speak.

Sometimes people who ponder Britten's work may feel that defense of their nation and its values leaves them no choice but to fight an aggressor. I think some such conclusions are right. Britten disagrees, but I have argued that the *War Requiem* itself is to a great extent independent of his commitment to a total pacifism of acts in that it is focused on emotional pacifism, a commitment that people engaged in a war of self-defense can and should maintain, although being at war makes it extremely difficult to maintain freedom from inner hatred and retributive anger. The insights of Britten's work, and of others like it, can inform deliberation about how to respond to an aggressor—at what point to respond, with what means, what limits, what ultimate goal. An emotional pacifist—someone who makes every effort possible to uproot aggression in his or her own personality and to move toward others in a spirit of love—will engage in a just war very differently from a person who sees no problem in aggression and violence. I have mentioned the way Beethoven's Ninth Symphony was connected by Riccardo Muti to the war in Ukraine—because it speaks of, and musically expresses, a spirit of universal joy and brotherhood that should animate patriots fighting for their freedom, in their conduct in war and their conception of how war should be ended. Something similar is true of Britten's more doubt-ridden and skeptical work: it can inform a spirit of brotherhood that sees value and beauty in human bodies and minds, and that remains steadfast in a determination not to permit humanity to be distorted and deformed by aggression, greed, and pride. If an aggressor is confronted in this spirit, without deflections into greed and retributivism, this increases the likelihood that after the conflict ends a solid peace may prevail—although Britten's work reminds us that the forces of aggression are buried deep in the human personality and are not likely to be permanently removed. Thus a spirit of vigilant warning—the spirit of both Owen and Britten—can and should inform such a conflict and its aftermath, preventing easy complacency and a heedless yielding to greed and narcissism.

In short: we should love one another, but also watch ourselves carefully: the "ram of Pride" awaits us all, even if caught for a time in a thicket. Britten's work, for me, strikes just the right note, combining active love with foreboding. May we all seek many ways to live in its spirit.

Bibliography

Associated Press. 1996. "Church of England Commission Says Hell Is Same—Only Different." January 17. https://web.archive.org/web/20210320053853/https://apnews.com/article/611c8aa8904dde105806f6c05485f995.

Bell, John, ed. 1985. *Wilfred Owen: Selected Letters*. Oxford, UK: Oxford University Press.

Bentham, Jeremy. 1823/2013. *Not Paul, but Jesus*. Project Gutenberg. https://www.gutenberg.org/ebooks/42984.

Blunden, Edmund. 1931/1963. "Appendix I Memoir, 1931, by Edmund Blunden." In *The Collected Poems of Wilfred Owen*, by Wilfred Owen, edited by C. Day. Lewis, 147–82. New Directions Paperbook. London: Chatto & Windus.

Boyd, Malcolm. 1968. "Britten, Verdi and the Requiem." *Tempo*, no. 86: 2–6.

Brett, Philip. 2006. "Auden's Britten." In *Music and Sexuality in Britten: Selected Essays*, edited by Philip Brett and George E. Haggerty. Berkeley: University of California Press: 186–3, 203.

Bridcut, John. 2006. *Britten's Children*. London: Faber & Faber.

Britten, Benjamin. 1962. *War Requiem: Op. 66, Full Orchestral Score*. Reprinted with corrections 2019. Boosey & Hawkes Masterworks Library. London: Boosey & Hawkes.

Britten, Benjamin, and Peter Pears. 2016. Ed. Vicki P. Stroeher, Nicholas Clark, and Jude Brimmer. *My Beloved Man: The Letters of Benjamin Britten and Peter Pears*. Aldeburgh Studies in Music 10. Woodbridge, UK: Boydell & Brewer.

Bullivant, Joanna. 2018. "'Practical Jokes': Britten and Auden's Our Hunting Fathers Revisited." In *Literary Britten: Words and Music in Benjamin Britten's Vocal Works*, edited by Kate Kennedy. Aldeburgh Studies in Music 13. Woodbridge, UK: Boydell & Brewer: 206–22.

Cameron, Paul. 1993. *Medical Consequences of What Homosexuals Do*. Colorado Springs, CO: Family Research Institute.

Carpenter, Humphrey. 1992. *Benjamin Britten: A Biography*. New York: Charles Scribner's Sons.

Chicago Symphony Orchestra (CSO). 2022. *Program Book—Muti Conducts Vivaldi & Handel Water Music*. Chicago: Chicago Symphony Orchestra. https://issuu.com/chicagosymphony/docs/wrap3_cso15_jan-feb22_issuu.

Collins, Wilkie. 1862/1994. *No Name*. Edited by Mark Ford. Penguin Classics. New York: Penguin Books.

Cooke, Deryck. 1988. *Gustav Mahler: An Introduction to His Music*. 2nd ed. Cambridge, UK: Cambridge University Press.

Cooke, Mervyn. 1996. *Britten: War Requiem*. Cambridge Music Handbooks. Cambridge, UK: Cambridge University Press.

Couderc, Gilles. 2013. "The *War Requiem*: Britten's Wilfred Owen Opera." *Arts of War and Peace* 1(1): 9–22.

Culshaw, John. 1982. *Putting the Record Straight: The Autobiography of John Culshaw*. New York: Viking Press.

Dalton, Dennis. 1993/2012. *Mahatma Gandhi: Nonviolent Power in Action*. Revised 3d edition. New York: Columbia University Press.

de Maupassant, Guy. 1888. *Le Rosier de Madame Husson*. Paris: Maison Quantin.

Devlin, Patrick. 1965. *The Enforcement of Morals*. Oxford, UK: Oxford University Press.

Downes, Stephen C. 2013. *After Mahler: Britten, Weill, Henze, and Romantic Redemption*. New York: Cambridge University Press.

Duncan, Ronald. 1937. *The Complete Pacifist*. Leicester, UK: Leicester Cooperative Printing Society Ltd.

Duncan, Ronald. 1981. *Working with Britten: A Personal Memoir*. Welcombe, UK: Rebel Press.

Elliott, Graham. 2006. *Benjamin Britten: The Spiritual Dimension*. Oxford Studies in British Church Music. New York: Oxford University Press.

Ellis, Havelock. 1900. "Sexual Inversion." In *Studies in the Psychology of Sex*. Vol. 2. London: University Press.

Evans, Peter. 1979. *The Music of Benjamin Britten*. Minneapolis: University of Minnesota Press.

Fischer-Dieskau, Dietrich. 1989. *Reverberations: The Memoirs of Dietrich Fischer-Dieskau*. Translated by Ruth Hein. New York: Fromm International Publishing Corporation.

Forster, E. M. 1971. *Maurice*. New York: W. W. Norton.

Foster, Michael. 2012. *"The Idea Was Good": The Story of Benjamin Britten's War Requiem*. Coventry, UK: Coventry Cathedral Books.

Fussell, Paul. 1975. *The Great War and Modern Memory*. Oxford, UK: Oxford University Press.

Gregg, Richard B. 1935/1959. *The Power of Nonviolence*. 2d rev. ed. New York: Schocken Books.

Hart, H. L. A. 1963. *Law, Liberty, and Morality*. Harry Camp Lectures at Stanford University. Stanford, CA: Stanford University Press.

Headington, Christopher. 1993. *Peter Pears: A Biography*. London: Faber & Faber.

Heaney, Seamus. 1995. *The Cure at Troy: A Version of Sophocles's Philoctetes*. New York: Noonday Press.

Hepburn, Ronald W. 1984. *"Wonder": And Other Essays: Eight Studies in Aesthetics and Neighbouring Fields.* Edinburgh: University of Edinburgh Press.

Hogwood, Ben. 2013. "Listening to Britten—*Seven Sonnets of Michelangelo*, Op. 22." *Good Morning Britten* (blog). August 29, 2013. https://goodmor ningbritten.wordpress.com/2013/08/29/listening-to-britten-seven-sonn ets-of-michelangelo-op-22.

Howard, Richard. 1962. *Ruined and Rebuilt: The Story of Coventry Cathedral 1939–1962.* Coventry, UK: Coventry Cathedral.

Hyde, H. Montgomery. 1956. *The Three Trials of Oscar Wilde.* New York: University Books.

Jerryson, Michael K. 2011. *Buddhist Fury: Religion and Violence in Southern Thailand.* Oxford, UK: Oxford University Press.

Jerryson, Michael K., and Mark Juergensmeyer, eds. 2010. *Buddhist Warfare.* Oxford, UK: Oxford University Press.

Johnson, Graham. 2017. *Britten, Voice and Piano: Lectures on the Vocal Music of Benjamin Britten.* London: Routledge.

Jones, Nigel. 2018. "Anthem for Groomed Youth." *The Spectator.* January 6. https://www.spectator.co.uk/article/anthem-for-groomed-youth.

Kafka, Franz. 1919. "In the Penal Colony," short story, many translations and editions.

Kennedy, Michael. 1961. Notes to *"Benjamin Britten, Jennifer Vyvyan, Norma Procter, Peter Pears, Emanuel School Boys" Chorus, Chorus of the Royal Opera House, Covent Garden, Orchestra of the Royal Opera House, Covent Garden— Spring Symphony.* London: Longmans, Green and Co.

Kennedy, Michael. 1981. *Britten.* The Master Musicians Series. London: J. M. Dent.

Kildea, Paul. 1999. "Britten, Auden and 'Otherness.'" In *The Cambridge Companion to Benjamin Britten*, edited by Mervyn Cooke. Cambridge Companions to Music. Cambridge, UK: Cambridge University Press: 36–53.

Kildea, Paul , ed. 2003. *Britten on Music.* New York: Oxford University Press.

Kildea, Paul. 2013. *Benjamin Britten: A Life in the Twentieth Century.* London: Allen Lane.

Kitcher, Philip. *Manuscript on Britten's War Requiem.* (forthcoming)

Lacey, Nicola. 2004. *A Life of H.L.A. Hart: The Nightmare and the Noble Dream.* Oxford, UK: Oxford University Press.

LaCroix, Alison L., Jonathan S. Masur, Martha C. Nussbaum, and Laura Weinrib, eds. *Cannons and Codes: Law, Literature, and America's Wars.* Oxford University Press, 2021.

Lee, Vernon. 1890. "A Wicked Voice." In *Hauntings.* Project Gutenberg. https://www.gutenberg.org/cache/epub/9956/pg9956.html.

Lessing, Gotthold Ephraim. 1766. *Laokoon: An Essay on the Limits of Painting and Poetry.* Translated by Edwin Allen McCormick. Baltimore: Johns Hopkins University Press, 1984.

Lewis, C. Day. 1963. "Introduction." In *The Collected Poems of Wilfred Owen*, by Wilfred Owen, edited by C. Day Lewis, 11–30. New Directions Paperbook. London: Chatto and Windus.

Lewis, Daniel. 2012. "Dietrich Fischer-Dieskau, Lyrical and Powerful Baritone, Dies at 86." *New York Times*, May 18, sec. Arts. https://www.nyti mes.com/2012/05/19/arts/music/dietrich-fischer-dieskau-german-barit one-dies-at-86.html.

Mahler, Gustav. 1979. *Selected Letters of Gustav Mahler*. Edited by Alma Mahler and Knud Martner. Rev. ed. and Translation. New York: Farrar, Straus, & Giroux.

Mayer, Elizabeth, and Peter Pears. 1943. Translations accompanying *Seven Sonnets of Michelangelo*. London: Boosey & Hawkes.

Mendelson, Edward. 1981. *Early Auden*. London: Faber & Faber.

Mill, John Stuart. 1869. *The Subjection of Women*. 1st ed. London: Longmans, Green, Reader & Dyer. Edited by Susan Moller Okin. Indianapolis: Hackett Publishing Company, 1988.

Mitchell, Donald. 1971. "'*Owen Wingrave* and the Sense of the Past: Some Reflections on Britten's Opera,' Liner Notes Accompanying the Complete Recording of the Opera Conducted by Britten." London Records, OSA 1291.

Mitchell, Donald. 1981/2000. *Britten and Auden in the Thirties: The Year 1936*. The T.S. Eliot Memorial Lectures Delivered at the University of Kent at Canterbury in November 1979. Reprint edition of Woodbridge, UK: The Boydell Press. Aldeburgh Studies in Music 5. London: Faber & Faber.

Mitchell, Donald. 1999. "Violent Climates." In *The Cambridge Companion to Benjamin Britten*, edited by Mervyn Cooke. Cambridge Companions to Music. Cambridge, UK: Cambridge University Press: 188–216.

Mitchell, Donald. 2004. "Pears, Sir Peter Neville Luard (1910–1986), Singer." *Oxford Dictionary of National Biography*, September. https://doi.org/ 10.1093/ref:odnb/39913.

Mitchell, Donald, and John Evans. 1978. *Benjamin Britten, 1913–1976: Pictures from a Life: A Pictorial Biography*. London: Faber & Faber.

Mitchell, Donald, and Philip Reed, eds. 1991. *Letters from a Life: The Selected Letters and Diaries of Benjamin Britten 1913–1976*. Vol. 1: 1923–39. London: Faber & Faber.

Mitchell, Donald, and Philip Reed, eds. 1996. Notes to *An American Overture King Arthur Suite: For Orchestra; The World of the Spirit*. Colchester, UK: Chandos.

Monsaingeon, Bruno. 2001. *Sviatoslav Richter: Notebooks and Conversations*. Translated by Stewart Spencer. London: Faber & Faber.

Norton, Rictor, ed. 1998a. *My Dear Boy: Gay Love Letters Through the Centuries*. San Francisco, CA: Leyland Publications.

Norton, Rictor. 1998b. "You Have Fixed My Life: The Gay Love Letters of Wilfred Owen to Siegfried Sassoon." Excerpts from *My Dear Boy: Gay Love*

Letters through the Centurie (1998), Edited by Rictor Norton." *Gay History and Literature*. 1998. https://rictornorton.co.uk/owen.htm.

Nussbaum, Martha C. 2001. *Upheavals of Thought: The Intelligence of Emotions*. New York: Cambridge University Press.

Nussbaum, Martha C. 2010. *From Disgust to Humanity: Sexual Orientation and Constitutional Law*. Inalienable Rights Series. New York: Oxford University Press.

Nussbaum, Martha C. 2016. *Anger and Forgiveness: Resentment, Generosity, Justice*. New York: Oxford University Press.

Nussbaum, Martha C. 2018a. "Mercy in Music." In *The Oxford Handbook of Western Music and Philosophy*, edited by Tomás McAuley, Nanette Nielsen, Jerrold Levinson, and Ariana Phillips-Hutton, 803–822. Oxford, UK: Oxford University Press.

Nussbaum, Martha C. 2018b. "From Anger to Love: Self-Purification and Political Resistance." In *To Shape a New World*, edited by Tommie Shelby and Brandon M. Terry. Cambridge, MA: Harvard University Press: 105–26.

Nussbaum, Martha C. 2021. *Citadels of Pride: Sexual Assault, Accountability, and Reconciliation*. New York: W.W. Norton.

Nussbaum, Martha C. 2022. *Justice for Animals: Our Collective Responsibility*. New York: Simon & Schuster.

Olito, Frank. 2021. "From Princess Diana to Prince Harry, Here Are 9 Times the Royal Family Showed Support for the LGBTQ Community." Insider. February 16. https://www.insider.com/royal-family-support-lgbtq-community-2019-6.

Orwell, George. 1942. "Pacifism and the War." *Partisan Review*: August–September, available at https://www.orwell.ru/library/articles/pacifism/english/e_patw.

Owen, Wilfred. 1963. *The Collected Poems of Wilfred Owen*. Edited by C. Day Lewis. New Directions Paperbook. London: Chatto & Windus.

Parliament of the United Kingdom. "Homosexual Offences." *Parliamentary Debates (Hansard)*. House of Lords, vol. 266. May 12, 1965. https://api.parliament.uk/historic-hansard/lords/1965/may/12/homosexual-offences.

Pears, Peter. "The Vocal Music." In *Benjamin Britten: A Commentary on His Works from a Group of Specialists*, edited by Donald Mitchell and Hans Keller, 59–74. New York: Philosophical Library, 1952.

Pyke, Cameron. 2009. "Shostakovich's Fourteenth Symphony: A Response to *War Requiem*." In *Benjamin Britten: New Perspectives on His Life and Works*, edited by Lucy Walker. Woodbridge, UK: The Boydell Press and the Britten-Pears Foundation: 27–45.

Reed, Philip. 1999. "Britten in the Cinema: Coal Face." In *The Cambridge Companion to Benjamin Britten*, edited by Mervyn Cooke. Cambridge Companions to Music. Cambridge, UK: Cambridge University Press: 54–78.

Romer v. Evans, 517 U.S. 620, 116 S. Ct. 1620 (1996).

Rupprecht, Philip . 2001. *Britten's Musical Language*. Music in the 20th Century. Cambridge, UK: Cambridge University Press.

Schopenhauer, Arthur. 1818–1844/1958. *The World as Will and Representation*. Translated by E. F. J. Payne. New York: Dover. Two volumes.

Schopenhauer, Arthur. 1840/2009. "Prize Essay on the Basis of Morals." In *The Two Fundamental Problems of Ethics*, edited and translated by Christopher Janaway. Schopenhauer, Arthur, 1788–1860. Works. English. 2009. Cambridge, UK: Cambridge University Press: 113–258.

Schultz, Bart. 2004. *Henry Sidgwick, Eye of the Universe: An Intellectual Biography*. Cambridge, UK: Cambridge University Press.

Shrock, Dennis. 2017. *Choral Monuments: Studies of Eleven Choral Masterworks*. New York: Oxford University Press.

Smith, Adam. 1776/1981–1982. *An Inquiry into the Nature and Causes of the Wealth of Nations*. Two volumes. Carmel, IN: Liberty Fund.

Steinberg, Leo. 1983. *The Sexuality of Christ in Renaissance Art and in Modern Oblivion*. 1st ed. New York: Pantheon Books.

Stevenson, Joseph. n.d. "Benjamin Britten: Our Hunting Fathers, Song Cycle for High Voice & Orchestra, Op. 8." AllMusic. n.d. https://www.allmusic. com/composition/our-hunting-fathers-song-cycle-for-high-voice-orches tra-op-8-mc0002373256.

Syme, Ronald. 1939. *The Roman Revolution*. London: Clarendon Press.

Symonds, John Addington. 1883. *A Problem in Greek Ethics*. Privately printed, available as an ebook at https://www.gutenberg.org/ebooks/32022.

Vickers, Justin. 2015. "Benjamin Britten's Silent 'Epilogue' to 'The Holy Sonnets of John Donne.'" *The Musical Times* 156 (No. 1933): 17–30.

Walker, Lucy. 2021. "Work of the Week 33. Tyco the Vegan." Britten Pears Arts. July 29. https://brittenpearsarts.org/news/work-of-the-week-33-tyco-the-vegan.

Warner, Michael. 2014. "Manning Up." In *American Guy: Masculinity in American Law and Literature*, edited by Saul Levmore and Martha C. Nussbaum. New York: Oxford University Press: 147–62.

Whitesell, Lloyd. 2013. "Love Knots." In *Rethinking Britten*, edited by Philip Rupprecht. New York: Oxford University Press: 40–59.

Wiebe, Heather. 2012. *Britten's Unquiet Pasts: Sound and Memory in Postwar Reconstruction*. Music since 1900. New York: Cambridge University Press.

Wiebe, Heather. 2015. "Discovering America: From Paul Bunyan to Peter Grimes." *Cambridge Opera Journal* 27 (2): 129–53.

Woolf, Virginia. 1938. *Three Guineas*. London: Hogarth Press.

List of Britten Works and Owen Poems

List of Britten Works Referenced
(chronological order)

Op. 4, Simple Symphony for strings (1934) (also version for string quartet)

Op. 8, *Our Hunting Fathers* for soprano or tenor and orchestra (words W. H. Auden) (1936)

_____, *Pacifist March* (1937)

_____, *The Company of Heaven* (1937)

_____, *Advance Democracy* (1938)

_____, *The World of the Spirit* (1938)

Op. 14, "Ballad of Heroes" for tenor or soprano, chorus and orchestra (words W. H. Auden and Randall Swingler) (1939)

Op. 17, *Paul Bunyan*, opera (libretto W. H. Auden) (1941, revised 1976)

Op. 18, *Les Illuminations*, for soprano or tenor and strings (words Arthur Rimbaud) (1939)

Op. 20, *Sinfonia da Requiem* (1940)

Op. 22, *Seven Sonnets of Michelangelo for tenor and piano* (1940)

Op. 28, "*A Ceremony of Carols* for trebles and harp" (1942)

Op. 33, *Peter Grimes*, opera (libretto Montagu Slater after George Crabbe) (1945)

Op. 33a, "Four Sea Interludes" from *Peter Grimes* (1945)

Op. 34, "Variations and Fugue on a Theme of Henry Purcell" ("The Young Person's Guide to the Orchestra") (1946)

Op. 35, *The Holy Sonnets of John Donne* for soprano or tenor and piano (1945)

Op. 37, *The Rape of Lucretia*," opera (libretto Ronald Duncan after André Obey) (1946, revised 1947)

Op. 39, *Albert Herring*, opera (libretto Eric Crozier after Guy de Maupassant) (1947)

Op. 40, "My beloved is mine" (Canticle I) for soprano or tenor and piano (words Francis Quarles) (1947)

Op. 42, "Saint Nicolas" for soloists, chorus, strings, piano (four hands), percussion and organ (1948)

Op. 44, Spring Symphony for soloists, mixed choir, children's choir and orchestra (1949)

Op. 46, "A Wedding Anthem" (Amo Ergo Sum) for soprano, tenor chorus and organ (words Ronald Duncan) (1949)

Op. 47, "Five Flower Songs" for SATB (Soprano Alto Tenor Bass) (1950)

Op. 50, *Billy Budd*, opera (libretto E. M. Forster and Eric Crozier after Hermann Melville) (1951, revised 1960)

Op. 51, "Abraham and Isaac" (Canticle II) for alto, tenor and piano (Chester miracle play) (1952)

Op. 53, *Gloriana*, opera (libretto William Plomer after Lytton Strachey) (1953)

Op. 57, *The Prince of the Pagodas*, ballet (1956)

Op. 60, "Nocturne" for tenor, 7 obbligato instruments and string orchestra, song cycle (1958)

Op. 65, Sonata for cello and piano (1961)

Op. 66, *War Requiem* (1961)

_____, "Jubilate Deo" (1961)

Op. 75, "Voices for Today" for boys' voices, chorus and organ "ad lib" (1965)

Op. 85, *Owen Wingrave*, opera (libretto Myfanwy Piper based on Henry James) (1970)

Op. 88, *Death in Venice*, opera (libretto Myfanwy Piper based on Thomas Mann) (1973)

List of Owen Poems Referenced
(alphabetical order)

Anthem for Doomed Youth ("What passing-bells for these who die as cattle?")

Apologia pro Poemate Meo ("I, too, saw God through mud")

At a Calvary Near the Ancre ("One ever hangs where shelled roads part")

But I Was Looking at the Permanent Stars ("Bugles sang, saddening the evening air)

Disabled ("He sat in a wheeled chair, waiting for dark")

Futility ("Move him into the sun")

Greater Love ("Red lips are not so red")

Insensibility ("Happy are men who yet before they are killed")

Maundy Thursday ("Between the brown hands of a server-lad")

Parable of the Old Men and the Young ("So Abram rose, and clave the wood, and went")

Preface ("This book is not about heroes")

S. I. W. ("Patting goodbye, doubtless they told the lad")

Sonnet: On Seeing a Piece of Our Heavy Artillery Brought into Action ("Be
    slowly lifted up, thou long black arm")
Strange Meeting ("It seemed that out of the battle I escaped")
The End ("After the blast of lightning from the east")
The Kind Ghosts ("She sleeps on soft, last breaths; but no ghost looms")
The Next War ("Out there, we've walked quite friendly up to Death")

Index

For the benefit of digital users, indexed terms that span two pages (e.g., 52–53) may, on occasion, appear on only one of those pages.